W9-BAV-672

CONGRESS
Its Contemporary Role

President Ford delivering his State of the Union Message before a Joint Session of Congress, January 15, 1975.
Photograph by Arthur Scott, Senate Photographer

16.00

CONGRESS
Its Contemporary Role

FIFTH EDITION

Ernest S. Griffith
Former Director of Legislative Reference Service
Library of Congress

Francis R. Valeo
Secretary
of the
United States Senate

with an Introduction by
Senator Mike Mansfield

New York: **NEW YORK UNIVERSITY PRESS**

1975

Copyright © 1975 by New York University

Library of Congress Catalog Card Number: 74-21660

ISBN: 0-8147-8779-7 (Cloth)
0-8147-8780-0 (Paper)

Manufactured in the United States of America

JK
1061
.G7
1975

CANISIUS COLLEGE LIBRARY
BUFFALO, N. Y.

PREFACE

The basic structure and purpose of this book remain those of the earlier editions. What this edition does is to update developments and to note and evaluate certain significant changes in the structure, mood, and role of Congress.

The changes which are taking place appear to be very deep-seated, if not irreversible. Of these the shift in emphasis and membership from rural to urban is the clearest. Perhaps, "suburban" or "metropolitan" is more precise—though in the past decade-and-a-half the preoccupation has been with the problems of the central city. That, in itself, is a partial response to another tidal change, the more general dispersal of the Negro population throughout the nation and its increased participation in the electoral process in every region.

The sustained resentment of Congress to the era of the "imperial" presidency is also noteworthy. It began, perhaps, as early as the third Roosevelt administration and reached a climax several decades later in the Nixon. Over the years, this resentment has been articulated very sharply at times. A more viable response to the continuing accretion of power in the presidency, however, has been the development of congressional staff services which give members and committees alike greater competence in confrontation with the Executive Branch. With skilled and adequate technical assistance, Congress is now in a better position to exercise oversight or review functions and to assume an affirmative or, at least a coordinate role in the determination of public policy. The natural consequence of the strengthening of *both* branches could be an evolving consensus which better serves the public interest.

Within Congress itself, a trend has been set in motion in the direction of the democratization of its processes. Whether this is permanent, or a swing of the pendulum, is too early to say. Whether, too, this diffusion of power and leadership in both Houses will lead to an outpouring of creative statesmanship or to increased frustration and delay is still an open question. It may be that greater voluntary party cohesion within the Congress will provide the means for a channeling of efforts into an integrated legislative program.

The entire Watergate interlude, hopefully, is an aberration in the longer range perspective of legislative–executive relations. If that is the case, it will have served to prove that the checks and balances of the Constitution are working. Not the least of their contributions is the catharsis that they have provided for a government which, having been taken too much for granted by the people, had begun to develop serious blights of irresponsibility, corruption, and abuse of power.

Not only the presidency, but also certain permanent agencies have suffered a loss of reputation in the Watergate era. Whether the executive bureaucracy is to be guided in the future by the President or Congress or by neither is still something of an open question. The possibility exists that with the restoration of a degree of equilibrium between the two branches, there may also come a period of cooperation. Together a President and a Congress as the elected agents of the people might exercise an effective control over the vast permanent Federal establishment which each, alone, has been unable to do. To some extent, the development of revenue sharing as a technique could contribute in this situation. If it serves to enhance the effective role of the states and localities in the making of administrative decisions, it will reduce the towering influence of the Federal bureaucracy. Militating against this, however, is the aid of outside pressure groups to entrenched bureaucratic favorites.

Both major political parties in varying degree seek adherents from a broad political spectrum. Pragmatism, rather than dogmatic ideology or strong partisanship, characterizes much of the membership in Congress as in well as the electorate. That is even more the case now than in the past. Nevertheless, the party caucuses in Congress, notably those of the Democrats, have grown in significance during the Nixon administrations. While the impact and durability of this change have not yet really been tested, it seems to be evoking a somewhat greater responsiveness of committee members to party consensus. The role of the Budget Committees, as provided for by the Congressional Budget and Impoundment Control Act of 1974, and its effect on the appropriating, spending, and taxing processes is untried at this writing. The purposes of the act seem laudable, but the timetable and structures which are set forth in the legislation are subject to considerable hazards.

We close with an appreciation to the Majority Leader, Senator Mansfield, for valuing the thought which went into this book enough to contribute an introduction. To Congressmen Bolling and Dorn and to Bruce Meredith of the House Appropriations Committee go our thanks for their helpful suggestions and insights.

ERNEST S. GRIFFITH
FRANCIS R. VALEO

Contents

INTRODUCTION

When Franklin D. Roosevelt was in his third term as President of the United States, I was elected for the first time to represent the Western district of Montana in the House of Representatives. By 1942, Roosevelt had already led the nation from the depths of the Great Depression into a modest economic recovery and then into World War II.

Roosevelt was not only a popular President, he also lifted the presidency to new heights of public acceptance. That was true at home and also among countless millions abroad where his name and style became the personification of America. Always the center of controversy, he gave the nation an aggressive leadership in the effort to overcome the depression and to win the war. He was surrounded by a host of talented associates in the Executive Branch whom he had brought or attracted to Washington. His administrations overwhelmed the Congress, the Supreme Court, and the permanent bureaucracy with bold innovations and incessant action. For all the years of his presidential incumbency, Roosevelt dominated the political life of the nation. His massive frame and leg braces, his smile and the resonant English with which he spoke to countless millions via radio became the hallmarks of an era.

Congress, on the whole, went along with the wishes of a highly popular President. It was often eager and rarely hostile to transferring to Roosevelt the powers which he requested and sometimes demanded. Only occasionally was there a sustained display of Congressional opposition, as when Roosevelt challenged the Supreme Court after his great electoral victory of 1936. When Congress did show reluctance to acquiesce in his requests, the President would deliver one of his famous "fireside chats." The nation would listen and respond, more often than not, with emphatic support. His popular base thus reaffirmed, he was not averse to moving, if necessary, without Congressional assent. He would do so by stretching his Constitutional powers or reviving some long forgotten law to justify a unilateral executive course of action. Frightened by the specter of revolution during the prolonged depression and by the rise of militaristic dictatorship in Europe and Asia, the people wanted action from their government. The Executive Branch was prepared to provide it and Congress went with the tides of the time.

Thus was set in motion a major shift in the fulcrum of power inside the Federal structure. Over the Roosevelt years, it was pushed far in the direction of Executive Branch supremacy. As I recall the era, Congress could have done little to have prevented this change even if it were of a mind to do so. The two Houses were aware, as the people of the nation were aware, of the need for Federal action to cope with the critical situation at home and abroad. However, Congress was not organized to comprehend the sudden deluge of domestic and international problems which had burst on the nation. Much less was it equipped, technically, to develop or even to evaluate policies for dealing with these problems. There was a scattering of individuals in Congress, of course, whose training and specialization made them equal or even superior to the best in the Executive Branch. Operating as individuals, however, they could be effective only in confronting minute aspects of the nation's problems. On the whole, the members of Congress were local in orientation, largely rural in outlook, with limited interest in issues beyond the reach of their home districts.

They were poorly paid, poorly housed, poorly staffed, and far less independent politically than is the case today.

The flow of emergency power to the presidency during the Roosevelt administrations became a quasi-fixed pattern in the Federal government. It was to continue almost unchecked for a quarter of a century after World War II. To be sure, the courts from time to time turned back unilateral Executive Branch actions. Occasionally, too, Congress refused to go along with some extreme presidential demand, rejecting, for example, President Truman's request for legislation to draft striking railroad workers into the army. Congress also began to develop in defense against continued Executive Branch encroachments new legislative devices such as the congressional veto to provide some limitation or post-check on the Executive Branch.

The Vietnamese War highlighted the great distance which we had come from a government of divided powers toward one of executive supremacy. As the war dragged on inconclusively year after year, the public began to grasp the fact that the Executive Branch had begun and continued a war without any but the vaguest Congressional sanction. From many quarters came demands for the termination of the involvement in Vietnam. Yet, even as popular hostility mounted against it, the war went on for several years. Congress began to examine in depth the alterations in the constitutional structure which had been accumulating for several decades and which lay at the bottom of the manner in which the war was undertaken and continued.

The Watergate affair and related events accelerated this process of reexamination. Whatever other factors entered into this sordid interlude, it was also, in part, the consequence of the tolerated growth of executive preeminence to a point where the entire constitutional structure of checks and balances had been placed in jeopardy.

That Congress has finally been able to begin to halt the erosion is due, in part, to its changing character. Members, today, are better-educated, more independent-minded and service-oriented than ever before. While the House and to a lesser degree the Senate remain substantially local if not rural in character, Congress as a whole is more aware of the national and international setting in which the Federal government functions. Party loyalty exists as in the past but it is not stifling. Many of the rules and rigid practices associated with Congress have been modified by reorganization laws, rules changes, and new concepts of leadership. There is, today, a greater equality, mobility, and distribution of power among members. Congress is far better staffed. It is not only able to obtain the facts that are necessary to judge the validity of presidential proposals and policies but, increasingly, to exercise oversight or review of executive departments and to originate and advance policies of its own.

What does this mean for the future? Does it signify not only the end of executive preponderance but also the ascendency of legislative government? There are some who might detect in current developments a trend in that direction. On the whole, however, it seems to me that what is involved at this time is more a recouping of abandoned or usurped congressional responsibilities. I am inclined to conclude with the authors that the pendulum will not swing all the way to a parliamentary system.

I think that that is all for the good. The continuing validity of the system of checks and balances has just been demonstrated in the denouement of the Watergate affair. A strong presidency remains as essential to that system and the stability and effective functioning of the Federal government as a competent Congress. Hopefully, out of the devastating experiences which led to the resignation of both a Vice President and a President, there will emerge a new era of mutual respect and cooperation in independence between the two branches which will better serve the interests of all of the people of the nation.

That this conclusion is also that of the writers of this fifth edition of *Congress: Its Contemporary Role* may be due, in part, to our shared experiences. Both authors have served the Congress in staff functions of various kinds since my arrival in Washington many years ago. Dr. Ernest S. Griffith, as Director of the Congressional Research Service of the Library of Congress for many years, and Francis R. Valeo, as a Senior Specialist and Chief of the Foreign Affairs Division in the same service, and subsequently in a succession of Senate posts culminating in his election as Secretary of the Senate, have had a unique vantage point. They have seen close-up the flow of power and responsibility between the branches as well as the changes within the Congress itself. In fact, as pioneer congressional professional staff, they have themselves played a part in the unfolding of these changes.

MIKE MANSFIELD
Majority Leader
United States Senate

Washington, D.C.
August 1974

CHAPTER 1

The Formal Constitutional Position of Congress

The constitutional position of Congress today is not primarily the product of formal amendment; nor is it primarily an outgrowth of changing judicial interpretation. It is, rather, a function of changing custom and practice—changes brought about on the one hand by the vast economic forces that reveal themselves in a transformed economy and on the other by the rise of other world systems which during World War II and for many years thereafter were in militant conflict. The emerging outlines of this informal constitution will be the principal theme of this work. Nevertheless, it is appropriate at the beginning to note the much less formidable changes produced by formal amendment and judicial interpretation.

Formal separation of powers is one of the three great principles of our Constitution. It used to be fashionable in academic circles to be critical of this principle, the criticism usually being coupled with an admiration for the parliamentary system and suggestions of various devices by which the American government could be made more like the British model. Critics did not always concede that installation of the parliamentary system by way of constitutional amendment was not practicable. They resorted, instead, to suggestions for various devices, institutional and otherwise, centering around more integrated executive–legislative relations on the one hand and greater party responsibility on the other.*

It is apparent that the argument that seemed most cogent to the architects of the Constitution in defense of separation of powers—that there was danger in the same man or body both making and executing the laws—now has quite different significance even though belief in the use of power to check power and hold it responsible is still valid.

We need focal points of leadership within Congress and without and we must see that this leadership is responsible. England, with its formal union of the legislature and the cabinet executive, is no more and no less in danger of a formal dictatorship than is the United States. The forces making for totalitarianism are not found primarily in the relationship between these two parts of the nation's government, except insofar as this relationship may put a premium upon a virtual dictatorship of the technically competent.** The dangers lie rather in external forces, in the power of the special interests, in the menace of enemies, in national disunity. Insofar as these factors are by-products of constitutions, they trace rather to multiparty systems fostered by proportional representation or to other divisive constitutional provisions which reflect in the legislature the nation's disunities.

The importance of separation of powers lies in its relationship to a menace to representative democracy already mentioned. This is the danger that the authority of technical competence as represented in the bureaucracy may transform an ostensibly democratic government into a dictatorship of the civil service behind the facade of a formal constitution. The great industrialized democracies of the world, including our own, have already gone some distance along this path. Yet close examination reveals that our Congress, perhaps alone among the legislative bodies of the world, has offered effective resistance to this trend. This it has done not merely in the

* Cf. chapters 5 and 16.
** Cf. chapter 6.

negative sense of picking and choosing among the proposals of the executive but by revealing a capacity for developing the necessary leadership to share in policy formulation or even itself to devise and adopt independent policies.

Stated more precisely, the contemporary genius of our American Constitution can be seen more accurately not so much in its safeguards against arbitrary action as in an affirmative insistence upon responsibility. Separation of powers has introduced a unique element into the relationship between Congress and the executive. The heart of the matter is that, by and large, neither the executive nor the legislative branch can operate irresponsibly for long in important matters. Always each is required, and must expect, to justify its action and its proposals before a constitutional equal. Irresponsible power is thus little known to our system. Even if power expresses itself in inaction rather than action, as is often alleged of Congress, the way lies open for the President to bring the popular will to bear upon the situation through the press and other public media.

This is the less important aspect of the picture. More important is the fact that the Congress can hold the Executive Branch accountable for administration and need not accept an executive program unless it believes it justified. Neither for that matter must the President follow Congress unless he in turn believes in a congressional measure, save only in the few instances in which a bill is passed over his veto. This necessity on the part of each to justify its conduct and its proposals before its constitutional equal is one of the really great principles which determine the nature of our government. Together with our Federal system and the single-member constituency, it makes for a system of government in which progress can take place in an atmosphere of common consent or at least of widespread acceptance. It is unifying rather than divisive. To trace the workings of this principle in its relationship to contemporary social and economic forces is to come close to a real understanding of congressional behavior.

In this context, it can readily be seen why the practice of presidential impoundment of congressionally approved expenditures raised serious congressional anxieties at the outset of the second Nixon administration. To be sure, this was hardly the first time that a President had refused to spend funds appropriated by the Congress. President Franklin D. Roosevelt used the device to shift spending from civilian purposes, to military as World War II closed in on the nation. In 1949, the Truman administration impounded $700 million of an appropriation to deny a congressionally directed expansion of the Air Force. It became apparent, however, that the Nixon administration intended not only to impound widely but to assert a Constitutional right to exercise what amounted to an "item veto," at least insofar as expenditures were concerned. Many of these impoundments were overthrown by action of the Courts. In 1974, the problem appeared on the way to resolution when Congress passed the Congressional Budget and Impoundment Control Act which allowed either House to reject a presidential impoundment by a simple majority vote.[1]

The clash over impoundment which ensued between the President and the Congress was inevitable sooner or later because there never was a clear separation of function or even of powers, as popularly understood, between the President and the Congress. The Constitution itself, with its checks and balances, has modified the purity of the theory of separation of powers. The legislative powers of the President and the executive powers of Congress in administration are well known for the most part. This latter power, for example, finds expression in the congressional insistence that standards and procedures in such administrative matters as personnel, organization, and purchasing in the executive department are to be prescribed by legislation. In truth, the constitutional synthesis deserves a better and more accurate title than either separation of powers or checks and balances. Institutionalized mutuality of responsibility on the part of coequals more nearly expresses the ideal situation.

Historically, legislative–executive relations have been fluid in the extreme. They have varied with persons, with issues, with the tempo of the time. On the whole, however, it has seemed as if certain inexorable forces had propelled our government, as they have other governments, more and more in the direction of executive dominance. In his presidential message of May 1822, Monroe characterized the legislative branch, "from the nature of its powers, all laws proceeding from it, and the manner of its appointment, its members being elected by the people," as by far the most important. In that year, the expenditure for Congress still exceeded that for the executive. Corwin put the situation as follows:

> The Constitution reflects the struggle between two conceptions of executive power: the conception that it ought always to be subordinate to the supreme legislative power, and the conception that it ought to be, within generous limits, autonomous and self-directing; or, in other terms, the idea that the people are *represented* in the legislative *versus* the idea that they are *embodied* in the executive. Nor has this struggle ever entirely ceased, although on the whole it is the latter theory which has prospered. . . . Taken by and large, the history of the presidency has been a history of aggrandizement.[2]

That such a development in the United States seems of late to have been arrested deserves most thoughtful examination. Whether this change is temporary remains to be seen. It may be only one of those cyclical changes in the locus of power between Congress and the President which we have witnessed in the past. It may on the other hand represent something more fundamental, one of those major developments arising from the introduction of some new factor of the first magnitude in our governance.

The structure of Congress remains in formal terms substantially unaltered from early days, except for the direct election of the senators, and the abolition of the Lame Duck Congress by the Twentieth Amendment. Both of these changes have had their principal effect in a sharpening of the accuracy of representation—important in an informal but positive fashion in the prestige and power of the body. The introduction of the direct primary into the structure of so many of the state governments has substantially affected the role of the parties in Congress.

Judicial interpretation has registered and to some extent facilitated certain broad changes in the respective positions of Congress and the President. It is worth noting that the great historical constitutional studies have been of the position of the presidency rather than of Congress. In part this may be because its story is more dramatic. The story of an upbuilding is more intriguing that the story of an erosion or decline. It would be an interesting and rewarding exercise to rewrite these same studies from the point of view of Congress.[3]

Among the constitutional changes which register a transfer of function from the Congress to the executive is the growth of delegated legislation within the extremely liberal metes and bounds set by the Supreme Court.[4] Let the delegation be according to defined limits; let it be essential for attaining the objective of the act; let it be recoverable; let it involve procedurally no violation of the "due process" and other clauses. Beyond these limits, there are apparently no other constitutional caveats against the delegation of congressional power. The Schechter case [5] ruling which blocked briefly the deluge of delegation of congressional power during the early years of the administration of Franklin D. Roosevelt has long since been conveniently interred. It should be noted in passing that a growth in delegated legislation is inevitable in a setting in which more and more legislation consists essentially of fixing objectives (rather than the passing of laws) and the creation of an agency to carry them out. The characteristic process of the latter is the type of continuous intervention which we have termed "adjustment."

Over against this tide of delegation to the executive is the advantage taken by Congress of the ambiguity of the Constitution in regard to the control over those matters which are central to the administrative process. Thus Congress has come to prescribe in some detail the organization, personnel practices, methods of accounting, budgetary procedure, purchasing and disposal, and many other similar areas commonly associated with executive power.*

Congress has occasionally written into statutes powers of removal other than by impeachment as in the instances of the Comptroller General and Members of the Board of Directors of the Tennessee Valley Authority. The Supreme Court has seesawed on this constitutional issue. The leading case in this connection is *Meyers v. United States* in 1926.[6] In that decision the Court voided a statute requiring Senate consent to removal of postmasters. Subsequently, the decision in the Humphrey Case and *Weiner v. United States* [7] admitted a congressional role by statute in removal and limitations on the President's powers of removal, notably with regard to regulatory commissions.

The examples of the General Accounting Office, the Government Printing Office, the Library of Congress, and the Botanic Garden reveal potential congressional administrative powers, despite some skepticism about their existence. In the so-called independent commissions there is obviously a twilight zone within which perhaps some congressional administrative power lurks. Apparently the full implications of congressional power to prescribe methods of removal have not been fully explored. In *United States v. Lovett*,[8] however,

---

* Cf. chapter 9 for a fuller discussion.

Congress is held subject to limitations in the use of the power of appropriations to force removals of individuals.

A succession of decisions (or the absence of ways to force a decision) has somewhat limited the investigating powers of Congress. The presidency apparently may refuse papers and possibly may ignore subpoenas, though these steps are seldom taken. Within an expanded field it may decline to answer questions. Appearances are voluntary. The presidency apparently may also transfer to his high officials something of his own immunities. Issues of this type which arose in loyalty investigations in the late 1940s and early 1950s are still unsolved, and their solutions are difficult to arrive at through judicial processes.

In the Ninety-third Congress, the issues arose again in acute and manifold form. After a great electoral victory, the second Nixon administration presided over a shortlived period of Executive Branch attitudes of superiority over Congress that bordered on the contemptuous. Unilateral presidential authority was claimed in regard to impoundment. At the same time the doctrine of executive privilege and the right to withhold information on the grounds of national security were extended arbitrarily to embrace virtually the entire Executive Branch of the government. Even relatively minor officials asserted the right to refuse to appear before the Congress.

The reaction of the Congress to these tendencies was immediate. In the Senate, several resolutions were adopted by the majority which were designed to provide organized resistance to what had come to be regarded as a dangerous unilateralism on the part of the presidency. Most significant, the majority was joined by the minority in establishing the Senate Select Committee on Presidential Campaign Activities with broad powers to investigate campaign practices during the 1972 presidential campaign. The committee's revelations regarding the Watergate affair wreaked devastation on the administration and was a precursor to the imprisonment of many of its key figures and, finally, the resignation of the

President. The constitutional question of the extent of the unilateral powers of the President to withhold information from Congress, however, remained unresolved.

Nevertheless, the usage of the investigatory power and other countermeasures served the purposes of Congress. A long period of general expansion of the independent sphere of the executive was brought to a halt. Much of the accumulation of this unilateral power had been derived from the President's functions in foreign relations, as commander-in-chief of the armed services, and as steward in emergencies because of the "nature of government." Such emergencies have included industrial disputes, crises in law enforcement, depressions, threats to national safety, and wars. Perhaps, the most sharply defined and extreme expression of this doctrine was the demand by Franklin Roosevelt in connection with the repeal of part of the Price Control Act:

> I ask the Congress to take this action by the first of October. Inaction on your part by that date will leave me with an inescapable responsibility to the people of this country to see to it that the war effort is no longer imperiled by threat of economic chaos.
>
> In the event that the Congress should fail to act, and act adequately, I shall accept the responsibility, and I will act.
>
> At the same time that fair prices are stabilized, wages can and will be stabilized also. This I will do.
>
> The President has the powers, under the Constitution and under Congressional acts, to take measures necessary to avert a disaster which would interfere with the winning of the war.
>
> I have given the most thoughtful consideration to meeting this issue without further reference to the Congress. I have determined, however, on this vital matter to consult with the Congress. . . .
>
> The American people can be sure that I will use my powers with a full sense of my responsibility to the Constitution and

to my country. The American people can also be sure that I shall not hesitate to use every power vested in me to accomplish the defeat of our enemies in any part of the world where our own safety demands such defeat.

When the war is won, the powers under which I act [9] automatically revert to the people—to whom they belong.

At that time, the validity of the projected action was not brought to a test. Congress complied, and the crisis was averted. If under the guise of an emergency, with Congress in actual session, a President had in fact the power Roosevelt claimed of setting aside a law by unilateral action, then, indeed, the position of Congress would be seriously and perhaps critically impaired. The nature of the world today is such that the claim of a national crisis can easily be advanced. Thus, the presidency in the hands of a man temperamentally inclined toward dictatorship would be a danger of the first magnitude.

In 1952, contending that an industry-wide strike constituted a national emergency, President Truman seized the steel mills. In the court actions that followed the government rested its case primarily on a President's inherent powers, with some support from his authority as commander-in-chief. The mills had extensive defense contracts. The Supreme Court ruled that the President had exceeded his powers, in that not only had Congress not authorized such seizure but had laid down other procedures.[10] Evidently there are limits even to the emergency powers of the presidency.

The Congress has been profoundly affected by the intervention of the Supreme Court in reapportionment in regard to state legislatures and Congress itself. In *Wesberry v. Sanders*,[11] the Court laid down the principle of "equal representation for equal numbers of people." As a result a very substantial number of hitherto rural seats have been transferred to urban and, even more, to suburban areas.

Yet, it should be emphasized again and again that it is by usage and not by formal amendment or judicial decision that the most far-reaching constitutional changes which involve Congress are taking place. These will be spelled out in greater detail later, but chiefly they lie within this area of legislative –executive relations. The role of Congress in international relations has changed. Treaties are less important when the executive takes actions in the nature of commitments which inexorably determine our future course. Agreements at Yalta, Potsdam, and Teheran, and the dispatching of combat forces to Korea under the Truman administration, to Indochina under the Kennedy administration, and to the Dominican Republic under the Johnson administration by unilateral executive decision—these and scores of other actions have reduced greatly the importance which at one time attached to the role of Congress in declaring war and ratifying treaties.

In the Congress and notably in the Senate, a belated attempt was made to reassert the role of Congress in foreign relations. A principal expression of this attempt to recoup power in foreign policy took the legislative form of the War Powers Resolution which was enacted over a presidential veto during the Ninety-third Congress. The resolution is designed to curb the use of "inherent" presidential powers by the Executive Branch to involve the nation in major military conflicts.* It received overwhelming bipartisan support in both houses.

The weapon of congressional investigation has also been sharpened and is growing sharper—be it poniard or meat ax. A committee is not merely an organ through which Congress seeks to assure executive responsibility in carrying out the intent of the law, it is also a source of profound influence on the exercise of administrative power in the area of its discretion. A committee is a coordinate locus of power with one or more executive departments, and with the specialization thereby implied it has always presented a formidable rival in the evolution of policy in its special area. Now that it has added to its arsenal the availability of permanent experts on its own staff, in the Congressional Research Service, the

* Cf. chapter 12.

General Accounting Office, and other congressional agencies in the process of formation, the decline in effective congressional oversight of the Executive Branch may be coming to an end.†

Neither the executive nor the Congress—and especially the Congress—has been organized to prepare and see through an integrated and harmonious policy. It was thought, for a time, that the Joint Economic Committee might contain the seeds of such integration in Congress, just as such agencies as the Office of Management and Budget and the Council of Economic advisors (and the Executive Office of the President generally) make possible in the Executive Branch such integrated planning as there is. However, the committee was inhibited from its beginnings in 1946 by its lack of power to introduce legislation. Moreover, the timing of the submission of the Economic Report has constituted a serious inhibiting factor of effective congressional response.*

Neither Congress, nor, for that matter, the Executive Branch, has conspicuously succeeded in this task of establishing cohesive policies. Yet, in a dispersive society and economy the need for integrating factors is obvious. The question was sharply illuminated in the Ninety-third Congress at a time of a serious shortage of fuel. In an address to the nation in 1974, speaking for the Democratic majority, the Senate Majority Leader pointed to the

> need to think ahead and begin to make the hard political choices between what is more important to the nation and what is less, between what is enduring and what is transitory. That is the full scale by which government intervention in the nation's economy, when it must take place should be measured. ... It seems to me that it would be helpful in this connection to bring together on a regular basis representatives of the executive branch and the legis-

* Cf. chapter 9 for a study of the nature of this oversight.

lative branch with those of industry, labor, and other areas of national life. The fusion of ideas and interests from these sources should help us to establish useful economic yard-sticks. . . .[12]

We may conclude at this point by indicating that a large measure of the greatness of our Constitution lies in its fluidity and adaptability. It allows much that matters in relationships to be determined by custom and usage, as changing social forces play upon government. Yet some features are permanent and of these none is more important than the separation of powers, which contains the deeper principle of the responsibility of power. This is the cornerstone of congressional-executive relations.[13]

NOTES

1. Lawsuits contested the contentions of the Nixon administration on impoundment, with members of Congress joining several of them. [See "Controversy over the Presidential Impoundment of Appropriated Funds," *Congressional Digest,* (Washington, D. C.) April 1973. pp. 99-128. The Congressional Budget and Impoundment Control Act, P.L. 93-344.]
2. Corwin, Edward S., *The President: Office and Powers* 4th ed., rev., (New York: New York University Press, 1957), p. 307.
3. Cf. Corwin, *The President: Office and Powers;* H. J. Laski, *The American Presidency* (London: Harper and Brothers, ca. 1940); W. E. Binkley, *The Powers of the President* (Garden City: Doubleday, 1940); *President and Congress* (New York: Knopf, 1947); Clinton Rossiter, *The American Presidency* (New York: Harcourt, Brace, 1956); Louis Fisher, *President and Congress* (New York: Free Press, 1972); Arthur M. Schlesinger, Jr., and Alfred de Grazia, *Congress and the Presidency: Their Role in Modern Times* (Washington: American Enterprise Institute for Public Policy Research, 1967); Woodrow Wilson, *Congressional Government; A Study in American Politics* (Boston, 1885)

(perhaps an exception, though it is more descriptive than historical).

4. See Carl B. Swisher, *Supreme Court in Modern Role*, rev. edit. (New York: New York University Press, 1965), chap. 2.

5. *Schechter Poultry Corp. v United States*, 295 U.S. 495 (1935).

6. 272 U.S. 52 (1926)

7. *Humphrey's Executor v. United States*, 295 U.S. 602 (1935).

8. 328 U.S. 303 (1946).

9. Cited in and discussed in Corwin, *The President: Office and Powers*, pp. 250-51.

10. *Sawyer v. Youngstown Sheet and Tube Company*, 343 U.S. 937 (1952).

11. 376 U. S. 1 (1964).

12. Senator Mansfield's interview on the state of Congress, *Congressional Record*, Washington, Feb. 7, 1974, p. S.1383.

13. We must note that the general problem of relationships between Congress and the Judiciary, especially the Supreme Court, has not been considered. From time to time, criticism of the latter has risen almost to fever pitch in legislative halls. Yet, never in recent decades has Congress taken any measures that would indicate that the majority of both houses shared this criticism. See Walter F. Murphy, *Congress and the Court* (Chicago: University of Chicago Press, 1962) and Herman F. Pritchett, *Congress versus the Supreme Court* (Minneapolis: University of Minnesota Press, 1961) for standard works on the subject. Following such periods, both branches have tended to temper their actions.

CHAPTER 2

The Members and Their Leaders

Characterizations of members of Congress have run the gamut from cartoons to statistics. The "typical" member has been pictured many times, but with somewhat more circumspection and respect of late. The "Claghorn" stereotype is badly dated. Members are probably less colorful than in the past, but more competent. In the Ninety-third Congress if the member were in the Senate, his average age was 55.3 years; in the House, 51.9 years. This age level has changed little in the past quarter of a century. A member is more often than not a lawyer, almost always a college graduate and a church member, native-born, a family man, extroverted, above average in height. He is not greatly dissimilar from the typical American of his years, albeit somewhat better educated, more likely to be service-motivated, and with far more interest in public affairs.

It is worthwhile to probe a bit more deeply at certain points, perhaps drawing some distinction between the man at the time of his first election and what the occupation itself subsequently does to him.

The post has become a full-time job, but usually without the financial security and with few of the amenities that normally in other walks of life attach to a post with comparable prestige and, more often than not, far less responsibility. As occupations of heavy responsibility go, congressional pay is poor. In 1973, only $6,500 separated the pay of the highest rank in the Federal Civil Service ($36,000) and a member of Congress ($42,500). A congressman is paid less than the Special Assistant to the Postmaster General.

We live in a society which puts a premium on job security, public deference, and character and ability. The occupation of a congressman stands up well in all but the desire for security. At this point it falls seriously short. So much is this true that certain occupations are effectively disqualified as significant sources of recruitment of congressional candidates. Election so breaks the rhythm of the pursuit of certain careers that failure in reelection makes it almost impossible for members of Congress to take up where they left off. A small businessman, for example, would find it hard to break away for a term or two in Congress and then return to his business. So, too, would a small farmer, unless he had a son at exactly the right age to step into the breach. A labor leader must be continuously at his job, or the competition for promotion and preference that is characteristic of such a career will quickly seize upon his vacancy—and rarely if ever could he successfully reenter after a lapse of years. Employees of firms, business or manufacturing, are not usually encouraged to take part in politics in the sense of running for office and, even if allowed to run, must usually resign their posts if elected. Most professions are similarly handicapped. Doctors and dentists become rusty, and others take over their practice. Teachers are expected to be nonpolitical, except possibly college professors.

On the other hand, there are certain occupations in which job security either is not a factor or is enhanced by service in Congress. The unemployed rich can find it a constructive outlet for their talents. Large-scale farmers can employ farm managers, at least temporarily. Housewives are not likely to be unoccupied even if eventually defeated for reelection. Retired businessmen, military officers, civil servants, if they retire early enough to assume the vigor of a campaign, are obviously eligible. So are journalists, because service in Congress can be of subsequent assistance in a return to their profession. College professors, especially in the social sciences, attain considerable glamor as well as experience through political success. Bankers may be granted leaves of absence, if they run on an approved conservative platform.

Above all, lawyers find even candidacy for Congress an asset, and election usually brings an enhanced reputation and usually additional clients to the firm. Add to this two facts: that the lawyer usually chooses his profession in the first place because of his interest in public affairs, and the further fact that analytic ability, the balancing of evidence, capacity for advocacy are all assets in the congressional setting as well as part of a lawyer's stock-in-trade. It is not surprising that 50.8 percent of the membership of the House and 68 percent of the Senate came from the legal profession in the Ninety-third Congress.

Finally, there is a category of eligibility that cuts across all of the others, in the sense that it is usually a dimension of them: whatever their occupational origins, candidates are for the most part also politicians. In other words, in any community, district, or state, there is a certain nucleus of persons interested in party organization, campaigns, government, and the powers, if not the favors, involved therein. In this group are some that make a career of officeholding, elective or appointive. Hence, a number of congressmen list their earlier occupations as "public official." Whether the candidate is already an official or not, usually he belongs to this inner circle of the politically active. It should be noted in this connection that insecurity of tenure may be more apparent than real, inasmuch as the number of defeated congressmen that appear later among the presidential or gubernatorial or mayoralty appointees is not inconsiderable. Others find themselves employed in or by private business, as lobbyists, or as experts in wending their way in the maze of the appropriate bureaucracy.

Certain personal qualities, while not universal, are so obviously assets that they may be largely presumed among members. The successful type is usually the extrovert, genuinely interested in people, able to project himself affirmatively into the thinking of groups (nationality, religious, occupational), gregarious, a "joiner," a churchgoer. Of late, emphasis upon intellectual acuity seems to be rising in the scale, as the complexity of the nation's problems have borne in on the electorate.[1]

What happens to these men and women after they are elected, or, even more, after they are repeatedly reelected? What does service in Congress do to a man's personality and character? It is a truism to say that it depends upon the man himself whether the good or the evil factors prevail in this occupational conditioning. Most likely it is something of both, for there are both occupational hazards and occupational constructs.

On the minus side, there is not the slightest doubt that the pace itself is terrific—too great, in fact, if there are inherent instabilities in a man's personality. Irritability in committee hearings is one very human reaction to this pace. Escapism of one sort or another is ever present as a temptation—escape from fatigue, escape from pressure. Surprisingly only a very small number have become alcoholics, at least in recent years. Perhaps the principal "escape" is for the member simply to give up the fight for serious accomplishment, to drift along with the party or committee leadership, and to cultivate his constituency.

In addition to the hectic pace are the hazards of having to seem understanding of all the individuals and groups who constantly seek special favors in the form of jobs, intervention with the administration, or support of or opposition to pending legislation. Probably much if not most of this response is "front"; back of it all, the member, more often than not, will follow his judgment and his conscience, albeit frequently behind a smoke screen of apparent sympathy with the point of view urged upon him. These pressures constantly tilt the scales in the direction of being all things to all men, and only the valiant and the thick-skinned can completely hold out. After all, the member is a *representative,* and "going along" on a minor matter may assure success on a major one, including reelection to continue the fight for the right. He is, after all, in Congress to get things done, and compromise is a necessary tactic in situations in which men honestly differ.

In the third place, there is the ever present danger of a dulling of the ethical edge of a man. At what point does a gift become a bribe—when it is valued at five dollars or five hundred? Does a liberal honorarium to make a speech before an organization constitute a commitment to the organization's program? If not, does subconscious appreciation work in the same direction? What constitutes conflict of interest? Stock ownership that preceded candidacy? The employment of a member of his family by a certain firm? What are legitimate expenses on travel accounts? What is a fair use of the congressional frank? Should a law firm in which a member retains membership take a fee in connection with a private immigration bill, or any other legislative matter? What obligations arise out of campaign contributions and testimonial dinners? The authors have been present at many discussions of questions of this type among members, and have been impressed with the seriousness of many of these discussions. One member will accept a lunch but not a dinner. One will take gifts worth less than five dollars and return the others. Another returns all gifts. The problems involved are far from easy. Where does courtesy end and influence begin? Where is influence legitimate and where "undue?" All the wiles of the social lobby, all the devices of presents and subtle suggestions of favors to come, all the apparent friendships which are not friendships—these and a hundred other matters render impossible a sharp line between "mine and thine," between prerogatives of office and its exploitation, between the public interest and betrayal of the public trust. To some extent, all public officials are exposed to the same conflicts of public and personal interests. For the congressman, however, his daily life is a constant round of temptations, not so much to overt malfeasance, but to blurred ethics.

The lines of propriety have been drawn more tightly in recent years. In the wake of several scandals, both houses have established committees on ethics and have provided some form of public disclosure of the fiscal affairs of members and congressional staffs. While the limited adequacy of this disclosure has been the subject of some criticism, the fact is that the Congress, on the whole, has gone considerably further in this direction than either the executive or the judicial branches where, of course, many of the same temptations of conflict between the public and personal interests exist. Bills have been considered in recent years which would establish uniform standards for the three branches, but to date have not been enacted.

In addition, contributions to congressional election campaigns along with presidential are now subject to very detailed public disclosure under the Federal Election Campaign Act of 1971. (1a) So exacting and demanding are the requirements of the law that they could serve to discourage informal and local larticipation in the management and support of political campaigns. Should that prove to be the case, it might in due course modify the characteristics of the "typical" candidate.

There is another side of the ledger that is impressive. Once in Congress, the average member usually gains greatly in his appreciation of the nature of the public interest. More will be said concerning this later.* At this point it is enough to say that the transition is usually from an earlier identification of the public interest with the economic prosperity of the group or groups most strongly represented in his constituency; to a second stage in which he also sees the cogency of the "other side" in these economic struggles; to a third stage in which

* Cf. chapter 10.

larger considerations of general prosperity, human rights, demeanor of the nation, and the strength of freedom become influential in decisions. His education as a congressman, because he has the experience of serving as a congressman, is well on its way when he senses that no *one* principle ever exhausts the meaning of a situation, that most decisions involve a conflict of principles, most of them good. He turns from principles to the consequences as a basis for his decisions.

His experience as a member quickly teaches him the desirability of specializing. Even a first-term member is listened to, if he discusses a subject on which he is or has become an authority. The committee system advances this aspect of his education, especially in the House. The genius of the body lies in the conscientious and thorough nature of its committee work, not in glamor and drama of floor debate or in the emergence of great national figures. If a House member will limit the scope of his efforts, he will find himself with time to do well in his sector. He will be respected by his colleagues and his views will carry weight with them. After several terms of growth, his advocacy or opposition may be all but decisive within the limited, though important, sphere he has set for himself.

The genius of the Senate is of another character; its ethos affects a man in a somewhat different fashion. For one thing, he is much more visible than a House member. A senator is one of a hundred. The press and airways, ever on the alert for presidential material, are able to cover this more limited field more thoroughly. Debating time is longer and divided among far fewer people. A senator is more likely to be a committee or subcommittee chairman, and much earlier in his career. He has a larger staff than a House member to take from him more of the burdensome detail. The very name by which he is called, "Senator," carries with it role-playing implications which are flattering, demanding, and sobering.

He seeks acceptance by his colleagues as well as his constituents. Beyond personal competence, such acceptance is dependent on his readiness to follow the rules—the rules of conscientious work, team play, mutual respect, an underlying integrity of purpose even though this latter may inevitably be tinctured with ambition. In a sense he must take himself seriously, as seriously as the high office he holds demands—but with a certain lightness of touch which signifies a human being who gives credit to his colleagues for sincerity, even though they differ with him and must from time to time make compromises to ensure that their state will have experienced senators if and when they run for reelection. "The Senate has men who primarily investigate the executive branch, men who speak to the society at large, men who specialize in a wide variety of substantive areas. . . ." [3]

In other words, the House member thinks of himself as a "Representative," the senator as a statesman, and all the mores and the network of procedures, organization, and custom call upon him to play this role. The great majority not only play it, but in the playing of it become the role they play.

One further factor should be noted, the senator's constituency is likely to be more diversified than that of the House member. He is subjected to a broader set of experiences and pressures, and consequently he is more likely to search for an urban–rural consensus or a business–labor consensus. It is this factor, together with the time lag in House reapportionment, that in part accounts for the more "liberal" record of the upper body in recent decades. It also accounts, in part, for the extraordinary number of candidates for the presidency who have come from the Senate in recent years. In the past quarter century, of the dozen Presidents or principal opponents in the presidential elections, nine had previous service in that body.

No one can know scores and hundreds of members of Congerss intimately without coming to understand them, and out of this understanding come to respect them. They are constantly on the firing line. The good they do is often obscured or ignored; the evil never wants for a reporter or critic. They wish to be better than they are, but the exigencies of the political scene, the importunities of the self-seeking, the group dispersiveness of the body politic set metes and bounds to the utopian. The realist must be content to do what he can, and that is not inconsiderable.

The transition is a natural one from a view of Congress as a collection of individuals to an analysis of the role played by its leadership. Where and whence are its leaders and its centers of power?

Consider first another aspect of the member as an individual. In one sense he is independent of leadership or of centers of power. Few are the sanctions that his colleagues or party leaders can impose on him in his own district or state. Within Congress as a body they can to a certain extent punish his insubordination, temerity, or maverick tendency—but, so long as he appears solicitous for his constituents, such punishment can rarely penetrate his reelection campaign. Then, too, in a sense the member is without responsibility to the national public, but is responsible to his constituents.* This creates the setting for a leadership relatively decentralized and inchoate.

Yet leadership there is, basically, because the individual is almost completely dependent upon others to get things done —whether for his district, state, or nation. Team play is necessary, and there must be a captain. Accommodation and compromise there must be, and these usually imply a broker. Carrying conviction there must be, and this very fact may well make each and every member in a sense a leader. In other words, a member must, to a very considerable extent, be an "organization man" and by generally accepted, though not binding, techniques must work his way into positions in which he can attain more and more of his objectives.

---

* The word "responsible" is used here in the sense of accountability. If the term "responsible" is used as a synonym of "self-disciplined, thoughtful, and conscientious," then, as a matter of conscience, he can be highly "responsible" nationally. Yet even this latter does not necessarily imply acceptance of leadership.

Both houses have customs and traditions which have been worked out over the years. The customs are generally functional. They are designed to promote comity and to make accomplishments possible. In the House, in particular, the new member is closely watched in this regard. Without sacrifice of conscience or constituency, will he "go along" with the leadership where possible? Does he specialize? Does he refrain from brashness? If so, after a term or two, he will find himself entrusted with those as yet minor responsibilities which are nevertheless the sure mark of favor on the part of those in power. Gradually his influence will increase, even though he may have to wait a long time for a committee chairmanship. In the Senate, recognition may come more quickly, for there are fewer to divide power. Under both the Johnson and Mansfield leaderships efforts were made to hasten further the process of full incorporation of new members into the mainstream of Senate activity. Senator Scott as Minority Leader followed suit. Younger members were added in their first terms to prestigious committees including the Steering and Policy Committees, the principal party leadership committees. Mansfield, in particular, exhorted the new members not only to recognize the equalizing element of "one-member, one vote" but to act on it in all Senate business.

In both houses, nevertheless, great store is placed upon willingness to make the necessary compromises to permit accomplishment, and upon mutual support on matters which are important to certain members but not to all.[4]

Where then is leadership and power centered? On really major issues, leadership from within the government is found in an interplay of the President, the relevant cabinet member, or member of the White House staff, the party leaderships in Congress, the responsible committee chairmen, and even isolated members with a strong stake in the results or an authoritative competence in the subject field. In other words, a major issue evokes the full panoply of the various centers of power and influence. The interplay is "political" in the best sense, often leading to an end result or decision which marks a large measure of consensus.

Regional or local issues on the other hand follow a somewhat different pattern. This is the sphere of "logrolling," as with the rivers and harbors, or "pork barrel" bills. Such measures are often collections of relatively minor items strung together with a specious unity; or they may be separate though still minor items, whose sponsors, on behalf of their constituencies, cash in on previously acquired or potential credit with their congressional colleagues. Requests for help from a fellow-member are often very difficult to refuse, if the item in question is something involving his district. Some major regional issues, especially in agriculture, follow much the same pattern on a larger scale. Trades are in order as between commodity spokesmen or even with larger and implicitly alien groups such as labor or mining. In measures of these types, leadership is scattered and decentralized. Spokesmen in Congress and lobbyists outside provide the dynamics and engineer the tactics looking toward success in behalf of their respective constituents or clienteles. The interaction among the members of a state delegation is often noticeable. Countervailing forces are of course present in all of the foregoing.*

In the case of issues which are of a specialized or technical nature, leadership is usually the prerogative of the relevant committee and of individual members who have mastered the facts underlying the issues and the probable consequences of the proposed change. The organizational and party leadership also play a role here in terms of providing the necessary priority in scheduling, but its active support is seldom needed.

Finally there are the issues of continuity. The widening of a previously approved social security program, the continuance of foreign aid, the granting of additional powers to the former Bureau of Narcotics, improvement in the working conditions of civil servants, a raising of the ceiling on the national debt,

---

* See chapter 10 for a fuller discussion.

authorization of new weapon systems, will serve as samples. This is the sphere in which the initative usually rests with the executive departments and agencies. The role of Congress is usually to serve as a board of review of such proposals and occasionally as their initiator.

Leadership may thus be thought of as a series of interlocking systems with power fairly well distributed. Within Congress are three such "systems," the party hierarchy, the committee hierarchy, and the specialized and distributed power and prestige of those who are authorities in particular fields. External to Congress are the Executive Branch, the lobbyists, and the local party organizations.

Within Congress, what kind of *person* is the leader? Usually he is one who recognizes a measure of individuality, a zone of freedom, as necessary to the rank and file of members. He is a man with a sense of the national interest, often an overriding sense. He is the one who can speak in accents which usually are close to the central point in the range of views of his colleagues. He rarely behaves autocratically in little things, and only within limits in great things and then almost always when the public interest dictates. He builds up a sizable reserve of good will by assisting members when he can, and draws upon this reserve when the occasion warrants. He evokes admiration for his skill and sureness of touch, for his sense of fair play and his hard work.

He may become an autocrat, and this may bring rebellion, as with Speaker Cannon and in more recent times with certain committee chairmen and, just before his election as Vice President, against Lyndon B. Johnson. He may be inept, or even tired and old, in which event he is likely sooner or later to be replaced in one way or another. Yet, in general, those chosen by their parties and those surviving election hazards until they attain committee seniority are far more likely than not to be *effective* and to exercise their power responsibly.

Provisionally, it is fair to say that the leadership and power structure of Congress are such that they offer ample opportunity for individual members to get things done, even if they belong to the minority party. Often, majority and minority leaders in the House or the Senate or chairmen and ranking minority members will team on issues in which they are in accord. In any event, the third leadership system, that of the technically competent specialists, is still open to minority members in a setting in which national loyalty and considerations of the public interest so often transcend party lines when the chips are down. Such a structure is peculiarly adaptable to the needs of an age of multiplicity of issues of extremely varied character. Such an age demands a similar variation in the patterns of decision-making.[5]

NOTES

1. Nelson W. Polsby, *Congress and the Presidency* (Englewood Cliffs; Prentice-Hall, 1964), p. 40. Polsby also calls attention to the prevalence of home-state interest, politicking, and coalition-building. See Donald R. Mathews, *U.S. Senators and Their World* (Chapel Hill: University of North Carolina Press, 1960) for a detailed analysis of the senators' backgrounds.
2. P.L. 92-225
3. Allen Drury's novel, *Advise and Consent* (Garden City: Doubleday, 1959) is a portrait of the Senate in action. See also William S. White's interesting and informal books: *Citadel* (New York: Harpers, 1956) and *Home Place: The Story of the House of Representatives* (Boston: Houghton Mifflin, 1965). Both authors were well acquainted with the Congress during the post-World War II period of the Texas leadership of Rayburn and Johnson.
4. For a sophisticated and thorough study of these customs as they affect the House, see Richard F. Fenno, Jr., "The Internal Distribution of Influence: The House," in David B. Truman, ed., *The Congress and America's Future* (Englewood Cliffs: Prentice-Hall, 1965), pp. 70-76.
5. A perceptive study of the individual member of the House and his experiences is found in Clem Miller, *Member of the House* (New York Scribner, 1962). A comparable insight into the

world of the individual senator is *You and Your Senator*, by
Vance Hartke (New York: Coward-McCann Inc., 1970); *Dirk-
sen, Portrait of a Public Man*, by Neil MacNeil (New York: The
World Publishing Co., 1970); *LBJ, The Exercise of Power*, by
Evans and Novak, New York: The New American Library,
1966.

CHAPTER 3

The Internal Organization
of Congress

Organization and procedure have always been vital factors in the efficient operation of any legislative body. They are central in this day and age, for the business of legislatures has multiplied beyond all reckoning. The opportunities for both service to the public interest and its betrayal have correspondingly increased. Organization and procedure are at least influential in determining whether service or betrayal shall prevail. The spate of books on Congress contain such a wealth of illuminating detail on its internal organization that repetition is quite unwarranted. Therefore, at this point certain observations are merely offered that may be helpful in understanding the broad spirit and purpose, rather than the details, of Congress in its corporate capacity.

There are certain determining factors that must preface any such overall understanding. There are 435 members of the House and 100 of the Senate. They must share whatever time is available. In recent years, Congress has operated virtually on a year-round basis. Nevertheless, floor time in the Senate has averaged but 1,200 hours a year and, in the House, only 770 hours. Much of this time, moreover, is consumed in quorums and roll calls.

The House at least must be organized for floor action so as to limit debate. On the whole, it has done this well and in practice tends to be more expeditious than the Senate. The latter, on the other hand, emphasizing other values, has tended to pride itself on unlimited debate in the final stages of the legislative process. Even in the Senate, however, the increasing work load has cut into this concept. In the past decade, for example, resort has been had more and more frequently to the rule of cloture which, if it can be applied, acts to cut off debate. Cloture has been attempted on more than fifty occasions in the past decade; compared with a total of only twenty-five attempts in the previous forty years. Between 1962 and 1972 cloture was applied successfully eight times. Prior to 1960, it was successfully used only four times.

Both houses are engaged in a constant and, to a considerable extent, a losing struggle against the avalanche of business which the complexities, crises, and political insistences of the present day have produced. The quantitative aspect of the problem is the less acute. More serious is the qualitative. The quantitative has found a measure of solution in the floor rules, in additions to staff, and in division of labor among committees and subcommittees. However, it is the qualitative aspect that even more strikingly finds expression in the committee organization. The standing committee is the chief instrument by which Congress enlists specialization to confront complexity. It is interesting to note that the British House of Commons in the Seventeenth century approached this problem in a similar fashion. Its procedures have since evolved in a fundamentally different fashion. Committees now play a minor role in the House of Commons, largely in examination of bills for soundness of detail. Legislation itself emanates from the "government"—in practice largely from the permanent officials of the civil service. These latter provide the element of specialization. Cabinet committees still exist, but their contemporary role and influence are unclear.

Another generally operative factor in influencing congressional procedure is the tendency on the part of most members to seek reelection. An incumbent runs for reelection on his record. His challenger usually has a clean slate on the issues. In the circumstances, the challenge of reelection often seems like a game in which a member avoids offending and caters to the desires of the maximum number of economic, racial, religious, or other groups as represented in his constituency. This reflects itself in congressional procedures. On the positive side, it appears in the introduction of many bills, in insertions in the *Congressional Record,* in speeches on (and off) the floor, in deferential treatment of witnesses in committee hearings, and, of course, in numerous activities not directly related to either organization or procedure.

On the negative side, various devices are used to avoid offense. This practical necessity has given rise to the development of procedural devices whereby an elected representative, desirous of serving the broader public interest, can avoid taking positions publicly on issues strongly felt by minorities in his constituency if the positions are regarded by the representative as not in line with the general welfare.

For many years the Rules Committee has occasionally performed this role in the House by blocking measures from reaching the floor or forcing changes in them as they emerge from the standing committee. Over the years, the committee has found justification for this particular course of action in its belief that certain measures with strong pressures behind them were nevertheless not in the public interest and when—this is the important aspect—it had reason to suppose that the House shared the Rules Committee's and not the standing committee's view. Yet, because of organized pressure—pressure perhaps of veterans' organizations, of labor, of business, of racial minorities, of the aged (it matters not which)—many members would be faced with the alternatives of severe political reprisals or a vote against their convictions if the measure reached the floor. In these circumstances the measure would probably pass, to the detriment of what the Rules Committee conceived to be the broader public interest. In this connection, it should be noted that political courage, like any other kind, is not a commodity in unlimited supply.

In performing this role for the House, the Rules Committee has from time to time exacted a price. The power to spare the House the hard choices on some occasions is also the power to thwart the will of the House majority on others. Various devices have been developed to curb arbitrary tendencies in the Rules Committee. The principal among these has been the power to enlarge its membership, to "pack" it, so to speak, with members partial to the position of the Speaker. Various rules such as Calendar Wednesday, the discharge petition, and the twenty-one-day rule have also been provided to get matters on the floor after prolonged delays in the Rules Committee, but these have rarely been used.[1]

For many years after World War II, the committee sometimes appeared as the bane of existence of House members and a House leadership predisposed to liberal social legislation. In the Ninety-third Congress, however, political changes brought control of the committee back into harmony with the majority leadership and the Speaker. On the other hand, the liberalized committee began to encounter increasing difficulty on the floor with its actions on legislation.

A power comparable to that of the House Rules Committee is not exercised anywhere in the Senate. To some degree, the Majority Policy Committee has served as a clearing house for legislation on its way to consideration on the floor and occasionally minor or special interest bills have been held up at that checkpoint. It has been the contention of the Senate Leadership, however, that the Policy Committee does not block measures of major significance, duly reported from legislative committees.

Congress is an institution in which power and position are highly valued and seniority is the principal avenue to the achievement of both. Oddly enough, seniority has never been a formal rule governing designation of chairmen or even membership of committees. As a custom, however, its grip on the Congress has been a powerful one. This ritual practice in both houses may be in the process of change. The Democratic Steering Committee of the Senate, for example, has considered other factors in making assignments and has chosen candidates for committees by secret ballot whenever there is a conflict of requests for assignment. In the early 1970s, it became the practice in both houses to go through the procedure of designation of committee chairmen by party caucus and then by clear-cut election on the floor.

The innovation has served as a reminder to those holding power in committees that power is derived not from years of service but from the party structure in Congress and, in the end, from each House itself.

Seniority, of course, is likely to remain a spirit which pervades the behavior of members. This is especially the case in the House. Because of the size of the body, respect for seniority is a road to more rapid recognition. Older members appreciate the seeking of advice on the part of new members. This does not mean that a first termer is not listened to in committee or even on the floor if he is really master of his subject, has something to say, and is not merely seeking prominence. After one or two years, during which his colleagues have taken his measure, he may be entrusted with a subcommittee chairmanship dealing with some problem close to his heart or even with the chairmanship of a special committee. By these devices many of the admitted disadvantages connected with rigid adherence to seniority are overcome. An unprecedented event happened with the incoming Congress in 1975. The 75 new Democrats in the House met with the old committee chairmen who gave an account of their stewardship, before the majority were re-elected.

The practice of seniority is not confined to Congress. Church and educational hierarchies, labor unions, business, and all institutions have their experience with the phenomenon. Nevertheless, of all the criticisms of Congress from outside its own membership, that of the seniority rule is perhaps the most universal.[2] The term "senility rule" has even been used occasionally.

If one is an advocate of responsible and disciplined party government, the seniority rule can readily be seen as an obstacle. It is not so much that the committee chairmen frequently and sharply diverge from "party line" votes. Goodwin has shown that such divergence, while present, is certainly not as great as is usually supposed.[3] What is more significant is that the rule insures a rival network of power and leadership. At the same time, it tends to overlap a third center of leadership, that of the subject matter specialist.

A more serious charge is that seniority has overweighted the distribution of power in the direction of conservatism. This charge is not always made with full cognizance of the ideological fulcrum of the Congress as a whole. Whatever their personal outlook, chairmen tend to bend with the tides in Congress. In any event, failure to do so is an invitation to eventual ineffectuality, circumvention, and removal.

Health and age considerations have also been raised in connection with criticism of the seniority practice. These have been subject to remedy by adaptation, though in varying degree and not in every instance.[4] It should be borne in mind, however, that a constituency, by vote, can always retire a member of Congress for age, health, or any other reason, and often does so. This contrasts with the public's inability to control the age and health factor as it involves other Federal officials, for example, the justices of the courts.

If he will exercise it wisely, a chairman has great power. Chairmen usually call meetings apart from those which committees may schedule at regular intervals. They often name the staff and assign their duties. They have priority in questioning witnesses and usually assume floor leadership on reported bills. They are members of conference committees. They name the subcommittees and strongly influence the selection and priority of agendas. As presiding officers, they may rule as to quorums, points of order, and other matters. They have very considerable opportunity to penalize individual committee members if they wish to use it. In the House, they have usually been able, at least until recently, to resist the assignment or transfer of a member to their committees.

In the great majority of instances these powers are exercised with at least the tacit concurrence of, or after consultation with, the membership. Decisions are often submitted to vote. In such cases, no adaptation is necessary other than that which the chairman himself voluntarily exercises.

In most committees with heavy agendas, the subcommittee device is freely used, and this gives to a number of other members the chance to exercise substantial leadership. Furthermore, its role in mitigating the evils of the seniority rule is obvious.

Nevertheless, where the chairman is out of tune with the majority of his committee, or even the parent body, and is obdurate or autocratic in the use of his powers, he can constitute a very serious roadblock, for, as has been already mentioned, his powers are very great. Yet, a number of remedies are open. By law a majority of a committee can do almost anything within the function of the chairman, provided it can find a chance to vote on the issues. A revolt in the House Government Operations Committee in the Eighty-third Congress transferred most of the powers from its chairman to subcommittees. If the chairman—or the committee as a whole, for that matter —is out of harmony with the will of its parent body or its party leadership, other adaptations are available. A bill can be referred to a more friendly committee. A special committee can be set up and the standing committee bypassed. The discharge rule can be invoked. To cite an extreme case, the Civil Rights Act of 1957 bypassed altogether the Senate Judiciary Committee and after the bill had passed the House was considered directly on the floor of the Senate.

The Legislative Reorganization Act of 1970 [5] has served to bulwark the rights of individual members against arbitrary behavior by a committee chairman. Under that act, the procedures of both Houses are revised (1) to facilitate calling of special meetings of committees by a majority, (2) to require filing of approved committee reports within seven days, (3) to prohibit use of general proxies,[6] (4) to give members time to file minority or individual views on committee reports, and (5) to permit calling of witnesses by the committee minority.

Adaptations of these types have gone far toward mitigating the evils and disadvantages of the seniority rule. It is at this point that another approach is relevant. Evils there are and evils there always will be, but what are the alternatives? The more usual proposals call for selection of chairmen either by the party machinery or by vote of the committee. In either instance the ever-present struggle for power is intensified. Basically, members of Congress generally favor removing to the sphere of automatic operation a matter as controversial, as likely to produce personal animosities, as unpredictable in its results, as susceptible of clandestine or even sinister forces as the election of committee chairmen. Add to these negative arguments against drastic alternatives the affirmative consideration of guaranteed long experience under seniority and there is every indication that Congress would far rather approach the problem by adaptations than by drastic change.

A type of alternative which has been proposed that would bypass these dangers and at the same time might mitigate some of the evils of the seniority system would appear to be to limit the term of the chairman to eight or ten years. At the expiration of this period he would be succeeded by the second in length of service. Still another approach suggests rotating chairmanships within and amongst committees. Such proposals have never really been taken seriously outside of academic circles. In Congress, they are generally passed off as impractical or self-defeating in their dismissal of experience and even as somewhat demeaning.

Centers of power are necessary in any body that would accomplish things, and the desideratum is that this power be responsibly exercised. When it becomes too concentrated or too arbitrary, as in the case of Speaker Joseph G. Cannon in 1910, there is revolt; but new centers necessarily arise. As of today, power is fairly well diffused, though the Speaker of the House and the Majority Leader of the Senate, partly in their own right and partly because of their close relations, inevitably, with the President, are among the most powerful single members. They, as well as the minority Leaders, are butteressed by fairly effective party whip organization.[7]

Party policy committees have also been developing as centers of power, for a quarter of a century in the Senate and of late in the House. Until recently, however, the House Democrats had been reluctant to crystallize too much formal party activity, caucus or otherwise, so as not to exacerbate the North–South cleavage. With the decline of the significance of that cleavage a more formidable party structure is beginning to emerge.

It can be seen in the increased influence of the party caucus and in the change in the manner of reaching preliminary decisions on Democratic committee assignments. Formerly, this authority was vested solely in the Democratic members of the House Ways and Means Committee. In the Ninety-third Congress, the selecting group was enlarged to include the Speaker, the Majority Leader and the Chairman of the Democratic Caucus. The Ninety-fourth Congress witnessed still another change with the power to make Committee assignments being vested in the new Steering and Policy Committee of the Caucus.

Within his own bailiwick, a House committee chairman ordinarily has had his way in blocking legislation, and often in promoting it as well. Senate chairmen are not in quite the same situation. Not only are they subject to leadership exhortation and other forms of party persuasion but the rules of the Senate readily permit challenges to arbitrariness by subject specialists directly on the Senate floor.*

---

* I.e., Committee blocked legislation can be introduced as a nongermane amendment to any bill.

The House Rules Committee obviously remains a powerful force. It may refuse to report out a bill unless discharged by a petition signed by a majority of the House or unless the bill is called under a special procedure on "Calendar Wednesday," if luck of location favors the bill. The committee may grant any one of several types of rule, certain of which are favorable and others unfavorable to the prospects of a given measure. It can make a favorable rule conditional upon an amendment which it favors. A rule as used here, by the way, for those who are not familiar with the term, is the regulation stipulating the kind, the control, and the extent of floor debate on a given measure.[8] The rule under which a bill is reported may be influential in or even determinative of the subsequent action. Thus a rule forbidding floor amendment, especially in tax bills, can be a means of preventing raids by special interests or safeguarding tax benefits for special groups written into the bill by the committee.[9]

These rules are near the heart of the way the House organizes the final stages in the legislative consideration of a given measure. The Senate, incidentally, is much less formal or rigid. Its principal traffic manager, as noted, is not the Committee on Rules and Administration but its majority leadership and the Policy Committee.

One of the traditional functions attributed to Congress is the illumination of issues with the consequent education of the public. It is doubtful whether this objective has figured very much in any conscious fashion in the evolution of congressional organization and procedure. Nevertheless, the accord given to the right of the minority to be heard, expressed in such a fashion as the usual equal division of time in floor debate in the House and the almost unlimited facilities for discussion in the Senate; the value put upon dramatization in hearings, through the custom of securing "headliners" as witnesses; the emphasis on open hearings written into the Reorganization Act of 1946 and reinforced thereafter, notably in the Reorganization Act of 1970—all these are evidence that a consciousness of the values inherent in education of the electorate has not been without its influence.

Many years ago, proposals for a good organization and procedure were set forth in an earlier book of one of the authors. [10] They included the following principles:

(1) Time for reflection.

(2) Time and opportunity for public reaction.

(3) Full public debate to be confined to essentials.

(4) Proportionate consideration, as between measures, and as between clauses within a specific measure.

(5) Respect for opposition and minorities.

(6) Opportunities for detailed amendment.

(7) Facility. Delays other than those contemplated under (1) and (2) must not be allowed in this day and age.

(8) Clarity of ultimate phraseology.

(9) No "riders" or irrelevancies.

(10) All private or special legislation should be relegated to subordinate legislation in one of the departments.

(11) Regular opportunity for questioning administrators.

(12) Supervision of subordinate legislation, providing where appropriate for delegated legislation to "lie on the table" for a stated period.

(13) Use of *ad hoc* commissions.

To a greater or lesser extent the various reforms which were set forth in the two legislative reorganization acts and the changes adopted in procedures and practices of both Houses are classifiable under these thirteen principles.

Political parties are the basis for the organization of Congress but they play a less important role in the substantive work of Congress. From an organizational standpoint, they determine the organization of the two Houses, including membership of the committees, notably the number of positions allocated to the majority and minority respectively. In determining committee slates, their influence is limited by the seniority convention and the tradition that a member once on a committee remains there, if he so wills. Modifications of this convention and tradition necessarily take place when a majority party becomes the minority and occasionally under other circumstances when deemed appropriate. Rarely is removal from a committee an instrument of party discipline, though transfer to a more desirable committee may be a party reward.

Committee assignments are made by caucus committees chosen by the party leadership and the party caucus.[11] Assistance to a member in his reelection, geography, suitability, endorsements, his own desires are all factors.[12] Among the Senate Democrats the custom is long established of designating each new member to at least one major committee of his preference.

It has been said that "The power of the President has been institutionalized; the powers of the congressional committees and their chairmen have been institutionalized; but the power of the central leaders of Congress remains personal, *ad hoc*, and transitory." [13] Notwithstanding tendencies to strengthen party leadership, the observation remains accurate.

Organization and procedure are woven into a seamless fabric through all the aspects of congressional activity. Some aspects are sharply criticized; others are highly praised. Neither praise nor blame is attempted here. Where organization is defective, adaptation and custom frequently come to the rescue. The use of the special committee and subcommittee to mitigate the handicaps of the seniority rule has already been mentioned. So with many another device. Things are not always what they seem. Nor are smoothness and speed of operation by any means the highest rung on the hierarchical ladder of values. Given things as they are—the nature of the electorate, the size of Congress, the complexity, number, and magnitude of the issues—Congressional organization and procedure do not come off badly, especially when it is borne in mind that failure to act may in some instances be a deliberately chosen wiser course, with procedural devices the instrument for making such failure to act practicable.

NOTES

1. "Calendar Wednesday" is a rarely used provision of the House Rules which permits the various committees to call up for floor consideration any bills or resolutions which would otherwise not be privileged. The last invocation of this rule occurred in 1962. Under the "Discharge Rule," the signatures of 218 members can act to discharge the Rules Committee and bring legislation directly to the floor and make it the pending business until resolved. In the Eighty-first Congress, the "twenty-one-day Rule" authorized the call-up of any public bill from the floor on the second or fourth Monday of each month, which had been blocked in the Rules Committee for twenty-one days. The rule was abolished two years later. An authoritative general treatment of the Rules Committee is to be found in James A. Robinson, *The House Rules Committee* (New York: Bobbs-Merrill, 1963).

2. For an extended discussion of seniority as it appears to members themselves, see Charles L. Clapp. *The Congressman: His Work as He Sees It* (Washington: Brookings Institution, 1963), pp. 221-34.

3. See George Goodwin, Jr., "The Seniority System in Congress," *American Political Science Review* (June 1959), pp. 412-436, for this, and many other interesting facts concerning the rule.

4. Such adaptation was forthcoming in the House Foreign Affairs Committee when health factors stood in the way of full activity on the part of Representatives Eaton and Chiperfield, its two Republican Chairmen in the last two decades. Both of them delegated major responsibility to colleagues junior to themselves. Senator Green voluntarily relinquished the chairmanship of the Senate Foreign Relations Committee when he was over ninety.

   During Senator McKellar's old age, Senator Hayden took over the burden of the work of the Senate Appropriations Committee. In turn, as his own stamina grew less, he divided the powers of the Committee generously among subcommittee chairmen.

5. 84 Stat. 1140.

6. Under a general proxy, a committee member, not in attendance, permits the chairman or some other designee to exercise his vote, not merely on a specific issue but on any issue coming before the committee.

7. See Randall B. Ripley, "The Party Whip Organizations in the United States House of Representatives," *American Political Science Review* (September 1964), pp. 561-76.

8. See J. A. Robinson, "The Role of the Rules Committee in Arranging the Program of the United States House of Representatives," *Western Political Quarterly,* (September 1959), pp. 653-69. Robinson's *The House Rules Committee* (Indianapolis: Bobbs-Merrill, 1963) is the standard work on the subject.

9. For an excellent study of the Rules Committee's views of its role and other aspects, see Robert L. Peabody, "The Enlarged Rules Committee" in Robert L. Peabody and Nelson W. Polsby, eds., *New Perspectives on the House of Representatives* (Chicago: Rand-McNally, 1963), chap. 6.

10. Ernest S. Griffith, *The Impasse of Democracy* (New York: Harrison Hilton Books, 1939) pp. 144 ff.

11. The Selecting Committees are as follows:
Senate Democrats—Steering Committee
Senate Republicans—Committee on Committees
House Democrats—Democratic Steering and Policy Committee.
House Republicans—Committee on Committees

12. Samuel P. Huntington, "Congressional Response to the Twentieth Century," in David B. Truman, *The Congress and America's Future* (Englewood Cliffs: Prentice-Hall, 1965), p. 22.

13. For a concrete study of the process in the House, since modified, see Nicholas A. Masters, "Committee Assignments," *American Political Science Review* (June 1961), pp. 345-57.

CHAPTER 4

Executive–Legislative Relations: The Weapons in the Struggle

Far more attention has been paid to the clashes, rivalries, and differences between the Executive Branch in general, and the President in particular, on the one hand and Congress on the other, than to their cooperation. We must grant that it is sociologically inherent that two coordinate centers of power operating in a common area will be jealous of each other and will each strive to gain the ascendancy. But it is also psychologically true that there will be accommodation when the shared end is great enough to command a common loyalty or urgent enough to force a solution. If the persons involved are public-spirited, naturally friendly, and broad-gauged—and more often than not the President, the department heads, and the congressmen are all three—the government becomes workable. Their mutually independent positions also have this advantage, that each usually is required to convince the other—always a humbling and wholesome experience—before effective action can be taken.

A closer awareness of the inner workings of our government would differentiate between the presidency and the bureaucracy. The former faces some of the same problems faced by Congress in controlling the latter. This is especially true insofar as both look toward economies. It is also true, though in a lesser degree, in matters of policy. So vast is our government and so readily may a bureau whirl in its own orbit that the White House finds much the same need for watchfulness and coordination over a bureau's activity that is felt by the concerned committee of Congress. When a bureau also has its protectors and advocates within Congress, the latter rather than the President may find itself calling the tune. Under such circumstances the difficulties may multiply for both.

In matters of policy insofar as it is distinct from administration the struggle is chiefly between Congress and the presidency. In this struggle each branch has a number of weapons. Of the President's formal constitutional powers, Corwin and others have written ably and at length. The veto power and the power of appointment (with the derivative lever of patronage) are the most obvious. Only under exceptional circumstances is the veto overridden. Two-thirds votes are hard to come by in issues controversial enough to have been subjected to veto in the first place. Moreover, members have been known to vote for a particular measure for political reasons, knowing that it would be vetoed.

The use of patronage as a lever to obtain compliance has been somewhat exaggerated. In extremely close situations on measures important to the administration, patronage may turn the trick. On the other hand, patronage can also operate in reverse. A large number of appointees even within the classified service go through the form of presenting a letter of congressional endorsement. Such letters do not ordinarily constitute patronage, for rare is the constituent whose hostility to the congressman has been so cogently expressed that he will be denied such a letter if he requests it. Genuine pressure exercised by a member in behalf of someone especially favored is another thing and results in the type of appointment for which some *quid pro quo* is often expected by the agency—even if it is no more than a measure of good will on the part of the member. This may be expressed when legislation or an appropriation of interest to the department making the appointment is up for consideration.

It should be borne in mind that patronage is as often geographic as it is personal in the sense that there is considerable discretion in the military, the environmental agencies, the post office, and elsewhere in the location of new construction. If not too blatant, this can occasionally be effective in securing support for or opposition to certain measures regarded as important by the Executive Branch. It takes the form of subtle threats of withdrawal as well as implied promises of benefits to a given state or district. Logrolling and the pork barrel exist also in the executive, but their actual extent in both branches is likely to be overestimated.

Occasionally the President diverts, or leaves unused, funds appropriated for some specific purpose of which he does not approve. This practice, known as impoundment, invariably leaves Congress with a sense of impotence or frustration; although, if economy has been promoted thereby, the objection may be somewhat muted. The weapon of impoundment had been used sparingly for many years without much more than grumblings of irritation from Congress. However, when President Nixon, after his landslide victory in 1972, made clear his intention to "impound" virtually at random, the reaction in Congress was immediate and vehement. Members of Congress even joined state officials in court tests of the constitutionality of the President's position. At the same time efforts were made in Congress to delineate by law a procedure to curb the President's insistence on his unilateral right to impound. These efforts crystallized in the Congressional Budget and Impoundment Control Act of 1974 whereby one or the other House was given the power of a reverse veto over any executive impoundment.

Somewhat akin to impoundment is the selective enforcement of laws or selective carrying out of programs when Congress fails to appropriate the amount that the executive has proposed as adequate for the total activity of an agency. If the cut has been drastic, it is often suspected in Congress that the agency then selects for curtailment those items likely to result in the greatest public outcry and, hence, the greatest tactic is the addition by the department of a "sweetener," that is, some popular program to unpopular legislation in an effort to gain overall approval.

There is another type of weapon against which Congress can do but little. This is the fait accompli, most evident in the President's power as commander-in-chief of the armed services, but not unknown in his other functions. It is a dangerous weapon and can rebound badly if not used sparingly and when it is reasonably clear that there will be ultimate vindication in the results of the action.

The technique of the fait accompli as used in the conflict in Indochina in the end progressively brought about a direct confrontation between the two branches. Eventually, it led to the enactment, over the President's veto, of the War Powers Resolution which seeks to assure a congressional role in the basic decisions of war and peace by defining the limits of the President's power to act unilaterally in employing the armed forces of the United States.*

The President has not been conspicuously successful in singling out individual congressmen for attack. Within his own party, even Franklin Roosevelt could not claim real victory in his attempted "purges." Truman seldom attempted such a purge in Congress, not even with its "Dixiecrat" members.** Eisenhower indicated his disapproval of members not by overt attack but by lukewarmness of support. The Congressional dislikes of both Johnson and Nixon found their way into the press, but neither President engaged in prolonged public feuds with any member. When the President attacks a member of the opposite party by name, the public enjoys it, as it enjoys any good scrap, but probably this does not greatly affect the future of the particular member. It may even build

---

* Cf chapter twelve for the full treatment of this resolution.

** An exception was his successful effort to oust Representative Slaughter of Missouri, but this was in Truman's own home district.

him up to a prominence he would not otherwise have enjoyed.

The prestige of the President and his office is enormous. Even members of the opposition party cannot help being influenced somewhat by these factors, if and when they are called into council at the White House. President Johnson brought the techniques of direct and personal persuasion to an all-time high, a practice which in the end provoked hostility on the part of various members who felt that an attempt was being made to "sell them a bill of goods" notably on the use of the armed forces in the Dominican Republic and in Vietnam.

The President can command the headlines at any time. Franklin Roosevelt devoted more time and attention to the press than to Congress and he was not alone in this respect. If a President has a message for the people and a capacity to deliver it, a radio-TV audience is assured. The televised press conferences of Eisenhower and, even more, Kennedy were very effective. Under a skilled President, the use of the media in the marshaling of public opinion in his support against a recalcitrant Congress is almost irresistible. But there are limits. A President may find his efforts ineffective or counter-productive if he appeals on issues in which the public is not very much interested, or if the public fundamentally differs, as on Truman's call for repeal of the Taft-Hartley Act, or if the public is sharply divided as with President Johnson's efforts to justify the course of military–diplomatic action which he pursued in Vietnam. Fundamental to the effective use of public opinion by the President against Congress is the degree of confidence or "credibility" which he enjoys at any given moment. In the absence of a substantial level of popular support, whatever his skills as a propagandist they are likely to prove unavailing.

Finally, it should be noted that the Executive Branch has had until relatively recently a preponderance of access to facts, both because of bureaucracy's continuity of experience in dealing with problems and because of its extensive expert research facilities. Thus, Congress had great difficulty in formulating an intelligent alternative policy on many issues. It was this superior command of information more than any other one factor that for many years gave the executive-legislative struggle the appearance of a losing battle for the latter. "It [Congress] can violently disturb, but it cannot often fathom, the waters of the sea in which the bigger fish of the civil service swim and feed." So wrote Woodrow Wilson in his *Congressional Government.*[1]

But Congress likewise is not without formidable weapons in the struggle. Chief among these are the appropriating and investigating powers. Appropriations are not merely concerned with economy in management. They are used in important fashions to indicate likes and dislikes of persons and policies in particular agencies and activities. Congress can increase an appropriation beyond the figures requested in an effort to bring about a reformulation of priorities. Perhaps, more often it is in the reductions that the significant policy guidance is given. In the Ninety-third Congress both edges of the weapon were in use. On the one hand Congress upped the availability of funds for social and environmental purposes. At the same time, appropriations for military and foreign policy purposes were decreased. In this fashion, a growing public concern with the domestic state of the nation was signalled through Congress to the Executive Branch.

The weapon of Congressional investigation may be used either by a standing committee (or subcommittee) or by a special committee created for a particular purpose. In any event, it is a matter of great concern when its focus of attention is directed toward the Executive Branch. The fear of an investigation influences, if it does not dominate, bureau practice. Even a question asked by a single member in a speech on the floor can be enough to change or head off certain administrative decisions. Many investigations are actually the expanded questionings of a single member. The practice of naming as chairman of a special investigating committee the member who first urged it (provided he is of the majority party) is a standing invitation to the alert to make such proposals.

Investigations of the Executive Branch are only a minority of the total number of Congressional inquiries. The largest single group consists of inquiries into problems, the outcome of which may be to give form to legislation. A heroic effort was made under the Reorganization Act of 1946 (Public Law 601, Seventy-ninth Congress) to regularize or systematize Congressional investigations. It was formally provided in the act that a watchful oversight of the appropriate agency or agencies was to be one of the major functions of the various standing committees. By this means it was hoped that a principal reason for the rash of special committees would be removed. To a considerable extent this hope has been realized. In the second session of the Eighty-first Congress, for example, out of the sixteen special investigations authorized, only five were entrusted to special committees. In the second session of the Eighty-third Congress, the number had risen to thirty-nine, but only six were by special or select committees. The remainder of the investigations were handled by the standing committees. In the second session of the Eighty-sixth Congress, there were nine such special investigating committees, but two of these were quite minor. In the first session of the Eighty-ninth Congress the number of special committees sank to two—on the Aging and on the Reorganization of Congress. The Senate and House continued their Select Committees on Small Business, however, and the former added a permanent Select Committee on Standards and Conduct.

Some tendencies to expansion had reappeared by the Ninety-third Congress. Still, the number of significant special or select committees operative at any one time did not exceed ten, and the total included what had become more or less permanent committees, on Small Business, Aging, and Standards and Conduct.

Investigations, whether by special or standing committees,

range all the way from the frankly punitive to those specifically designed to advance the interests of a particular department. Where the agency investigated is sure of its ground, it naturally does what it can to convert the investigation into a forum for its vindication or to gain support and understanding. Where the chairman and committee are hostile or irresponsible, the hearings may become a battle of wits, with the executive even refusing relevant papers or records. Conflict between the branches reached unprecedented peaks during the McCarthy loyalty investigations of the Truman–Eisenhower administrations and in the inquiries in the Watergate affair and related matters of the Nixon administration. In the latter case, Congress even went so far as to enact special legislation, and the committees went to the courts to obtain documentation from the Executive Branch.

The President's resistance to Congress was based on contentions of executive privilege as it involved the preservation of the "stature" of the presidency, or National Security, notably where the Central Intelligence Agency was involved. In earlier confrontations of a similar nature as, for example, during the loyalty inquiries of the 1950s, previously mentioned, the Executive Branch laid stress on the confidentiality of many of its papers, especially personnel records. In addition, where the Federal Bureau of Investigation was involved, an additional reason for secrecy was advanced. It was alleged that disclosure of the papers would imperil the methods by which the FBI obtained much of its information. Congress refused to accept the rationale advanced by the Executive Branch either in the Watergate affair or in the loyalty inquiries. It sought with varying success for ways and means to breach the wall of secrecy.

In general, contests of power between the two branches, arising out of investigations, have not been fought in the courts. In *McGrain v. Daugherty* in 1927,[2] involving the Teapot Dome Scandal and the Congressional investigation of Attorney General Daugherty and his office, the Supreme Court made the nearest approach to a flat recognition of the fitness and propriety of the investigative process in relation to the supervisory power of Congress over executive administration. The Court, however, went only so far as to declare the investigation of the attorney general necessary and proper on the ground that the information requested was needed for the efficient exercise of the legislative function. The Court said:

> We are of opinion that the power of inquiry—with process to enforce it—is an essential and appropriate auxiliary to the legislative function. It was so regarded and employed in American legislatures before the Constitution was framed and ratified. Both houses of Congress took this view of it early in their history—the House of Representatives with the approving votes of Mr. Madison and other members whose service in the convention which framed the Constitution gives special significance to their action—and both houses have employed the power accordingly up to the present time. The acts of 1798 and 1857, judged by the comprehensive terms, were intended to recognize the existence of this power in both houses and to enable them to employ it "more effectually" than before. So, when their practice in the matter is appraised according to the circumstances in which it was begun and to those in which it has been continued, it falls nothing short of a practical construction, long continued, of the constitutional provisions respecting their powers, and therefore should be taken as fixing the meaning of those provisions, if otherwise doubtful.
>
> We are further of opinion that the provisions are not of doubtful meaning, but, as was held by this Court in the cases we have reviewed, are intended to be effectively exercised, and therefore to carry with them such auxiliary powers as are necessary and appropriate to that end. While the power to exact information in aid of the legislative function was not involved in those cases, the rule of interpretation applied there is applicable here. A legislative body cannot legislate

CANISIUS COLLEGE LIBRARY
BUFFALO, N. Y.

wisely or effectively in the absence of information respecting the conditions which the legislation is intended to affect or change; and where the legislative body does not itself possess the requisite information—which not infrequently is true— recourse must be had to others who do possess it. Experience has taught that mere requests for such information often are unavailing, and also that information which is volunteered is not always accurate or complete; so some means of compulsion are essential to obtain what is needed. All this was true before and when the Constitution was framed and adopted. In that period the power of inquiry—with enforcing process —was regarded and employed as a necessary and appropriate attribute of the power to legislate—indeed, was treated as inhering in it. Thus there is ample warrant for thinking, as we do, that the constitutional provisions which commit the legislative function to the two houses are intended to include this attribute to the end that the function may be effectively exercised.[3]

Since that historic decision, the courts have made additional delineations of the congressional investigatory power. An authoritative summarization by Frank B. Horne of the Legislative Reference Service (now the Congressional Research Service) of the Library of Congress notes the following:

(a) That the scope of a congressional investigation is as broad as the legislative purpose requires.

(b) That the subpoena of a duly authorized investigatory committee of Congress is no more restricted that that of a grand jury.

(c) That the right of a legislative body to demand and receive, from the Executive Branch, information and papers which it deems pertinent to the legislative process is established.

(d) That this established right has been vigorously asserted at times by the Congress of the United States against the President and executive officers.

(e) That the President and the executive officers have vigorously opposed such asserted right on the basis of the fundamental doctrine of separation of powers of the executive, legislative, and judicial branches of the Federal Government.

(f) That the Congress has merely asserted its right to obtain information without attempting to enforce it.

(g) That the Congress has never attempted to invoke against executive officers the law which provides that every person who, having been summoned by either House to give testimony or to produce papers upon a matter under inquiry, willfully makes default, is criminally liable.[4]

All of these factors were present in the stark confrontation between President Nixon and the Senate Committee on the Watergate affair and between the President and the House Judiciary Committee when considering his impeachment. In the first case, the Senate group under Chairman Sam Ervin sought at one and the same time to negotiate with the White House the transfer of presidential documentation in the form of recording tapes while at the same time asserting in the courts the constitutional right of the Senate to demand this documentation. In the second case, the courts made available to the committee information obtained in grand jury proceedings which the President had sought to deny it.

Having dealt at length with the constitutional problems presented by executive refusals, it should be added that such refusals are the exception. In general, the executive complies with requests for data or responses to questions. In any event, Congress has numerous indirect sanctions with which to punish a noncooperative administrative agency or department.

That congressional investigations, if constructively handled, can be enormously useful has no stronger witnesses than the Teapot Dome story after World War I and the Truman War Investigating Committee in World War II. Here were examples of how the very independence of Congress prevented any whitewashing of financial scandals and permitted a genuine watchdog function. In the same fashion, the Watergate investigation probed deeply and relentlessly into the darker recesses of our electoral processes and set the stage for changes in campaign practices. Significantly, this investigation was devoid of partisan bickering. In general, the congressional investigation, in addition to other roles, performs the function of the question hour in the British House of Commons, and performs it considerably better.

The occasion of confirmation of presidential appointments is often used by Congress to indicate attitudes and even to obtain implied commitments. Thus, Attorney General Elliot Richardson gave as one of his reasons for resigning from the Nixon cabinet his inability to carry out a pledge to the Judiciary Committee at the time of confirmation, to protect the independence of the Special Prosecutor in the Watergate affair. Congressional fears of radicalism, executive usurpation, special interests, and dislikes of particular aspects of foreign or other policies are frequently voiced at the time a name is up for consideration; these attitudes are not without their effect, even if the nominee is in fact confirmed.

"Senatorial courtesy," the practice by which appointees are "cleared" in advance by the President is a special case—resulting for practical purposes in appointments by the senators (or occasionally by majority members of the House*, of officials whose duties are within the bounds of a single state. It may be regarded as something of an offset against the President's use of patronage to obtain his will. Such "courtesy" is influential but not usually decisive in appointments to positions of national scope.

There is a type of congressional influence which is not well understood by the public and which is difficult to ferret out in all its ramifications. This is found in the informal but direct relationships set up between certain members or committees and particular bureaus or persons in the executive. The ties

* Cf. chapter 5 for other aspects.

are various. Sometimes the bureau chief involved is one originally recommended by a member of Congress. Sometimes assiduous cultivation of a particular committee or friendship arising out of common interests is responsible. Perhaps the bureau itself was originally the creation of a particular committee and was designed to carry out the economic or other interest represented by the members. Frequently these "sub-systems" are found at the sub-committee level. "Government by whirlpools" characterizes much of the Washington scene.

One cannot live in Washington for long without being conscious that it has these whirlpools or centers of activity focusing on particular problems. The persons who are thus active—in agriculture, in energy, in labor, in foreign trade, and the parts thereof—are variously composed. Some are civil servants, some are active members of the appropriate committees in the House and Senate, some are lobbyists, some are unofficial research authorities, connected perhaps with the Brookings Institution or with one of the universities, or even entirely private individuals. Perhaps special correspondents of newspapers are included. These people in their various permutations and combinations are continually ..meeting in each other's offices, at various clubs, lunching together, and participating in legislative hearings or serving on important but obscure committees set up within the departments. Among such human beings interested in a common problem, ideas are bound to emerge —ideas for programs, ideas for strategy. . . .

. . . There is nothing really mysterious about this sort of government. It is essentially "of men" and these men behave very naturally. "Who says what to whom, and what is the reaction?" This question, if we could obtain enough answers, would capture the spirit, the genius of our own or any government. It is our opinion that ordinarily the relationship among these men—legislators, administrators, lobbyists, scholars—who are interested in a common problem can be a much more real relationship than the relationship between congressmen generally or between administrators generally. In other words, he who would understand the prevailing pattern of our present governmental behavior, instead of studying the formal institutions or even generalizations in the relationships between these institutions or organs, important though all these are, may possibly obtain a better picture of the way things really happen if he would study these "whirlpools" of special social interest and problems.[5]

It is this type of congressional–bureaucratic relationship that underlies the reluctance of Congress, at times, to give department heads effective control over their bureau chiefs. The first Hoover Commission pointed to this situation as handicapping effective control by the President over much of the administration. Moreover, the independent commissions with terms of office overlapping presidential elections were created in this fashion originally so as to be not entirely beholden to presidential favor. The Watergate investigation in its revelation of the manipulation of the bureaucracy for political purposes underscored the wisdom of even these limited congressional checks on arbitrary administrative power in the White House.

Illustrative of the fashion in which bureaus with congressional connections can circumvent or even defy presidential intent is the position of the Engineer Corps of the Department of the Army. The Engineer Corps and its twin or rival, the Bureau of Reclamation, are the great construction agencies of the Federal Government. The secret of the power of these agencies lies in the value to a district or state of the construction and subsequent operation of such water resources projects. The power of both of these agencies is probably exceeded by that of the Federal Highway Administration. This latter has an immense largesse at its disposal. Together with the state highway agencies it subsidizes, the contractors who perform the construction, and the automobile industry and drivers who use the end product, it constitutes a whirlpool of tremendous power.

In other words, insofar as there is a struggle between Congress and the President, it is an oversimplification to say that the latter can count on all the agencies and bureaus siding with him, even though he may have appointed the chief or the majority of the commissioners. Many an agency has its way of bypassing the chief executive and working with those in Congress whose interests parallel its own. In fact, a strong case can be made out that we actually have "four-way" government instead of the classic tripartite. Congress, the presidency, the bureacracy, and the judiciary are the four. A full understanding would require close examination of the relationship of each of these with the others.[6]

The power of impeachment is normally among the weapons of Congress—it has been invoked only twice against officers of the Executive Branch—once against the President, and once against the secretary of war. Both instances resulted in acquittals. Again, in the wake of the Senate and court revelations regarding Watergate, the pressures for impeachment of President Nixon rose to precipitous levels. In early 1974, the House Judiciary Committee was directed to consider the question. A protracted struggle developed almost at once between the President and the committee over the constitutional dimensions of this power of the House of Representatives. Such questions were raised as to what constituted an impeachable offense and the extent of the right of the President to withhold subpoenaed documentation from the committee under his obligation to "protect the Presidency." The questions were widely discussed but had not been resolved when the resignation of President Nixon rendered them moot.

Among the weapons which Congress commands in its struggle with the Executive Branch is the General Accounting Office. The Legislative Reorganization Act of 1946 places an affirmative responsibility on the agency (Section 206) as follows:

The Comptroller General is authorized and directed to make an expenditure analysis of each agency in the Executive Branch of the Government (including Government corporations) which, in the opinion of the Comptroller General, will enable Congress to determine whether public funds have been economically and efficiently administered and expended. Reports on such analyses shall be submitted by the Comptroller General, from time to time, to the Committees on Expenditures (i.e., Government Operations), to the Appropriations Committee, and to the legislative committees having jurisdiction over legislation relating to the operations of the respective agencies, of the two Houses.[7]

The Legislative Reorganization Act of 1970 added to the expanding powers of the Comptroller General, authorizing him on his own initiative or on Congressional request, to make cost-benefiit studies of government programs and activities. Pursuant to the two reorganization acts, Congress has called increasingly on the General Accounting Office to go beyond routine fiscal audits into deep probes of bureaucratic programs and management practices. The agency also supplies special staff support to committees for a multiplicity of studies and investigations. In this connection its operations sometimes parallel those of the Congressional Research Service of the Library of Congress.

By its ready response to Congressional needs, the General Accounting Office has earned the title of "Watchdog of Congress." [8]
The intimacy between the two bodies is substantial and growing. While there has been some criticism of this development,[9] the fact is that a great need existed for professional and technical competence to support the Congress effectively and the General Accounting Office has been willing and able to supply it.

Through the use of its investigatory powers, Congress is

discovering, of late, that many of its handicaps in the struggle with the Executive Branch are of its own making. Over the years, there have been vast delegations of authority to the Executive Branch, notably under the pressure of "national emergencies." The emergencies disappear in time but the delegations remain on the statute books, to be used subsequently by the Executive Branch at times of its own choosing. Over the past forty years these delegations have acted, in the words of the Senate Special Committee on the Termination of the National Emergency, to equip the President without further leave of the Congress to "seize property; organize and control the means of production, seize commodities; assign military forces abroad, institute martial law; seize and control all transportation and communication; regulate the operation of private enterprise; restrict travel; and, in a plethora of particular ways, control the lives of all American citizens. . . . For forty years freedom and governmental procedures guaranteed by the Constitution have, in various degrees, been abridged by laws brought into force by states of national emergency."[9]

Increasingly Congress is writing statutory time limits in legislation which delegates power to the Executive Branch. This acts to circumvent a possible presidential veto of future efforts to recapture a delegated power. It also inhibits the accumulation of a pool of delegated powers by the Executive Branch. It may well be that an amendment of the Constitution is emerging by which any withdrawal of powers granted the President shall not be subjected to veto, if Congress so decides.

Akin to this development is the extension of the use of concurrent resolutions, a type of legislative action which is not subject to presidential veto. Provisions are made in the original statute for subsequent amendment by concurrent resolution. It is worthy of note that in some regular legislation it is provided that powers granted may be terminated in this fashion.

A few statutes provide that certain administrative actions are to be subject to review by a congressional committee. Certain real estate transactions of the armed services, for example, have been so restricted. In 1965 President Johnson vetoed a bill on the grounds of dubious constitutionality which would have required the approval of the Armed Service Committee for the closing of military bases. The Omnibus Rivers and Harbors Act of 1965 in authorizing smaller water resource projects (costing under $10,000,000) required the specific approval of the Public Works Committees of both Houses prior to spending on a specific project. The President, claiming that this was a derogation of his authority, announced his intention of non-use and to seek repeal. The appropriations bill for the Department of Defense for fiscal year 1956 contained a proviso requiring approval of the committee chairmen prior to the department's divesting itself of a business activity by turning it over to a private concern. President Eisenhower, through the attorney general, challenged the constitutionality of this and indicated his intention of ignoring it. In all these and similar instances, Congress is in search of a flexible device under which detailed administrative acts may be subject to review without having to be made the subject of special legislation.

Occasionally, Congress or one House of Congress, passes a "sense" resolution which, in effect, gives vent to attitudes on a given subject. These are often signals flashed to the Executive Branch, especially in international policy, which show the mood of Congress. Such resolutions are not binding on the executive, but they can be warnings of gathering storms or encouragements, as the case may be. The power to speak out in this fashion is still capable of considerable development, notably with regard to foreign policy. This will be discussed further when we consider the role of Congress in international affairs.*

Finally, one should note the acquisition by Congress of a fairly substantial permanent professional staff. As noted, the General Accounting Office has been greatly expanded. So, too, has the Congressional Research Service. In addition, a new

* Cf. chapter 12.

Office of Technology Assessment and the Joint Staff of the Joint Study Committee on Budget Control have been established. The professional staffs available to members in their offices or on committees have also grown in size. No longer is it so difficult for Congress itself to analyze the proposals of the Executive—and, if it sees fit, to formulate alternative policies.**

Thus are checks and balances and the means to bring them into play evolving in practice, revealing ramifications often unforeseen and striving to assure that irresponsible power will not be exercised under the Constitution. Certainly, the use of these weapons is often complicated. For example, it is always dangerous, though not necessarily harmful, for a bureau to have two masters. Yet, there are compensations, and usages have arisen whereby cooperation may modify conflict. To these we next turn.

NOTES

1. Woodrow Wilson, *Congressional Government* (Boston: Houghton Mifflin, 1885), p. 27.
2. 273 U.S. 135.
3. Quoted from a manuscript entitled "Subpoenaing Files from an Executive Department," prepared by Frank B. Horne, Legislative Reference Service, Library of Congress, May 26, 1949.
4. Senate Document 99, 83d Congress, second session, Congressional Power of Investigation, p. 21. The document develops the points in some detail.
5. Griffith, *The Impasse of Democracy*, p. 182.
6. In this connection, see Richard E. Neustadt, "Politicians and Bureaucrats," in David B. Truman, ed., *The Congress and America's Future* (Englewood Cliffs: Prentice-Hall, 1965), pp. 102-20; Peter Woll, *American Bureaucracy* (New York: Norton, 1963).

**Cf. chapter 6 for an extended discussion of congressional staff services.

7. Congressional Quarterly Service. *Guide to the Congress of the United States* . . . , Washington, D. C. p. 441.

8. See reference to Eliot Stanley, "The General Accounting Office, One-Eyed Watchdog," ibid., p. 445.

9. Quoted by Ronald Goldfarb in "The Permanent State of Emergency," *Washington Post,* Jan. 6, 1974. p. B4.

CHAPTER 5

Cooperation in Executive–Legislative Relations

Separation of powers largely precludes the type of semi-enforced cooperation which parliaments such as the British enjoy, thanks to the sanction of dissolution in the hands of the prime minister and the power of the party to deny candidacy to a recalcitrant member. There are sanctions or weapons in the hands of both the President and Congress available for the one over against the other, as we have already seen. Yet, each branch preserves substantial zones of independence. Thus there must be a voluntary element in working together which arises out of inner convictions—such as a common loyalty to nation and party and a common desire to support those measures which will result in re-election or a common belief in the soundness of specific means and ends. The President and his party mates in Congress do share a common electoral interest, but this is less than would be supposed—in part because they have different constituencies and in part because of the value the voters place on independence whether of a President or a Congressman. During the twentieth century we as a people have come to have a comparatively weak sense of party loyalty or solidarity. In practice our national parties are loose federations of local organizations, and neither cohesive nor integrated. Least of all would they think of or be able to wield all-powerful sanctions. Moreover, supraparty considerations, especially a common loyalty to the national interest, are frequently more powerful factors than party loyalty. Especially is this so because the points of view of the two parties on major issues are often indistinguishable. Hence, even for party cooperation we are again thrown back largely upon voluntary elements, of which the skill of the President in exercising qualities of leadership is one of the greatest. The constitution itself prescribes certain procedures making for executive–legislative cooperation, though many of these have usually been regarded as falling into the more hostile category of checks and balances. For example, the power of the Senate to confirm appointments does result in a constant flow into key political posts in the administration of men who have in some measure the confidence of the Legislative Branch. When we consider that a number of such appointees have also had to be cleared with the senators of their home states, and were frequently recommended by them, the scales are weighted still more strongly in the direction of cooperation. Moreover, one might almost say that at long last the requirement of a two-thirds vote in treaty ratification has come to be regarded, not as obstructive, but as an invitation for the President to seek the Senate's cooperation even in the stages of treaty negotiation—its "advice" as well as its "consent." Similarly the possibility of a presidential veto in connection with many important measures has brought consultation and compromise prior to passage that have forestalled the veto.

The presidential message has grown enormously in the frequency of its use and probably also in the attention paid to it by Congress. It has come to be an expected element in leadership, especially at the outset of a session and at the time of national crisis.

Laws have also made contributions to the devices potentially favoring free cooperation. Under the Legislative Reorganization Act of 1946, for example, the most systematic attempt in history was made to see that the committees of Congress corresponded to the agencies and structure of the Executive Branch. Furthermore, under the terms of the act, each of these committees was charged with "watchfulness" over the corresponding agency or agencies. This results in some cases in invitations to the agency or agencies to come in and tell their story to the committee—without a set agenda and without formal consideration of a bill. Relations between committee members and staffs on the one side and high officials of the Executive Branch on the other have extended considerably beyond their institutionalization in committee procedures.

Ingenuity with an assist from a benevolent Supreme Court (In *Sibbach v. Wilson & Co.*, 312 U.S. 1 [1941]) has brought into being a device of considerable promise. This is a kind of legislative veto over details of executive administrative action in areas in which it is desirable to introduce much greater flexibility than is feasible in ordinary legislation and at the same time permit Congress to exercise a measure of control. The principal case has been in the field of executive reorganization. Under the Reorganization Act of 1949 plans for reorganizing the Executive Branch, submitted by the President, were subject to disapproval by either House of Congress during a period of sixty days by a majority vote of its total membership. Similar powers of disapproval appeared in subsequent extensions of the reorganization act.[1]

Departments and agencies maintain liaison offices for contact with Congress. The number of persons engaged in this effort to promote the Executive Branch's legislative interests or to assist members of Congress, has increased greatly. As early as 1963, more than 700 persons were involved in legislative liaison.

Liaison personnel have become to a considerable extent the eyes and ears of the White House and the departments on Capitol Hill, somewhat offsetting the subsystem relationships between bureau chiefs and members and even direct confrontations between the President and the leaders of Congress.[7] Indeed, one of the chief complaints, notably of Republican members of Congress during the Nixon administration was their inability to get to see the President.

At the top level, however, there are still conferences between the President and the leadership of his party and the opposition in Congress. No one can read the White House appointment list, moreover, without realizing that there is a highly flexible use of conferences with members of Congress on matters of mutual interest—with the initiative divided between the two branches. Chairmen of important committees do have conferences in person and by telephone with the President and his most intimate aides with respect to legislative programs.

It is not at all certain that a formalizing of the various types of contact which exist between the Executive Branch and Congress would necessarily increase the measure of cooperation which in practice is now achieved. Flexibility is a strongly favorable factor in assuring the reality of these relationships. Moreover, by present means those in the opposition party can also be called in council. This is especially important in a Congress in which the two branches are controlled by opposite parties. Flexibility also permits the neutralizing of some of the less fortunate results of seniority which would not be the case under formalized arrangements. In any event, consultations between the White House and Congress are a practice with an influence that only those close to the situation can fully appreciate. It is worthy of comment that Presidential Assistant Lawrence O'Brien saw to it during the Kennedy and Johnson administrations that all new members of Congress had ample opportunity for direct dialogue with the President. Under Nixon the practice was not pursued with comparable vigor.

If conferences between the President and members of Congress are significant, so also are conferences between cabinet and other members of the administration and appropriate Congressmen. These occur frequently, and this network of informal liaison is one of the keys to the successful operation of our Constitution.

In most committees the practice has grown up of referring

relevant bills to the appropriate departments for comment prior to action. In minor legislation, an unfavorable report from a department is likely to be decisive. A favorable report, however, carries no corresponding assurance, unless it falls within the "whirlpool" pattern already discussed.* In such instances, when the interests of a bureau and a pressure group correspond to the predilections of a number of the committee members, the probability of passage is greatly increased. It is this type of situation which is often one of the best illustrations of the previously mentioned situation in which the relationship between a bureau and a committee can be more significant than between the bureau and the presidency.

Of growing importance also are conferences at the "staff level," between employees of members of Congress or the congressional committees and key men in the administration. The two-way flow of advice and opinion, of information as to administrative problems and information as to congressional attitude, is prolific in its contribution to understanding. Staffs of the Appropriations Committees come to learn which agency budget officers they can trust as sources of information. The General Accounting Office necessarily is in contact with untold numbers of Executive Branch employees. Analysts on the staff of the Congressional Research Service make it a point to check with representatives of the departments—a check often designed to make certain that the account given of the official administration point of view is in fact accurate, though the treatment of that point of view in a report often includes not only a critique of it but also a presentation and analysis of alternatives.

Congress has come to frown on the earlier practice of leaning heavily on experts borrowed from the executive to staff its committees. In any clash of loyalties the permanent connection might well prevail and the preference now is for professional technicians who are directly or indirectly associated

*Cf. chapter 4.

with the Legislative Branch. On the other hand, a proviso of the Legislative Reorganization Act of 1946 has been abolished that required a year's interval before a former member of the professional staff of a committee could take a job with the executive. A modest flow of personnel to the Executive Branch from Congress and its committee staffs takes place, in part to make it possible for the agencies to understand Congress better and in part doubtless to capitalize on Congressional experience and connections. A similar hiring in the other direction is not unusual. Many former Executive Branch employees are found in Congressional offices, committees, and in the supporting congressional agencies. In the long run, the practice of interchange can be helpful. Congress still operates to a great extent on informal understandings and usages, and the factor of exchange of personnel is likely to influence cooperation.

The use of members of Congress as representatives at international and other conferences is an important device making for cooperation. This is better considered at length in connection with the congressional role in international affairs. At this point, it is enough to call attention to its potentialities in other fields as well. The technique of the joint legislative-executive commission utilized in the Temporary National Economic Committee, the two Commissions on the Organization of the Executive Branch (the Hoover Commissions), and the Commission on Intergovernmental Relations is growing, notwithstanding an initial timidity of the executive and its reluctance to share deliberations because of the "complicating" nature of congressional participation. Some examples of joint commissions in which appointees from the Congress have participated during the decade 1963–73 include:

- American Revolution Bicentennial Commission
- Federal Council on the Arts and Humanities

- President's Commission on the Assassination of President Kennedy
- Presidential Election Campaign Fund Advisory Board
- Commission on the Organization of the Government for the Conduct of Foreign Policy

Patronage has been deplored, and rightly so, as undermining the integrity and quality of the civil service. It is doubtful whether such contribution as patronage may make to better understanding between the two branches really compensates for this damage. It does presumably purchase a measure of cooperation in some congressional circles through fear of its loss, but whether cooperation won in this fashion is in the public interest is problematical. Other rewards for party regularity fall into the same category. A reverse twist takes the form of what might be termed "executive patronage" whereby decisions on personnel selection or other matters are influenced by a desire to establish a better rapport with a key member of Congress or committee without any pressure being exercised from the Congress. It ought to be appreciated, perhaps more than it is, that responsible government is not served in either case.

The influence of the President is very great indeed. Upon his nationwide election, upon his incomparable command of the mediums of communication, upon the glamor surrounding him as the head of a great nation, upon his superior command of information, upon all these and many other factors, the President may rely when he wishes to exert his personal influence with Congress in behalf of a particular course of action. Surely these factors are enough; more would introduce elements making for the operation of less worthy motives on the part of congressmen. These motives in the end may be self-defeating in that their cumulative effect might so lower the quality of representative government as to render it less capable of performing its roles of critic and generator of alternative policies.

A sense of urgency has been with the Federal government almost incessantly since the Great Depression. Anyone reading the record must have been deeply impressed with the readiness of Congress to rise to the occasion—first, with the antidepression measures of the mid-1930s, then with measures during our period of belligerent neutrality, then with actions throughout the years of World War II, the postwar reconstruction, European rehabilitation and foreign aid, the Cold War, the crisis of Korea and the spread of Cold War to Asia, Indochina, and most recently, in reactions to the U.S. rapprochements with China and the Soviet Union. One does not have to subscribe to the specific scenario of policy which was followed in any of these episodes in order to recognize that congressional cooperation with the Executive Branch was forthcoming, often, one might add, perhaps on the basis of a too-ready acceptance of the authority of the latter. Measures by executive fiat might have been quicker but that they would have been sounder and would have obtained that measure of popular acceptance accompanying congressional discussion and decision seems highly unlikely. Indeed, when the direction of policy by the Executive Branch did increasingly take the opposite tack of avoiding a congressional input, as in Southeast Asia and the later years of the Indochina war, the consequences for the nation bordered on the disastrous.

When there is no urgency in a given field, the normal pattern should be a wait for concurrent majorities to reveal themselves. Our country and our people are, in fact, not less well off economically and otherwise than those nations whose problem of executive–legislative cooperation has been solved by the domination of the executive.[3]

Nevertheless, proposals working toward greater free cooperation between the two branches as between equals are in order. Chiefly these call for the formalizing of devices which have operated in informal fashion, and for increasing the use of ones which thus far have been employed only occasionally.

Corwin and Hyneman would establish joint councils. The

Corwin proposal [4] calls for reconstruction of the cabinet so as to contain the leading members of a joint legislative council. Heads of departments and agencies would be members only as the occasion demands. The Hyneman proposal [5] calls for a central council selected by the President. It would have the function of formulating the program of the government and directing its execution. Membership would include a small group from Congress, some of the key administrators, and probably a few men of great standing who held no other formal governmental office.

The LaFollette-Monroney Committee [6] had several devices of this type presented to it, and in its *Report* recommended the formation of a joint legislative and executive council tied in with a strengthening of party responsibility. The congressional members would consist of the majority policy committees of the two houses with the occasional inclusion of the minority policy committees. In addition, the *Report* laid great stress upon a committee structure of Congress which paralleled the administrative structure of the executive.

Senator Kefauver was in a long tradition of advocates of bringing members of the cabinet on to the floor of the houses for questioning, thus extending to the whole Congress (with the by-product of a wider publicity) a device now used by the committees. Opposition to and support of such a measure exists in both Congress and the executive. An interesting variant of this proposal was presented to the House Select Committee on Committees [7] of the Ninety-third Congress. It called for the designation of a deputy secretary by the Executive Department to sit "as a member of the House, to take part in debate, to be available to questioning and to have the right to ask questions."

Lasswell proposes the formation of national security committees within Congress (made up of representatives of appropriate other committees), the chairmen of which might sit with the National Security Council. [8]

Paralleling the relationships between the President's Council of Economic Advisers and the Joint Committee on the Economic Report, Wallace Parks suggested a joint committee on foreign economic policy, also to receive a report from the executive.[9]

Much attention has focused, of late, on more vigorous pursuit of the congressional oversight function as a means of inducing greater cooperation between the branches or, in any event, of insuring a greater degree of congressional control. The proposals which were examined by the House Select Committee on Committees [10] included an enlarged role for the Government Operations Committee, a Congressional Advisory Committee for each executive department, creation of a Special Oversight Committee, establishment of a Committee on Budget Control, and creation of a separate oversight subcommittee on each standing committee. For the most part, these proposals have been known for many years. The trend is toward strengthening the role of the individual committee and sustaining its efforts by making more staff assistance directly available or indirectly through the Congressional Research Service and other agencies of Congress.

One of the most interesting developments has been the annual "president's program." This really started with President Truman. It was consolidated under Eisenhower. Kennedy, Johnson, and Nixon have followed the same general practice. The program has centered in the three messages, on the "State of the Union," the Budget, and the Economic Report, to which has now been added a fourth, the "State of the World." Items proposed in these messages are then normally followed by administration-drafted bills. An interesting by-product has been the leverage these procedures give the President not only in the press and Congress but even over his departments and agencies.

Why has Congress generally not resented these programs? Several factors are operative at this point. In the first place, the great majority of items had been before Congress for a number of years. Many, indeed, are of congressional origin.

Presidential endorsement became a matter to some extent of timing, the identification of the right moment for throwing the weight of the office back of a proposal. In the second place, Congress with its increasingly developed and available expertise has felt much more secure in dealing with such recommendations. It is able to regard them as yardsticks, to be screened, amended, rejected, substituted for, or accepted, after hearings and analysis. In these circumstances, especially as there is nothing to prevent Congress from adding items, if it wishes, the "President's program" nonetheless plays a most convenient role in furnishing an outline agenda for the session. Back of the messages may well lie very considerable informal consultations with key congressmen, a give and take which furnishes the initial step in consensus building.

With the tacit acceptance of the "President's program" in the aforementioned roles, new importance attaches itself to the congressional role in "incubating" ideas which later find their way into the aforesaid program. The earlier introduction of bills on a subject by individual members, the eventual inquiries and scheduling of hearings on the part of committees, the reporting out or even the passage of a measure in one house—all are part of this clearly identifiable congressional role. Issues are illuminated, support is developed, alternatives are explored—all very important steps preparatory to the day on which the President makes a given measure his own. The leadership function is thus seen as a much more diffused one than is popularly supposed.

In conclusion, be it noted that much more has been accomplished already in the direction of cooperation than is generally supposed. This cooperation is not of the rubber-stamp character allegedly realized at certain times in our national history. Nor is it the reluctant cooperation induced by bribing or bludgeoning. Usages of cooperation somewhat haphazardly acquired, however, might crumble in a less favorable climate. It is this hazard, among other considerations, that has led so many political thinkers to call for a strengthening of party discipline as an instrument of party responsibility and to call for party responsibility as a means of enacting an integrated national program. At present, the more informal, freer system allows for flexibility to match the great variables in the case—variables in persons in key positions, variables in subject matter, variables in the degree of crisis, variables as to whether the party of the President is or is not in control of one or both houses of Congress. The burden of proof, it seems to us, lies with those who would straitjacket the institutional arrangements. In the end, such proposals may prove self-defeating.

NOTES

1. The Reorganization Act, 63 Stat 203 as amended in 1971 (85 Stat. 574) expired on April 1, 1973. Efforts to renew it so far in both the Senate and the House of Representatives appeared to have been frustrated by the strain in the relations between President Nixon and the Congress, growing out of the Watergate Affair.
2. See the very interesting article in the *Public Administration Review* on March 1966, pp. 14-24, by G. Russell Pipe.
3. Too much should not be read into this statement. All that is really meant is that certainly the burden of proof lies with the other side to isolate and evaluate this factor in a situation of multiple causation.
4. Corwin, *The President: Office and Powers*, pp. 297 ff.
5. Charles S. Hyneman, *Bureaucracy in a Democracy* (New York: Harper, 1950), pp. 571 ff.
6. Joint Committee on the Organization of Congress. Established under House Concurrent Resolution 18, Seventy-ninth Congress, 1st session.
7. Joint Committee on the Organization of Congress, *Suggestions for Strengthening Congress* (Joint Committee Print, Seventy-ninth Congress, second session, June 1946), (Washington, D.C.: United States Government Printing Office, 1946), pp. 43-45.

8. Harold D. Lasswell, *National Security and Individual Freedom* (New York: McGraw-Hill, 1950), pp. 106 ff.

9. Wallace Parks, *United States Administration of Its International Economic Affairs* (Baltimore: The Johns Hopkins Press, 1951).

10. House of Representatives. Select Committee on Committees. *Committee Organization in the House.* Invited Working Papers, Volume 2, pp. 710-722.

CHAPTER 6

The Congressional Response
to a Technical Age

The principal difficulty faced by Congress in carrying out its contemplated functions may be put in question form. How can a group of nonspecialists, elected as representatives of the electorate, really function in a specialized and technological age. For surely no one will deny that the overwhelming majority of the great problems facing the government are complex to such a degree that the most skilled specialization and the most profound wisdom are none too great to deal with them. It is this factor that in most industrialized nations has given the major impetus to a growing bureaucratic domination of government.

The effects of the multiplication of problems and of their growing complexity have revealed themselves largely in three ways. They have increased the demand upon the members' time by the individual constituent; they have forced an adaptation in the direction of specialization and reliance upon expertise; and they have created a dispersiveness in the electorate that has reflected itself in the rise of the pressure group and in an erosion of congressional party responsibility. In all probability each of these trends is irreversible, given separation of powers and our present election system. Fortunately, there are advantages as well as disadvantages to the general welfare in these developments.

Until the end of the Civil War there were seldom more than two or three major issues facing a given Congress. The rest of the world kept its distance for much of the time, though even a slight interference tended to be felt deeply by the self-conscious rising nationalism of the young republic. Slavery was an issue, complex it is true, but maturing over many decades. The detailed development of governmental functions was largely a state and local matter. Continuous intervention in economic and other matters—apart from the tariff—was almost unknown. The opening up of the public domain was perhaps the only exception.

Let us examine somewhat more closely the implications of this relatively simple state of affairs in the spheres already noted. In the first place, the necessary attention to individual constituents consisted largely (after Andrew Jackson's time) of attention to job seekers and, occasionally, land grabbers. Districts possessed less than half the population of the present districts, even toward the end of the period. The number of voting constituents was further cut in half by the absence of woman suffrage. In many states the Negro was disfranchised even after the War between the States. Difficulties in transportation precluded visits to Washington on the part of all save the relatively well-to-do few. Congress was in session only a few months of the year. Members were not granted secretarial help, nor did they need it till well on in the century. In other words, the members of Congress had the time to spend in thought and deliberation on issues. At the same time the really major issues were few, usually slow in maturing, and predominantly nontechnical in nature.

It was this nontechnical character of public questions that lent itself to their resolution largely in an atmosphere of "principle" or party loyalty. The average member knew, or thought he knew, the answers. Where principles were not immediately forthcoming party supplied them. Party cohesiveness was practicable in an age of few, but persistent, major issues. Debate was leisurely, but in spite of this frequently resulted in more heat than light. To this day, many are still somewhat under the illusion that a single principle exhausts the meaning of a given issue; there were few then who doubted it. Debates marked the clash of principles, which gave them a certain aura of moral quality, but they contained much less of a truly objective, factual nature than is evident today.*

Pressure groups existed, but the average constituency, even the average state, was relatively homogeneous. North versus South, commerce versus manufacturing, debtor versus creditor—these were the relatively simple cleavages that translated themselves into national policy, and seldom did a given member need to suffer from political schizophrenia. The intricate crisscrossing of conflicting groups of today's era of statism was not present to complicate at one and the same time a legislator's conscience and his reelection. The party machinery was more influential than the committee in major decisions, even though the committee system was a relatively early adaptation to the need for detailed preliminary consideration of measures.

The contrast with the present day is tremendous. Congress functions in a different world. By the second or third decade of the twentieth century, labor and agriculture and the veterans had learned the lesson that business had learned earlier: that political action can be a powerful weapon in the arsenal of economic struggle. Laissez faire, even in the lip service paid to it, crumbled before the hard realities of the 1930s, as did isolation in the 1940s. The United States became a great power in the world arena; by 1945 it found itself at least potentially "the" great power; in 1960 it shared its world influence with a competitive rival of similar magnitude. In 1970, other potential rivals had appeared on the distant horizon.

---

* Here again the expansion westward, with the problems and policies associated with the public domain, may be regarded as an exception.

The result of these and other forces was revolutionary in the legislative field. Governmental regulation in some fashion or other extended to every business and labor union; government controls reached most of the farmers; government contracts could make or break thousands of firms; veterans' benefits in one form or another probably touched the majority of families; government projects and construction were forthcoming with increasing largesse.

The first and most obvious effect of this was in the changed relationship between a member of Congress and his constituents. While still with him, no longer were the importunities of job seekers the major relationship of this sort. Perhaps the majority of the voters had an individual economic stake, not merely in the legislation before Congress, but in the fashion in which laws already passed were being administered. In fact, law in the sense of a generalized rule of conduct was no longer the characteristic governmental expression. Laws of the present day—at least the more important ones—characteristically set an objective, create (or designate) an agency to attain that objective, and define the metes and bounds of the agency's conduct. Then they leave it to the agency to administer or adjust in the light of the objective, the specified sector (usually economic) of national life by some process of continuous intervention. Great discretion is often allowed the agency in particular cases. In such a process countless individuals are affected. To these individuals their member of Congress often appears as the only human element in a faceless monster known as government, providentially placed both geographically and in the hierarchy of authority to intervene in their behalf. It is this type of activity which today the member finds particularly time-consuming. True, his power in these matters is greatly exaggerated; his effort to upset normal administrative processes often is even more exaggerated, when it exists at all. But the constituent by letter, telephone, or in person asks or demands help. Constituencies in the House now average about 500,000; in the Senate, almost 4,400,000. Women as well as men vote; racial barriers have crumbled. Modern travel and a greatly improved standard of living bring people to Washington in astronomical numbers. Students are encouraged to write to their congressman for information and to visit him when in the city. Individual claims for attention vary. A member may be asked to appear before a regulatory commission, to obtain funds to dredge a harbor, to change the route of a highway, to inquire about the cause for delay of a pension, to obtain an exception to the rules governing Federal aid to a local housing project, to support an effort to secure a contract, to protest a questionnaire sent a business firm, to appear as a witness in a labor dispute before a Federal mediator, to obtain a higher acreage quota for a particular crop, to "do something" to find a son or a husband missing in Indochina.

Certain deeper meanings of this type of activity in the direction of preservation of localism will be left for later analysis.* The emphasis at this point is on the demands made upon a member's time and attention as the result of the tremendous increase in the span of governmental activity, and to call attention to the fact that the portion of the demand here discussed bears little relationship to the member's responsibilities for national policy. He does, it is true, learn something of the workings of particular measures from these constituent requests, but the chief effect is the sheer time consumed, time necessarily subtracted from the consideration of general policy. Quantitatively, it is not too easy to set a figure, but some earlier studies have indicated that it was not unusual for a member to devote up to eighty percent of his time to dealings with his constituents. On the other hand, more recent studies would put the average between twenty-five and thirty percent—probably indicating an increasing reliance upon office staff.[1] Most of what has been said has been on the assumption that members of Congress should concern themselves primarily with legislative tasks. This is true, but the other

* Cf. chapter 15.

side should not be downgraded. In a government as complex as ours, surely there is much to be said for the individual citizen having an advocate in his behalf, if he feels in some fashion helpless before a gigantic bureaucracy. To serve in this manner is by no means the least important function of a congressman.

Adaptations to this situation are numerous and relatively obvious. Members work longer hours, and Congress remains in session for more of the year—though other factors must bear primary responsibility for the latter. Office staffs have grown considerably. Departments have established liaison offices and information bureaus to simplify the problems of contact. Questions of concern to constituents dealt with by the Congressional Research Service have grown from 1,250 to about 6,500 a month in the last two decades. Writers and administrative aides may help with the congressman's statements and letters. He develops techniques of courteous refusal. Yet, when all is said and done, the problem of the demands on time remains unsurmounted and is probably insurmountable. More often than not, the demands are met by cuts into the time others normally allot to family.

Alleviations are possible as, for example, in the voting of home rule for the District of Columbia. Some hope may lie in the appointment of an "ombudsman," following Scandinavian precedent, to whom congressmen may refer many of the complaints which he and his staff now investigate. Such an agent of Congress could take these matters up with the executive agency and report back to the member.[2] Actually, all congressional offices do have one or more employees who perform this function and most agencies and departments maintain units to respond to them. Another hopeful possibility is the establishment of a consultative service in Congress on office management under the Legislative Reorganization Act of 1970.[3] In both houses, the initial usages of automated data processing are in operation, with back-up services available in the Library of Congress.

Most serious, because more fundamental, are problems of

complexity and magnitude in the legislative output itself. The great difficulty is not even the fact that in a given session of Congress there are forty or fifty major issues. It is rather what is inherent in the nature of the issues themselves. The measures proposed are often urgent; they are almost invariably far-reaching, but obscure in their derivative or secondary effects; they are often drastic in their primary impact, but in a complex and disturbing way; they are highly specialized; they may involve a multitude of principles, often conflicting; they always involve a quantity of facts for background. All this is only to say that they are a reflection of a specialized, but interlocked, technical age whose social and economic and political structure is intricate, sensitive, dynamic, and at the same time scarcely understood even by the wisest and the best informed of men.

Here, for example, is a partial and highly selective list of really major issues and measures that faced the Ninety-second Congress. In international relations and national security these included contributions to the Asian Development Bank and to the Inter-American Bank, Foreign Aid, Strategic Arms Limitation Interim Agreement, ABM (Anti-Ballistic Missile) Treaty, continuance of Radio Free Europe and Radio Liberty International, Wheat and Coffee Agreements, Revision of Status of Okinawa, Seabed Arms Control Treaty, Disposals from Stockpiled Scarce Materials, The Military Budget, Pay and Benefit Adjustments for Military Personnel.

On the home front, the list was very long and included, in addition to numerous appropriations measures, questions involving:

Agricultural subsidies
School lunches and child nutrition programs
Aircraft piracy control
Handgun controls.
A whole range of legislation involving the government of the
    District of Columbia
Economic opportunity measures

Wage and price controls
School aid
Lowering voting age to eighteen
Protection of presidential candidates
Black lung benefits
Health research and community mental health programs
Indian benefits measures
Minimum wage rates
Manpower development and training
Strengthening national park, wilderness, and
    recreational programs
Pollution control
Whale killing prohibitions
Space administration authorization
Rail passenger subsidies
Drug and alcohol rehabilitation for veterans

In this setting of dynamic and complex demands on Congress, the changes in Congress have been profound and far-reaching during recent years. Actually, the last three decades have been but the climax to a trend that was already noticeable during the latter part of the last century, and certain congressional adaptations trace to this period or even earlier. For convenience, we may group the adaptations under three interrelated headings: procedural changes, a growth in specialization, and an increasing reliance upon technical experts.

The whole question of congressional procedure has received excellent descriptive and analytic treatment in the writings of Cannon, Luce, Galloway, Riddick, and others, and need not detain us here save for a few observations. In both House and Senate, it is steeped in precedent, and a member who masters it has elements of effectiveness denied to the uninitiated. The House by its tendency to divide time equally between supporters and opponents of a measure, the Senate by its virtually unlimited debate—these bear eloquent witness to our overriding belief in the rights of minorities to be heard and in the efficacy of discussion. In the House, the minority is occasionally of the opinion that the more rigid limitations set by the House on total debate place it at a disadvantage as compared with the Senate. In the latter the rules more than compensate for any disadvantages facing the minority in the House. Whether the invitation to delays and filibusters of the Senate is too high a price to pay in comparison with the greater possibilities of order and expeditiousness of the House is a matter of opinion. The House does manage to transact an enormous amount of business, considering its size. Neither house has mastered fully the problem of the congestion of business toward the end of the session.

The Legislative Reorganization Act of 1970 made some adjustments to procedures. These involved additional protection of the rights of individual members in both Houses, in committee and on the floor, with some new possibilities of delays. However, the role of the party leaders was also strengthened, assuring greater expeditiousness at least in those cases where both parties were prepared to act.

In the House, the time wasted in routine quorum calls and roll calls was cut by procedural changes and also by the introduction of mechanical voting.[4]

Deserving of somewhat more attention is the increasing tendency of Congress toward division of labor and specialization within its own membership. The most obvious expression is in the committee system. Among the changes brought in by the Reorganization Act of 1946 was the replacing of the old committee structure by fewer and, in the Senate, smaller committees. In this fashion, it was expected that the average member would find himself on one or two committees only. In the ensuing years, the number of assignments has multiplied and committee specializations have again overlapped.[5] This has led the House to establish a special committee to examine the question once again. A similar concern has appeared in the Senate. The question is being examined there, however, by the regular committees. The Reorganization Act of 1946 did bring a higher degree of specialization within the membership. The need to specialize has become so evident that it has been spoken of as "a norm of legislative behavior." [6] By one means or another there is naturally some gravitation on the part of an individual member toward the committee whose subject matter he already knows best, or is most interested in, or which deals with the problems which mean most to his district or state. These three provisos frequently coincide and reinforce each other in a given instance, and after a modest amount of service a member may find himself looked upon as an "authority" on a given subject among his colleagues. Deference will be paid then not only to his membership on the committee responsible for a given measure but also to his substantive knowledge.[7] It is thus that the individual member often attains influence as well as power.

So the habit prevails, on the one hand of reluctance to go counter to a committee recommendation, on the other of looking to different people for guidance on different subjects. This cuts squarely across party membership and is one of the factors which tends to prevent its strengthening. It is the instinctive as well as rational triumph of knowledge in a technical age. It operates within a committee as well as between the committee members and the Congress as a whole. It may operate, and frequently does—in the respect paid to a well-informed member who is not a member of the relevant committee at all.

All of the foregoing is written in full knowledge of the extent to which clientele interests are concentrated in certain committees. It is probable that such committees find their bills more frequently subject to floor amendment. Yet, a bipartisan committee recommendation by the great majority of a committee is rarely altered or revised on the floor, especially of the House. Where eighty percent or more of a committee are in agreement, a bill which reaches the floor is rarely denied passage, although at least in the Senate it may still be amended significantly.

As noted, through the same tendency toward specialization,

subcommittees have continued to proliferate, and also special or select committees, though to a lesser extent than before. The former as well as the latter are frequently galvanized into life to secure intensive examination of a given problem. Each makes it possible to utilize as chairman a member of special talent. Such a member might under seniority have had to wait years before having the opportunity to contribute through his peculiar qualifications in a given area by serving as chairman of the appropriate standing committee.

The third major adaptation of Congress to the problems of a technological age lies in its use of experts outside its own membership. The story is an interesting and important one, extending in its implications far into executive–legislative relations, the role of lobbies, and the prospects for representative government itself. Because the story is less familiar than that of the other adaptations, it will be told at greater length.

Toward the end of the nineteenth century, questions and problems concerning business and industry came to the fore. The establishment of the Interstate Commerce Commission and the passage of the Sherman Antitrust Act illustrated the trend. With the presidency of Theodore Roosevelt, the extent of such concern with economic life grew more marked, and Woodrow Wilson's "New Freedom" put the seal on the development.

The congressional response to the pressure of these problems was not to rely on its own native equipment, as it tended to rely in the earlier period of its existence, but to call on experts from the interests involved for advice. Characteristically, though not exclusively, this took the form of a major development of the committee hearing as an institutional device to bring such experience to bear upon pending problems and legislation. Thus, reliance on the experts connected with the special interests was not nearly the sinister affair that might be inferred. Legislation was often the product of conflicting interests, each of which had the opportunity of appearing before the committee. Where there was no apparent conflict, it was nevertheless part of the American mores to believe that what benefited business or agriculture benefited the nation as a whole. Thus, there was no inner conflict in a member's mind between the special interest and the general good. This method seemed right and proper for another reason also. The majority of Congressmen were (and still are) lawyers, and to a lawyer truth emerges from a battle of protagonists. Undoubtedly, this strengthened greatly the use and prestige of the hearing, which was for the lawyer member the courtroom in which he and his colleagues served, as it were, as judge and jury. If in connection with the appearance of a particular witness a member occasionally forgot his normal role and became prosecuting attorney or the counsel for the defense, who shall say that this, too, was not part of a way of dealing with problems which was an expression of his customary occupational thinking.

Even when the time came at which the representatives of organized labor marshaled experts as able as those of industry or agriculture, the result still fell considerably short of presenting a complete and unbiased picture. This held true, even though the belief that the general welfare equaled the sum of the welfares of the special groups showed something of the same tenacity as a kind of "group utilitarianism" which the individualistic utilitarianism of Adam Smith and Bentham possessed. In this earlier form the general welfare was equated to the sum total of individual desires. The flaw in both individual and group utilitarianism was the same. Just as there were conflicts between individuals in which general welfare not only did not coincide with the triumph of the stronger over the weaker but might be something quite different from the desires of either or even a compromise between the two, so in the larger group conflicts and relationships there was often a public interest identifiable that was something other than the victory of one side or the other, or other than even a compromise between these two. Third, fourth, and fifth parties entered in.

The over-all interest of the consumer was surely part of the total picture that was of concern to Congress; so also were national strength and the interest of future generations.

Under these circumstances it is not surprising that eventually experts other than those from the special interests came to be called upon and in the end to be accorded an influence as great as or greater than the latter. In the first instance these were most often spokesmen from the Executive Branch.

The turning point came with the election of Franklin Roosevelt to the presidency in 1933. Industry and finance were flat on their respective backs and to a considerable extent discredited in the public's mind as well as uncertain in their own minds. The outlooks of organized labor and organized agriculture were still extremely limited and were confined almost entirely to preoccupation with solutions for their own particular problems without much reference to the economy as a whole. With one accord these groups turned to government for the answers.

The problems were real. The new brain trust and the old bureaus ground out a program to meet them. Measure after measure of major importance went from the White House to Capitol Hill. Many of them were quite gratuitously labeled "must" legislation, for Congress had more or less lost any momentum of policy formulation it once possessed and was ready for strong and informed leadership. Gigantic research and action bureaus grew almost overnight and generated still further legislation. The evidence concerning the first two or three years of the New Deal would indicate that fully eighty percent of the important legislation was for practical purposes White House and bureau generated (and, much of it, drafted as well), rather than originating in Congress itself. This still held true even if there were included as a congressional product that which resulted from the prodding and counsel of experts of the special interests and other sources.

This was a development more important and far-reaching than might at first be supposed. Under the parliamentary system of government there had come to be a worldwide trend in the industrialized nations in the direction of executive bureacratic dominance. In Great Britain, for example, behind the facade of the cabinet were the permanent civil servants, tirelessly and ceaselessly advising the individual ministers as regards indicated legislation on the basis of their (the civil servants') study and experience. Except for certain trends in the electorate, tidal in their nature, which reflected themselves in shifts in party allegiance and a consequent shift in general direction in a limited number of spheres of legislation, the permanent officials matured virtually all the legislative proposals, and, with the concurrence of the parliamentary leaders (i.e., the cabinet), were able to secure their enactment. This left to Parliament as a whole only a bit of polishing and now and again a delay or a rejection.

These were the days in which many writers, including the senior author, predicted that a similar set of usages would emerge behind the facade of our own Constitution. We saw Congress reduced largely to a ratifying role, with the executive in an ascendancy, based ultimately upon the superior technical competence of its personnel. As in Great Britain, so in our own country these expert-devised programs would be pushed by a partisan executive with the various devices of party discipline at his command.

Actually, the net result was not too greatly different from reliance upon the representation of the special interests, for the latter on a broad scale transferred much of their attention to the Executive Branch, often by fostering the establishment of bureaus in the Executive Branch, which became their respective spokesmen. These bureaus in turn generated legislative proposals more or less agreeable to their respective clienteles. Hence, new, but still unappreciated, conflicts took place in the resultant legislation. This particular defect must be reserved for special analysis later.* Other defects or short-

*Cf. chapters 9 and 10.

comings of the transferrence were more immediately noticeable.

At the end of a decade Congress had become increasingly
restless. Many factors were involved, among them an institutional jealousy and, more important, a feeling that all was not
well in a setting in which the number of unemployed was still
over 10,000,000 in spite of all the effort. There was also present
a strong feeling of frustration and resentment, in that the
executive seemed to have most of the chips in the form of
vastly greater research facilities, at times approaching a kind
of monopoly. Almost the only alternative experts available to
Congress were the still considerably discredited specialists
and representatives from commercial and industrial circles.
More fundamentally there had come to be a sincere and
genuine appreciation that reliance upon the executive for fact
finding and analysis had also some serious limitations.

In the first place, the President was elected in a political
campaign. The heads of the agencies were mostly his partisan
appointees. By the very nature of the democratic process,
declarations of policy were made in the course of such a
campaign that constituted the surface reason for subsequent
legislative proposals. Similar public policy declarations would
be made during the years following an election, not only by
the President, but also by his appointees. It soon came to be
noted in Congress that the findings and testimony of the
experts from the several agencies were almost invariably such
as to constitute an endorsement of these publicly assumed
positions of the political chief. This might be cause as well as
effect, of course, for the chief might well have taken the
position in question because he had become familiar with the
facts and analyses of his experts; but this was not always so.
Often the roles were reversed.

In an address by Luther Gulick there was a memorable
characterization of government research. He took his
audience in imagination to a huge room whose walls were
covered with files and pigeonholes labeled "Facts." In and out

of the room came and went a continuous procession of men carrying sheets of paper. When the men came in, their sheets were blank, save for the conclusions. Diligent search would then be made among the files and pigeonholes for facts which would add up to the preconceived conclusions. Such facts, when found, were duly entered, and, with the documents thus prepared to the satisfaction of the researcher, he would leave the room. This, said Gulick, was "government research"—of sorts, no doubt, but a characterization with a sufficient element of truth in it to evoke an appreciative response from his listeners.

Conversely, those in Congress who held positions on issues other than those held by the executive found themselves severely limited both in inquiry and in debate. Leaks from dissenters within the executive, private research organizations, special interests—these were hardly a match for the mass of facts and figures presented by an executive cloaked with the aura of the "public interest" and monolithic in its rejoinders to any criticism.

A second weakness lay more within the bureaus themselves than in the political pronouncements of their chiefs and the President. This was the very human tendency to stay in a rut, or to find it dificult to change one's mind once a position had been assumed. While prevalent in all walks of life and in all varieties of bureaucrat, it was and is especially dangerous if and when it is found in the armed services. A legislative body is peculiarly weak in this area of policy because to the mysteries of the technical are added the further mysteries of the secrecy that surround so much that may be basic to a wise decision. Yet, the legislative body cannot and dare not delegate all responsibility in this area. Witness, for example, the reliance the French Chamber of Deputies placed upon the Maginot Line on advice of its general staff and the near-fatal consequences thereof. Witness, too, the early near unanimous preendorsement of President Johnson's decision to commence direct combat in Vietnam in the Tonkin Gulf resolution and the unforeseen consequences thereof. The real question at this point is not so much whether a given expert in the Executive Branch is right or wrong in a particular instance but whether there are authoritative alternatives that merit consideration along with the executive viewpoint.

In the third place, a bureaucrat normally recommends policies that do not involve diminution of his own staff and powers. This is not unnatural, nor need the sinister or selfish motives of "empire building," present at times, necessarily be brought into the picture for its understanding. Each chief who is worth his salt believes in the objectives of his agency. Therefore, it normally follows that, given a larger staff or given extended powers to enable him to control more of the factors influencing the attainment of these objectives, he feels that he can do a better job. This is not itself an evil, provided that he is required to justify his recommendations before a body commanding authoritative technical competence and one which, at the same time, has no vested interest in such tendencies. If the congressional committee which, under the usages of our Constitution, has the primary responsibility to pass judgment on the request does not itself have in its own membership or in the alternative sources of information and analysis open to it a roughly comparable competence in the specific field in question, it is naturally at a very considerable disadvantage in passing judgment on the request for greater staff or greater powers. The result may be as great an evil, if a Congress rejects all such requests out of a blind resentment, as it is if a Congress is an unwitting dupe in granting them. The fact that Congress in practice has avoided either of these extremes does not remove the danger of falling measurably short of the best decision in a given instance through lack of mastery of subject matter.

Here then were at least three defects in predominant reliance upon executive research, analysis, recommendations, and expertness—defects which Congress felt were occurring, if not universally, at least with sufficient frequency to cast considerable doubt on even apparently well-documented proposals. Congress was frankly uneasy, and this uneasiness grew steadily until it crystallized in the mid-1940s into the beginning of a major expansion of Congress's own staff agencies.

These staff agencies marked a third stage in the development of the use of *expertise* in the meeting of the challenge of technology and specialization to the effectiveness of representative government. Not that such use of staffs of its own was unknown to Congress before the 1940s. It had long been customary, especially in a major congressional investigation, for a committee of Congress to assemble for the purpose an *ad hoc* staff often of very great technical competence. However, the quality of such staffs was not always uniformly high. Their temporary nature contained its own limitations. Furthermore, a laudable desire for economy often led to a congressional committee's borrowing such experts from the Executive Branch. The latter was usually quite ready to loan, inasmuch as something regarding the future course of the lending agency was often the subject under discussion. On the other hand, over the years certain committees developed in their regular clerks persons of great professional competence and on a nonpartisan basis. The career of Marcellus Sheild, for twenty-nine years Clerk of the House Appropriations Committee, is one of the best known but is by no means unique. For many years, both houses had had in their offices of legislative counsel a skilled legislative drafting service. In 1926, the Joint Committee on Internal Revenue Taxation was set up and granted a professional staff of modest size. Over the ensuing years this staff functioned continuously as a high level congressional audit on Treasury proposals, not hesitating to bring forward documentary support for forms of taxation alternative to those advanced by the executive; or to challenge Treasury estimates of prospective revenues.

The first further tangible expression of this awakening desire of Congress for its own permanent professional staff was found in some modest increases in the appropriations for the

Legislative Reference Service of the Library of Congress in the early 1940s. The first top-flight experts (later to be known as "senior specialists") were appointed in the four fields of foreign relations, taxation, American law, and labor relations. It was in part the satisfactory initial experience with these men that led to the authorized extension of senior specialist appointments to all fields under the Legislative Reorganization Act of 1946.

This act marked the real birth of a full-fledged congressional staff. It was a major response to needs already indicated. The major provisions affected the offices of the legislative counsels, the standing committees, and the Legislative Reference Service. A separate act gave each senator an administrative assistant and authorized small staffs for the policy committees of the two parties. A provision was also included, expanding the investigatory role of the General Accounting Office at the behest of Congress. The standing committees were each allowed to engage up to four professional staff members at substantial salaries and "without regard to political affiliations and solely on the basis of fitness to perform the duties of the office. . . ."

While differing authorizing provisions were made for additional staffs for the Appropriations Committees of the two houses, each marked a substantial increase. The Legislative Reference Service (now the Congressional Research Service) was also greatly expanded over the next two decades. It was assigned three roles in the general scheme of things: supplementary aid to committees and primary aid to individual members and, most recently, a function in automatic data processing. Aid to committees was greatly expanded under the second legislative reorganization. The agency's functions were elaborated to include identification of emerging problems in a committee's sphere; the designation of a specific liaison person at a committee's request, and expansion of basic data status on national problems. Expressed in appropriation terms, the increase in total congressional staff aid of a research and reference character was striking. Standing committee staff appropriations increased from $944,280 for the fiscal year 1944, to $5,432,690 for 1956, to $6,054,335 for 1961 and to $15,870,665 in 1973. Appropriations for the offices of the legislative counsels of the two House increased from $83,000 in 1944, to $290,000 for 1956, to $416,950 for 1961, and to $1,432,375 in 1973, and for the Legislative Reference Service from $166,300 to $790,000 for 1951, to $1,061,000 for 1956, to $1,660,200 for 1961, to $2,524,000 for 1965, and to $10,927,000 for the re-named Congressional Research Service in 1973. A striking change also occurred in the appropriations for the General Accounting Office. In 1946 it was $39,236,000. By 1973, it had increased to $77,262,000. To these older research facilities, the Congress added an Office of Technology Assessment in 1972, with an initial appropriation of $2 million.[8] Still another specialized congressional agency was established, primarily, to serve new committees, one in the House and one in the Senate, on the Budget. These last two units overlap to some degree, the Congressional Research Service and the General Accounting Office, but the Director of the Service and the Comptroller General who heads the latter were made ex officio members of the Advisory Board of Office of Technology Assessment. Clearly they carry the concept of technical specialization on behalf of the Legislative Branch to a new degree of intensity. The first evolved in response to a realization of the inadequacy of the Executive Branch in dealing with long-range environmental problems. Consideration of the second was the congressional response to a growing assertion of unilateral executive control over fiscal matters and priorities in expenditures as well as to the leveling of charges of fiscal irresponsibility at the Congress during the Nixon administration.

The pattern of congressional staff work and utilization is still uneven—uneven as between members, between committees, between subject fields. The offices of the legislative counsels are well established. Their tenure and the essentially nonpartisan character of their staff are not in question. With the exception of a single year, the trend in the Congressional Research Service has been steadily upward for the last thirty-four years, if quantitative and qualitative use and the sums appropriated and transferred from committee funds are fair measurements. Its nonpartisanship and scholarly character have been recognized in Congress.

Staffs of the standing committees present a less clear but clarifying picture. Party considerations have played a part in some committees in determining personnel practices, although there were from the outset certain notable exceptions. The selection of the staff of the Foreign Relations Committee of the Senate, for example, has been free of political considerations since the outset. Others have had partisan overtones. By 1965, the long-continued Democratic majority and the tendency in many committees for the chairmen and majority party to monopolize the staff led to an intensified demand among many House Republicans for assured minority staffing. This practice has now become quite general in both houses. The Legislative Reorganization Act of 1970, which added two professional positions to the staff of each standing committee, also provided that the minority, as a matter of right, had authority to fill two professional positions if it chose to exercise the right.

Lawyers and journalists have been employed in considerable numbers, economists and subject specialists perhaps somewhat less so than would have been anticipated. However, the tradition of permanence soon made specialists of all of them. Staff members have been obtained on loan from the Congressional Research Service and the General Accounting Office and this has resulted in a significant integration of these groups in the work of certain committees in which this takes place.[9] An interesting recent trend in congressional staffing involves the effort to coordinate the work of the new research agencies, that is for science and technology and for budget control with the older units—General Accounting Office and the Congressional Research Service. In the establishing legislation for these two new agencies there is recognition of the dangers of fragmentation and duplication in a growing congressional establishment.

It is possible that in certain respects Congress may even be beginning to be overstaffed. In addition to the new congressional research agencies and the expansion of the older agencies as well as the permanent professional staffs of the committees, each session sees a number of special investigations, usually with temporary personnel, which tend to take on a permanency. The quality and purpose of these special investigations differ greatly. Some have been for purposes of patronage and politics; others have been led by persons of great ability. Some have allegedly been created in response to pressures and suggestions from the temporary staffs of expiring investigations so as to retain their congressional connections. The costs of such special investigations in the Senate increased from $170,268 in 1940 to $692,603 in 1947, $1,936,217 in 1954 to $4,361,956 in 1965, to almost $14 million in 1973. The increase is accounted for in part, by the fact that pay scales are higher and that staff is no longer freely borrowed from the administration, but the growth of investigations is the largest factor. It remains to be seen whether the Legislative Reorganization Act of 1970 with its emphasis on oversight investigations as a regular staff function will act to arrest the growth of special investigations.

More important has been the effect of staffing upon the total role of members of congress. For the purpose of the present discussion the staffs may be considered as constituting a single corps. The trends are unmistakable. For example, on every major and most minor issues one group or another is called upon to make an independent, objective study—called upon either by the appropriate committee as a whole or by the minority or by an individual member or members. Thus, there is introduced a "third force" of experts, usually designed as a corrective to the bias of the special interests and to any short comings in the substantive recommendations of the executive.

For the most part, this third force does not itself make recommendations. As regards the Congressional Research Service, for example, this is invariably the case. As regards the committee staffs in many and perhaps most instances, the staff objective is to present an unbiased total picture—neither hostile to nor in support of the picture presented by the Executive Branch or the special interests, but filling in the gaps, assessing the factual base, outlining possible alternative courses of action. Sometimes this operates in the direction of reinforcing, though usually in considerably amended form, the recommendations of the executive, as in the Marshall Plan, in repeated revisions of the Social Security Act, in various programs of Federal aid to the states, in tax legislation, in the SALT agreement and the ABM treaty and in many other subjects. Sometimes legislative staff activity contributes to a decision to postpone action to force a more thorough and impartial assessment of a situation by the executive. At other times, it aids Congress in developing an independent policy in the teeth of presidential opposition, as in the Taft-Hartley and Landrum-Griffin Acts and manpower programs and with regard to the cessation of U. S. military activity in Southeast Asia. At still other times, though this might not be acknowledged by the Executive, it has been a strong factor in bringing the latter to a definite change in the direction of its policy.

The respective contributions of the staff services and of the members themselves can never be accurately assessed in instances like the foregoing. Nevertheless, the indications are many that the enlargement and strengthening of the staffs of Congress have in fact been a major factor in arresting and probably reversing a trend that had set in in the United States as well as in every other industrialized nation. This is the trend in the direction of the ascendancy or even the virtually complete dominance of the bureaucracy over the Legislative Branch through the former's near-monopoly of the facts and the technical and specialized competence. Other legislative bodies—the British Parliament through its Royal Commissions, the Swedish Riksdag through its "remiss" and commission devices—do from time to time tap alternative expert sources. The new Japanese Diet and the German Bundestag have instituted legislative staff services on the American model that have great potentialities. Yet, by and large the Congress of the United States still remains the major legislative assembly of which it can unmistakably be said that its independent, creative functioning has grown steadily in the last twenty-five years or so. The time elapsed is naturally still too short to be certain that this will be a permanent achievement. The sudden withdrawal of public confidence from the Executive Branch after the Watergate affair has created a time of great testing for the continued validity of this observation. The people have turned to the Congress for a greater input of constructive leadership. It remains to be seen how well Congress can deliver on this heightened public expectation.

Congress is likely to continue to use the services of the experts of the executive but the trend is in the direction of executive personnel serving as witnesses only. For many years previously they had also been the advisers and consultants whose word had often carried the day. The change is seen in the end results. Where a witness from the executive has come unprepared, he may well find himself demolished in a committee hearing. Where his case is "solid," a consensus usually results. It is specialization on the part of members and staff alike that has increased the effectiveness of Congress in this connection.[10]

In a subtle fashion, the nature of many congressional hearings has changed. No longer are witnesses confined as they once were largely to representatives of special interests and of the Executive Branch. Specialists from the public at large are increasingly called in by invitation of the committees themselves. In a series of hearings on the war in Vietnam and on relations with China and other questions of foreign policy during the Ninety-first and Ninety-second Congresses, for example, the Senate Foreign Relations Committee assembled a formidable array of private experts on Asia whose televised comments day after day left the Executive Branch hard-pressed to justify the continuance of the policy of involvement. This procedure helped to bring closer the day when U.S. policy was revised to one of Vietnamization and withdrawal of U. S. forces. These and similar hearings develop into full-scale panels when the experts in question fall into differing schools of thought, and appear in discussions under committee auspices. The advice of professional staff well informed and up-to-date on developments in their field is invaluable in the selection of such witnesses.

Congress has thus mastered, or has provided itself with the tools to master, the problem of assuring itself of an unbiased, competent source of expert information and analysis. By the same token it appears to be in the process of mastering the problem of recapturing its constitutional role as an independent policy determiner—a self-respecting coequal of the Executive Branch, in practice its competent partner or its intelligent critic. Congress has done this without sacrificing its own standing as the elected representatives of the people. This has been no small contribution to the content of free governance in a complex and technical age.

It is worth summarizing the analysis thus far of legislative–executive relations. Reference was made at the outset of these relations as an "institutionalized mutual responsibility of coequals." In the light of the development of *expertise,* this characterization may now be given a richer meaning. The mutual responsibility is seen to be much more than that of coequal power in the formal sense. Power to be effective must be buttressed by knowledge and Congress now has this knowledge at its command. For either branch to have its way it must now convince the other as to the wisdom, operative as well as political, of a proposed course of action. This change has gone on when both branches have been under the control of the same and of different parties. That would suggest that the transition is not transient but enduring, not political but constitutional.

NOTES

1. Warren H. Butler, "Administering Congress: The Role of Staff," *Public Administration Review* (March 1966), p. 6.
2. Henry S. Reuss, "An 'Ombudsman' for America," *New York Times Magazine* (September 13, 1964), p. 30. Walter S. Gellhorn, *Ombudsmen and Others* (Cambridge: Harvard University Press, 1966).
3. Office of Placement and Office Management. (Title IV, P. L. 91-510, 84 Stat 1140).
4. Ibid., Title I.
5. The trend remains in the direction of two committees, usually pairing one of the third rank with one of the second rank. See Louis C. Gawthrop, "Changing Membership Patterns in House Committees," *American Political Science Review* (June 1966), pp. 366-73.
6. Herbert B. Asher, "Committees and the Norm of Specialization," *Annals of the American Academy of Political and Social Science*, Philadelphia, January 1974, p. 63.
7. Between one-fifth and one-quarter of the members of most committees have served ten years or more.
8. 86 Stat. 797. For an excellent analytic description of the Office of Technology Assessment see Anne Hessing Cahn and Joel Primack, "Technological Foresight for Congress," *Technology Review* (March/April 1973), pp. 41-48.
9. See Kenneth Kofmehl, *Professional Staffs of Congress* (West Lafayette: Purdue University Press, 1962).
10. Former Congressman and Undersecretary of Treasury Joseph Barr, in a public address, September 20, 1965, before the Washington Chapter of the American Society for Public Administration, commented that he had learned far more in his chosen field of international finance in his two years in the House than in his two graduate years at Harvard. Not only did he have the high order expertise of the members and staff of the Ways and Means Committee to call on, but he used freely the assistance available from the various agencies in Washington.

CHAPTER 7

Appropriations

For many decades the appropriating process has been almost the only point in the congressional agenda at which the program of the government passes in review in its totality. Here legislative intent can be enhanced and promoted; here also it can be hampered or strangled altogether. Economy and extravagance struggle. The pressure groups beat upon the committee doors. The executive masses its persuasion and its coerciveness, its facts and its subterfuges. The Appropriations Committees have the largest memberships and among the largest staffs of any of the standing committees. Their tasks are among the most difficult.

Some of these difficulties are patent. The sheer size of the total budget is one, for in fiscal 1975 it reached the staggering total of over $300 billion. Figures cease to have meaning and leave the average individual dazed. Should the budget be $10 billion more or perhaps $10 billion less? How is the worth of one program or purpose to be weighed against others? Close examination, apart from sampling here and there, is simply impossible in a situation of such unbelievable complexity. If appropriations are to be considered in detail, there are not days, weeks, and months enough to cover the ground. If it is in lump sums, who is to judge whether the amount is too much or too little to attain the end? Occasionally work-load measurements lend a color of objectivity to changes in size of staff; but these conditions are exceptional, and there is seldom assurance that the original base was itself a sound one. Whole sections of expenditures, especially in the military, are shrouded in secrecy and, at least until after the Vietnam experience, were accepted by Congress largely on faith. Occasionally, appropriations for functions declining in significance or largely obsolete are retained year after year at their old figure, principally for want of a substantive analysis of the work itself. Then, too, the approach employed by the executive retains the fiction of the equal importance of all items in the estimates, and what would be enormously valuable assistance from the Office of Management and Budget or the agency itself, in assessing priorities, is not forthcoming. Duplications, especially in research and intelligence, are covered up through emphasis on minor differences. Their detection is the more difficult because they usually fall within the province of different subcommittees of the Appropriations Committees of the two Houses and it is in the subcommittees that the detailed examination of estimates takes place. Pressures from the interests involved and from their congressional spokesmen are overtly and subtly exerted. At any time a spartan decision in the direction of economy on the part of the committee may be overthrown in a quick vote on the floor or more often by the committee of the other House, which may hold a different view. Moreover, a very large part of the budget either does not go through the regular appropriations process or is subject to appropriations review but cannot be cut. In the former category are certain programs which have come to be known as "backdoor" spending, because they are handled outside the appropriations process. The most important of these are entitlement legislation, where Congress enacts a requirement mandating the expenditure of funds. This includes social security, unemployment payments, interest on the debt, medical care for the aged, and retirement benefits for Federal employees. In these instances, the amount that is spent in any given year is "open ended," that is, it depends on outside circumstances (such as the condition of the economy and interest rates) rather than on congressional action.[1]

Spending also may be uncontrollable because of contractual commitments made by the Federal government. In any year, a sizable portion of the budget goes to the payment of obligations incurred in earlier years. Of the proposed expenditures of $304 billion for fiscal year 1975, it has been estimated that only $84 billion—barely 25 percent of the total was subject to any reduction by Congress short of a major policy change in existing legislation.

The Appropriations Committees are unlike any others in many respects. In the House the committee has normally been an "exclusive" one, membership on any other standing committee being exceptional in the extreme. The Reorganization Act of 1970 provided that, while senators could serve on two major committees, only one of them could be on the following committees: Appropriations, Armed Services, Finance, and Foreign Relations.

Specialization within the committees is the general rule. The committees of both Houses have elaborate subcommittee structures. It was customary for House members to serve on only one major and one minor subcommittee, but in 1974 the number of subcommittees was increased to three for most members. Customarily, the same staff member serves the same subcommittee year after year.

Continuity is highly important, as regards both members and staff. Often, members of the House Appropriations Committee are from "safe" districts and rarely change to other committees. Unlike the ordinary legislative standing committee, most of the business of the Appropriations Committee each year is "old" business. The agency presenting its estimates and the estimates themselves have a tradition and a content for the most part familiar over the years to those who have served on or served the subcommittee for long periods. The measure of an agency's officials and especially of its budget officer is taken, and action on their requests colored thereby. While the continuity has the virtue of cumulative experience, there is also the problem that it can encourage the retention of obsolete or contraproductive functions.

Members of the Appropriations Committee develop certain occupational characteristics. Conscientiousness and a thick skin exist in about equal proportions in the usual Appropriations Committee member. Notably in the House, the self-image of hard work and budget-cutting prevails. Norms of expected behavior include deference to seniority within a subcommittee, reciprocity based on specialization, nonpartisanship with exceptions.[2]

The Senate Appropriations Committee exhibits certain differences. The smaller membership of the Senate does not permit exclusive committee assignments, and hence the average senator can spend less time on details. On certain of the subcommittees there are three ex officio members from the appropriate standing committees serving as liaison. This holds true of Agriculture and Forestry, Post Office and Civil Service, Armed Services, Joint Committee on Atomic Energy, District of Columbia, Public Works, Foreign Relations, and Aeronautical and Space Sciences.

In the past, the Senate committees' consideration of an appropriation was more often than not delayed until after the House had acted. The pressure of business has been such in recent years that this course is increasingly impractical. Committee consideration, that is, the subcommittee hearings of public and private witnesses and initial markup, has become virtually simultaneous in the two Houses. In such instances, however, the Senate subcommittees do not report until after they have heard from the House. To a very considerable extent the Senate thus acts as a board of review, and its role in the appropriating process is somewhat circumscribed as a result. Frequently, the Senate is left at the end of a session with a week or two to consider a measure which has been in the House for months. The House Appropriations Committee, in turn, points to prior delays in authorizing committees as the root of the problem. From there the buck is passed to the Executive Branch which is charged with tardiness in coming to Congress with its specific budgetary proposals involving additional authorizations. However that may be, it has been necessary in recent years to resort time and again to what are called "continuing resolutions" to finance the regular operations of the government. Continuing resolutions are devices which permit agencies to spend funds (usually at the existing level) pending passage of a regular appropriation.

The practice has been most unsatisfactory. It has muddled the appropriating process, preventing rational review of programs. It has permitted agencies to continue functions which should be reduced or eliminated and prevented them from undertaking or expanding essential programs. It has rendered meaningless the legal June 30 closing for the next fiscal year. In the Congressional Budget Act of 1974, the start of the fiscal year was moved from July 1 to October 1. The main purpose was to provide additional time for legislative action on the budget, but the expectation also is that the shift in the fiscal calendar will reduce the reliance on continuing resolutions. Further remedy may come from another feature of the new law which sets a closing date (with exceptions in emergency circumstances) for the reporting of authorizations by legislative committees. It provides a timetable for all phases of the budget and appropriations process in order to avert a last-minute jam of appropriations.

Each year the Appropriations Committees and Congress set forth seemingly formidable total reductions of the budget as their basis for claims of substantial economies. Each year these claims are criticized by the executive as largely "bookkeeping" devices. Some reductions result from decisions to postpone previously authorized programs. If these are ultimately undertaken and completed, the economy involved is somewhat dubious—unless, indeed, they subsequently serve as deterrents of requests for still more programs. Other congressional-imposed economies are directives to shrink unspent balances. Some of the most substantial cuts represent lowered estimates on the part of the committees as to what will be needed for certain statutory expenditures, such as veterans' benefits or agricultural subsidies. These are accompanied by directives to the agency to bring in a supplemental or deficiency estimate, if experience shows the need. Supplemental and deficiency appropriations are of the magnitude of several billon dollars in the usual year. When all these items are taken into account, congressional economies are probably much more modest than usually claimed.

In the performance of their duties, the Appropriations Committees occasionally receive assistance in addition to that of their own staff. On request, the budgetary officers of the Executive Branch will make special studies. On the basis of the Reorganization Act of 1946, the General Accounting Office undertakes studies of the efficiency of agency operations. The GAO claimed that its endeavors to improve efficiency and other activity in the departments and agencies saved $284 million in fiscal year 1973. The audit reports of the General Accounting Office are also valuable in congressional consideration of subsequent agency requests. Tips about examples of waste and extravagance as well as maladministration are constantly received by the committees. Many of these are investigated prior to the hearings or form the subject of questions at the time of an agency's appearance.

Floor amendments to appropriation bills are fairly numerous, but the majority are defeated. The opposition party to the administration may at times use this occasion to dramatize some issue. While floor time is equally divided between the parties, the ranking majority and minority members of the Appropriations subcommittees usually act as joint proponents of their bills since they are almost invariably in substantial agreement by the time the measure reaches the floor.

Floor amendments customarily fall into three groups. The first group arises quite naturally from the fact that Members of

Congress do not always agree on matters of policy; an amendment is a means of expressing disagreement with the policy recommended by the Appropriations Committee. Consequently, proposals to increase or decrease the funds for a particular activity are ways in which the House or Senate as a whole may express a verdict on the activity. This is especially true in highly controversial issues, such as defense costs, the war in Indochina, foreign aid, social services, and the distribution of earmarked revenues as between highway construction and rapid transit. Amendments at this point, though expressed in money terms, really concern policy matters. Note especially the activity on the part of certain members for their favorite agencies.

Of another type are the "economy" amendments, offered either in succession on a number of estimates or as an overall cut on a percentage or lump-sum basis or otherwise. This type tends to be favored during periodic "economy" drives, and it has the attraction of enabling members to vote for savings in total spending when they are unwilling or unable to cut specific items. On the other hand, this method has been severely attacked as constituting the virtual abdication by Congress of its appropriating responsibilities because it does not consider the relative merits of programs or subject them to detailed review. It has been on the grounds of congressional irresponsibility that some Presidents have claimed the power to "impound" appropriated funds. In the past, Congress has criticized this practice but had stopped short of requiring that the President spend appropriated monies. The issue, however, was sharply drawn in the Ninety-third Congress when, provoked by an unprecedented amount of executive impoundments, Congress passed the Congressional Budget Act of 1974 to control presidential refusals to spend money. Under the new procedure, any presidential proposal to defer an expenditure is subject to veto by majority vote of either House while a proposal to rescind an appropriation cannot take effect unless approved by majority vote of both Houses.

An amendment of a third type is the effort of a member in behalf of a particular project for his own district. This is not dissimilar from the first type but is more essentially local in character. When such amendments succeed, as they do from time to time, they serve to "make a record" for the member.

Nor does the action of either House singly represent the final verdict. Time and again, conference committee action is decisive in controversial policy matters.

When finally passed, what do the appropriation measures singly and collectively express? Many things, for they often represent the real thinking of Congress on national policy as distinct from its frequent response to the special interest in substantive legislation.

For this very reason, there have been valiant efforts in the last few years to achieve an overall view at the fiscal policy level. The first of these was the legislative budget provided for under the Reorganization Act of 1946 whereby all receipts and expenditures were to be brought together for simultaneous fixing of targets. There were two major attempts to make the provision operative. For practical purposes, these must be written down as almost complete failures. The reasons lay deep in the fiscal timetable and to some extent in the nature of the appropriation process as then established.

During 1950, a new method was used to give an opportunity to register over-all fiscal policy. This was in the form of a single measure, an omnibus appropriation bill.* Changes in the revenue system were incorporated in a separate tax bill, but estimated total revenue figured largely in the floor discussions of appropriations. The most significant consequence of this innovation did not relate to the details of individual items but took the form of over-all reductions aiming at the total. These were first urged in the form of percentage cuts, applicable to all save certain items or agencies. There also passed the House

---

* Foreign aid and certain other items were continued in separate bills, but Congress was well aware of their general contour.

a provision forbiding the filling of all except a small fraction of vacancies as they arose.

Opinion is divided regarding whether the economy thereby effected compensated for the alleged abdication of congressional discretion and the presumed necessity of cuts in activities deemed important. The method itself had from time to time been applied to individual appropriations, in which an agency had been asked to absorb a cut or the cost of a new activity or its pay increases. The fact of the matter is that it is good for an agency to go through this type of wringer occasionally, provided it is not repeated too often and does not go too far, for it forces reexamination of the staffing of particular units regardless of vested interests and sacred cows. What eventuates is likely to be more streamlined as well as more economical.

The omnibus bill was dropped after the one session, and separate subcommittees again resumed preparation of separate bills for the various grand divisions of the government.

A more ambitious and complex effort to reform the appropriations process was enacted in 1974. New budget committees have been established in the House and Senate and, in addition, a Congressional Budget Office has been created to provide information and analyses on budget matters.

This new congressional budget process is to be given its first full application in the fiscal 1977 budget. It, therefore, is not possible to evaluate its impact at this writing. However, the act appears to signify the intent of Congress to take a more active and responsible role in determining the fiscal policy and program priorities of the United States.

The appropriating process is often Congress's corrective for that which, in default of such a corrective, would otherwise be deemed its legislative intent. To pass a law or grant an authorization does not complete the legislative action on a given subject. So intricate is the pattern of group pressures and trades that very frequently the laws and authorizations require "correction" through curtailed appropriations—or omitting an appropriation altogether—in order to register the real judgment of Congress. At other times, a curtailed appropriation represents something more personal with the committee, for departments and agencies and activities and the heads of each vary in popularity. If the committee strains too far the general opinion of the House, floor amendments are moved. Sometimes the "corrective" is more substantive, and directives or riders are introduced. But by and large, in spite of strains between the Appropriations Committees and the other standing committees, there is a widespread acceptance of the former and, often, a wish for them to be "hardboiled." They are one of the great restraining factors on Congress and the government as a whole.

To what extent these traditional practices will be modified by the Congressional Budget Act of 1974, to which reference has been made, is uncertain at this point. The introduction of two new committees, one in each House, to act as "umpires" between the conflicting claims of the committees of interest and as between them and the fiscal control committees may very well bring about substantial changes in the relationships of the power cores within Congress as well as in the Federal government itself. It remains to be seen if the Congress has at last found the means for an assertion of rational control over itself and over the finances of the government in a highly complex and technological era.

If the potential of this latest change is realized, Congress, more and more like the British Parliament, will begin to look at the budget not only as a means of expenditures control but also as an instrument of national planning. Nevertheless, the amounts and activities involved are too tremendous and far-flung to suppose that Congress as a whole, or even very many of its members, can grasp them in their totality. No one can master them in detail. What is involved is an overall program, vast and far-reaching—of defense, of welfare, of world outlook, of development of resources, of the political economy of a wealthy and powerful nation. It is as trustees of this program that the Appropriations Committees and Congress in their appropriating function have done their best to serve.

NOTES

1. See Arthur Smithies, *The Budgetary Process in the United States* (New York: McGraw-Hill, 1955), var.; R. A. Wallace, "Congressional Control of the Budget," *Midwest Journal of Political Science*, (May 1959), pp. 151-67.
2. See Richard F. Fenno, Jr., "The House Appropriations Committee as a Political System," *American Political Science Review* (June 1962), pp. 310-24, for an exceptional study of this aspect of the House Committee.

CHAPTER 8

Congressional Investigations

Congressional investigations play a multitude of roles.

The congressional investigation furnishes a basis of legislation. That is its time-tested function firmly supported by the members of Congress, the Judiciary, and, more or less, by the Executive Branch. The congressional investigation shares this legislative role, with research, with executive recommendations, with the presentments of individual members, with lobbyists, and others.

The investigation is also an instrument of oversight or congressional review of the Executive Branch. There are other instruments of this kind: the appropriations process, floor debate, and contacts both formal and informal. Many times the investigation finds itself operating in the prelegislative twilight zone in which the very fact of illumination influences conduct, sometimes rendering legislation unnecessary. Congressional speeches, on and off the floor, or even the mere introduction of a bill, may likewise bring about such a desired result. A by-product of the investigation is the education of the public, especially since the advent of the televised hearing. This role the investigation shares with floor debate, research reports, and constituent contacts. It also is one among many ways of sharpening the image of congressmen as conscientious and vigorous servants of the public interest, although on occasion the opposite effect may be produced. Either way, it can be a factor in the electoral process.

In other words the investigation is not unique in any of its roles; nor can one always say in any particular instance which of the various potential roles it is designed chiefly to serve, nor how many it will end by serving. It should be reiterated, however, that in theory at least, its prime function is related to legislation.

George Galloway observes the following in his work on the congressional legislative process:

> Aside from its informative and disciplinary functions, the congressional investigating committee is often used by group interests to exploit crisis situations, to expose and attack rival groups and practices, and to mobilize public opinion against opposing groups and the governmental agencies associated with them. . . .
>
> The scope and conduct of congressional investigations have been subjects of controversy throughout the history of the Republic. Their powers and procedures have been bitterly attacked and vigorously defended. . . . It is now well settled that the congressional committee of inquiry is a device appropriate for use in the performance by Congress of its legislative, supervisory, and informing functions.[1]

Again in a later work, Dr. Galloway calls attention to the "variety of practical uses" of investigations. "Their most important function has been to collect facts so as to enable committee members to make informed judgments regarding legislative proposals. . . . A second use of the hearing process is the safety valve function. . . . A third use . . . is as a political sounding board for the legislature, furnishing a barometer to gauge public opinion."[2]

The Reorganization Act of 1946[3] was an attempt to systematize the many congressional investigations by assigning the overseeing of certain agencies to appropriate standing committees. The act has had the effect of at least reducing the number of committees created especially to conduct investigations. Significantly, the Reorganization Act of 1970 made no additional changes of any great significance, except to strengthen the oversight function of the regular committees.

Attempts have been made to draw the line between an investigation and the ordinary committee inquiry and hearing, but without too much success. Occasionally an investigation will be ordered and separately financed without any hearings at all ensuing. A line can perhaps be drawn as to whether the investigation is conducted by a standing committee or by a special or select committee. Lines can also be drawn between inquiries requiring supplemental funds and those conducted by the permanent staff. Some investigations use the subpoena power; others do not even ask for it.

The truth of the matter is that the investigation in essence is a *process* and not a single, definable instrument. It lends itself to the performance of many functions. It is highly adaptable in the detail of its rituals. It is a most useful tool. According to whether they are narrowly or broadly defined, one may count up to several hundred investigations in a given session.

Some investigations are of persons. Most of these are by appropriate committees of the Senate, prior to action upon presidential nominations. Occasionally they take on the guise of witch hunts, and still more rarely are preludes to impeachment.

One of the most celebrated investigations in recent times was that of Gerald R. Ford as Vice President designee to succeed Spiro T. Agnew in the first application of the 25th Amendment. Under its terms, his confirmation by both houses was required. In the House, the Judiciary Committee was named to handle it in a regular referral. The same procedure was followed in the Senate except that the Committee on Rules was the designee, and only after lengthy consideration to determine whether or not the nomination presented a special situation requiring a special procedure.

Responsibility for oversight of the administration results in a number of investigations.* Some, such as the succession of investigations of the regulatory commissions by the House Interstate and Foreign Commerce Committee's Subcommittee on Legislative Oversight, the Special Committee on Federally Supported Research and Development Programs, and, more recently, those of Senator Proxmire's Appropriations Subcommittee into cost overruns in Defense Department procurement, and the Watergate affair, concern themselves rather widely with the conduct and functioning of entire units. Others, such as those concerned with the dismissal of General Douglas MacArthur by President Truman and President Nixon's firing of Archibald Cox, the Watergate Special Prosecutor, and the resignation of Attorney General Elliot Richardson, deal with single episodes or acts. Of this sort, too, was the investigation of the Pearl Harbor disaster more than three decades ago. These investigations can sometimes end by ranging widely if they uncover some vein of weakness in the structure of the Executive Branch.

Some inquiries arise in the course of the appropriations process, seeking economy or assurance of the execution of legislative intent. The Government Operations Committees, working closely with the General Accounting Office, have a continuous mandate, a roving commission to investigate almost anything in the administration that seems to need it.

Most frequent are the inquiries conducted in connection with regular legislative bills and ratification of treaties. These "hearings" are in some circles not considered investigations at all; but, if we are thinking in terms of a "process," they most certainly qualify.

Finally, there are the investigations of "problems." Organized crime, the hunt for Communists in government in the 1950s, the disarmament inquiries, racketeering in labor unions, tax-exempt foundations, private pension systems, inva-

---

* See chapters 4 and 9 for a fuller analysis of this aspect.

sions of privacy by the Federal government, the war in Vietnam, and Watergate and campaign financing practices, are among the most famous. Under this heading undoubtedly fall the annual inquiries as to the state of the nation's economic health by the Joint Economic Committee, and its widely ranging analyses of the major aspects of our political economy. The investigations of problems and the hearings on bills are largely interchangeable, for often it is the multiplicity of bills on a subject that leads to an investigation of a problem, and the existence of a problem is not infrequently recognized by focusing consideration upon a specific bill.

The investigation as "process" follows many patterns. Before considering variants, desirable or undesirable, it is a useful analytic tool to sketch the stages likely to be followed in the ideal full-fledged inquiry. First is a clear definition or demarcation of the problem or question. If a specific bill is under consideration, its content will serve initially as such a demarcation. If not, then the problem will be defined. This is followed by the allocation of staff, or the request for and the obtaining of additional funds for the expense of the inquiry. At about this stage, a request is often made to the Congressional Research Service or some other research source to conduct a preliminary "skirmishing" of available sources. If staff is to be added, a staff director, and, often, a minority counsel are selected and proceed to select additional staff. The next stage is the preliminary staff planning of the inquiry, which, when approved by the committee, establishes the basic approach of the investigation. A balanced panel consisting of a cross section of expert witnesses is then named. Questions to be explored in hearings are determined. These are questions of interest to the committee members or suggested by staff analysis. Prehearing conferences serve to focus the hearings. In the hearings themselves individual committee members develop particular points. Organizations concerned with the problem are invited to make their views known, although they seldom need an invitation. So also are appropriate agencies in the Executive Branch. Broad questions develop and staff or other research studies are commissioned thereon. Supplementary witnesses may be invited to appear to assist the committee. The committee holds a number of executive sessions in which the general outlines of the findings are first determined, and then reports and bills are drafted in detail. These are then presented to the parent body along with recommendations. If a bill results and is passed and sent to the other House, then the appropriate committee of the latter should (and often does) ask its staff to brief it on the nature, substance, and results of the investigation prior to its own considerations.

A surprising number of investigations conform in all essentials to the process as thus outlined. A large number of others fall short in one or more particulars, and it is these shortcomings that raise serious questions as to the process itself, and even as to the responsibility of Congress.

Some investigations range widely and irresponsibly. Some become mere "fishing expeditions." It was this type of excess that led to the case of *Watkins v. U.S.*,[4] in which the Court declared in succession that there must be a legislative purpose, that the purpose must be defined, that there is no general authority to investigate individuals or to expose for the sake of exposure, that inquiries "designed to 'punish' those investigated are indefensible," that witnesses have their constitutional rights which Congress must respect.[5] Yet in general the power of inquiry is coterminous with its legislative competence.[6]

Some committees have been known to "stack" witnesses, giving far more time and preferred positions to one side— usually the position held by the chairman—than to the other. Questions and treatment of witnesses may be motivated by headline hunting rather than a search for truth. Committee members may rely upon their immunities in making random or baseless charges. The rights of witnesses may be grossly infringed—although much less now than before Congress gave attention to the problem. Investigations may be punitive in intent, arising out of resentment at certain administrative decisions. The "prosecuting attorney approach" may badger witnesses unmercifully. These and other abuses have led many committees to adopt codes of fair procedure. The codes have many elements in common—the right to counsel, the right to defend oneself against charges, the obligation of members to treat witnesses with courtesy. On March 23, 1955, in the Doyle resolution, the House amended its standing rules to incorporate therein such a code for its investigations.[7]

The Legislative Reorganization Act of 1970 is silent on this point although it involves a number of changes in the committee structure of both Houses. That, in itself, would appear to be an indication that major abuse of the investigatory power is largely a thing of the past. Certainly, there were no charges of mistreatment of witnesses or other abusive practices in connection with the Senate Watergate investigation, which was of a nature that opened wide the possibility.

Criticism is occasionally voiced in the Executive Branch that committee staffs sometimes, during an investigation, exact as their price for support of a bill the inclusion of a specific point favored by a staff member, though opposed by the executive. The implication here is that the members themselves are too busy to master the details of the bill, and necessarily rely upon staff which, in turn, may have its own axes to grind. On the other hand, the staff member may well be speaking on the basis of what he knows of the members' real intent.

All of these criticisms are important. Yet they never affected more than a minority of the committees, although they obtained a far greater proportion of public attention. Meanwhile, be it instrument or process, the investigation will find the roles assigned to it a challenge to perform more adequately, skillfully, and responsibly. On balance, no one seriously advocates the abolition of the investigatory process or even its substantial curtailment.

A few supplementary observations are in order. For the most

part, the chairman makes or breaks an investigation; as Truman did when he headed the War Investigating Committee or Ervin did in the Watergate affair. He can pursue the investigation thoroughly and constructively. He can give each of the other committee members his chance to develop lines of questioning without reference to party. He can use staff intelligently and permit his colleagues to do the same. Above all, he can impart a "tone" to the whole proceedings that is worthy of the occasion.

The type of staff utilized makes a genuine difference. The most effective are those of professional competence, minimal partisanship, conscientious, and resistant to the intrusion of their own points of view into the procedure. In the type of investigation which is an extension of the particular interest and drive of the chairman, the committee counsel should ordinarily be one engaged for the occasion and in full sympathy with the chairman's intent. Partly because so many members of Congress are themselves lawyers and tend to give a juridical coloration to investigations, there is a disposition to use lawyers in this capacity rather more than subject specialists. To the latter, either on the committee staff or in the Congressional Research Service, is more frequently assigned the preparation of the staff research papers and other background work. If the staffs are mere recipients of patronage, they can be quite wasteful, for even though they may be potentially competent, much time must be spent on their own education.

There is the ever-present danger of distortion. The charge has also been made that some staff personnel may on occasion stimulate unnecessary investigations in order to retain employment. On the other side of the coin, many standing committees undoubtedly have continuing agenda and responsibilities in excess of the capacities of the professional staff members normally assigned to them. What may be lost in occasional overstaffing may be more than made up by the experience of these men who are retained year after year for a series of special investigations financed by *ad hoc* funds. This is undoubtedly a factor favoring the assignment of investigations to standing committees rather than to special committees, which latter, by the nature of their establishment, must recruit new and often inexperienced staff on a purely temporary basis. It is not surprising, therefore, to find these special committees occasionally borrowing on a reimbursable basis from the experienced and immediately useful staffs of other committees, the executive, the General Accounting Office, or the Congressional Research Service. Such staff members retain their earlier tenure, and return to their original agency when the committee no longer needs them. Many of these problems are, in effect, recognized in the Congressional Reorganization Act of 1970 which with its stress on the oversight or congressional review function of the standing committees has sought to minimize the use of special investigations.

In the House, a committee wishing to sponsor a special investigation requiring funds presents the case to the Committee on House Administration, in principle usually after clearing with the Speaker. The latter's opposition is usually tantamount to a veto, and his influence on what is to be investigated is one of his principal sources of power and influence. In the Senate any senator of the majority party can propose (in the form of an introduction of an establishing resolution) an investigation. This is subject to the consideration by the committee which would normally claim subject-matter jurisdiction.

More usual in the Senate is for a senator to work from within a standing committee and be named as chairman of a subcommittee to deal with the problem in question. In some committees such assignments are perennial, extended from Congress to Congress, with successive grants of funds.

In both Houses, it is usual for the member sponsoring a successful resolution setting up a special committee to be named chairman thereof. This adds to his prestige as well as his opportunity for service. It also widens considerably the committee-leadership base, supplementing the seniority rule by often drawing upon the rank and file for chairmen. Under rare and extraordinary circumstances, the party majority leaders may serve as chairmen, as they did in the full-dress investigations in space and astronautics following the advent of the first sputnik. More often than not, if the party leadership is persuaded as to the need of a special investigation it will also name the chairman, as was the case with Senator Ervin's designation as chairman of the special Watergate committee.

In conclusion, we repeat that the investigation has not one role, but several. It is a process, an instrument, if you will, to carry out a number of functions. It has grown greatly in frequency and prestige, as the agenda of Congress has multiplied many times, and as the problems facing the nation have grown in magnitude and complexity. Transitions are observable, chiefly in the direction of perfecting technique and safeguarding against abuses. Skill in questioning, focusing upon the relevant, buttressing by research at both the preparatory and the synthesizing stages, streamlining of press relations, increasing nonpartisanship, development of codes of fair and orderly procedure—these and other trends are making the congressional investigation a potent and dramatic instrument in governance. It is the major factor in legislative–executive relations, the major educator of the public in dramatizing issues (rivaled only by the President's press conference), one among several tools to serve as the basis for congressional decisions. As it makes further gains in responsibility and precision, the congressional investigation will appear more and more clearly as a vital part of the democratic process.

NOTES

1. George B. Galloway, *Legislative Process in Congress* (New York: Thomas Y. Crowell, 1953), pp. 487, 627.
2. George B. Galloway, *History of the House of Representatives* (New York: Thomas Y. Crowell, 1961), p. 89

3. Public Law 601, 79th Congress
4. 354 U.S. 178 (1957)
5. See "Congress v. the Courts: Limitations on Congressional Investigations," *University of Chicago Law Review,* Seminar 1957, pp. 740–45
6. See the reaffirmation of this concept in *Barenblatt v. U.S.* 360 U.S. 109 (1959)
7. See House Manual, Sec. 735, Rule XI, subsection h-q pp. 366-68 (1960). Attention is also called to the study of the McCarthy hearings in Alan Barth, *Government by Investigation* (New York: Viking, 1955). The book is a disturbing, though one-sided, account of the extravagances of the McCarthy era.

CHAPTER 9

Congress and Administration

Only the naive believe that Congress legislates and the President administers—that is, that our tripartite government observes a strict protocol and that each part stays out of the others' provinces. The founding fathers were well aware that their neat division of separation of powers into the legislative, executive, and judicial had been deliberately overlaid or complicated by the principle of checks and balances in the text of the Constitution. Informal usages have found many a further interstice in the formal document, until there are few major sectors of governance to which at least at some time or other both Congress and the President have not laid claim.

Yet, outside of Congress itself there has been surprisingly little criticism of the extent to which the executive has matured legislation, legislation which in its more or less finished form is sent to Congress, sometimes with an imperious expectation of enactment. Nor has there been much but rear guard criticism of the expanded powers of the bureaucracy to make "regulations" in great profuseness, for these have seemed an inevitable development from the very nature of present-day governance. Where these trends have been criticized, it has most frequently been by those who have objected to the substance and not to the process; Congress has itself had its share of criticism for passing the enabling legislation in the first place.

On the other hand, the ventures of Congress into what administrators customarily regard as their peculiar sphere have been subjected to widespread censure. This censure can take the form of intense but underbreath resentment on the part of the administrators. The gulf between that which Congress has operatively considered to be its role in administration and what the administrators in their candid moments are prepared to concede such a role to be is one of the most fundamental and pervasive conflicts in the whole national picture. It is not growing any the less with the years.

It has been correctly urged that the line between policy and administration is impossible to draw. Congressmen, no less than other students of the problem, are keenly aware of the extent to which many an administrator forms policy in his day-to-day decisions. This is especially true, for example, in actions of the regulatory commissions, but it occurs wherever discretion is implicitly or explicitly vested in an agency. The subject has been vigorously explored, not only in the journals and reviews but also in the committee hearings of Congress itself. It furnishes a measure of justification for much of the congressional interest in the kind of person administering even in the lower echelons. The fact is that Congress and especially its committees seek to bend the departments and agencies to their will. Reciprocally, departments and agencies seek to free themselves as far as possible from congressional control. The Forest Service, for example, attempted unsuccessfully to secure legislation which in effect would exempt the Eastern forests from the Wilderness Act, by substituting an administrative category of wild areas set up by the agency. In this they were supported by the timber interests.

The Constitution is both ambivalent and ambiguous on the congressional role in administration. It declares that the President shall be the seat of executive power; it gives confirmation of appointments and the appropriating function to Congress. In the several legislative powers entrusted to Congress it makes no stipulation of or sets no limit to the detail that may mark a law; and statutory detail is or may be carried so far that in effect it is administration. A watchful oversight or review of the work of the executive, especially in recent years, has been conceded to be an appropriate legislative function, but the differences are sharp and widespread on what is appropriate overseeing and, even more, what is correctly bracketed under the elusive concept of "control." The term, "monitoring," has become increasingly popular, though this is somewhat more limited. "To monitor means to test, to educate, to criticize, to publicize, to question, to compel explanations, to oversee performance, and thus to establish limits of tolerance and expectation." [1]

For our purposes, it may be useful to consider this subject under the three headings of control or supervision, standards, and specific decisions, and then consider each in turn.

The word "control" is popularly so loosely used that it is important at the outset to understand what is really meant.[2] We face in the bureaucracy a force of tremendous power—a force which, if it operates within legally prescribed limits and according to popular intent as reflected in the policies of elected officials and other media, can be an instrument of far-reaching effectiveness for the public interest. Conversely, it can become a Frankenstein monster, a law unto itself, interested largely in its own perpetuation and expansion. Some of the great post-revolutionary political conflicts in the People's Republic of China have centered on this issue. Many view the transformation of the original revolutionary zeal of Soviet communism into the present police state as of this character.

Then, too, there is the vitally important question of honesty and integrity. Controls internal and external can do much to assure that this tremendous machine does not fall into the hands of the unscrupulous, though the final verdict in these matters rests rather with the spiritual forces that so largely determine the mores of a people. In the popular mind, the problem of control involves efficient operation—that is, economy, effectiveness in performance of the several functions, coordination in the bureaucracy as a whole. With the growth in numbers, with the advent of so much that is discretionary in officialdom and so much that can vitally affect the individuals and groups with which officialdom deals, the bureaucracy has come to have very great political power of its own. All too frequently this is capable of influencing the very electoral process on which its control so largely depends. Moreover, in American eyes, there is a new and important element requiring control, an element of integrity which in times past has been largely taken for granted, but no longer can be so. Finally, much of policy determination itself is inherent in administration. For example, there is the power in foreign relations and in direction of the armed services to create major *faits accomplis*. Another example is the weight of authority which experience with problems gives to a government agency administering a field such as agriculture when it proposes new legislation. Thus, it becomes all too obvious that general policy as well as detail is a sphere in which the issue of control of the bureaucracy is vital. All these elements—legality, intent, honesty, integrity, efficiency, political power, loyalty, policy—are parts or aspects of the problem of control.

Limited roles in control are played also by the courts and the General Accounting Office, but our concern here is not with them, except insofar as the latter has recently considerably expanded its investigatory role in response to committee inquiries. The built-in controls of the "presidency," especially of the Office of Management and Budget, and of the Civil Service Commission, are also of major importance in any overall consideration, but are relevant here only in that they constitute the alternative instruments offered by those who criticize or resent the role of Congress.

Legality on the part of the administration is scarcely the responsibility of the Legislative Branch, nor does it claim it as such. The courts and the General Accounting Office are the normal enforcing agents, but occasionally a speech will charge illegality, or congressional investigations will uncover information which is sent to the attorney general or automatically alerts or spurs enforcement action, the Watergate Affair being a celebrated case in point. Committees or members will also raise questions on the basis of information received from the General Accounting Office or from the press or leaks within the Executive Branch.

Distortion of legislative intent is another matter. This is a province that Congress regards as peculiarly its own. Apart from amending the law, which is not likely to be too practicable a remedy because of the probability of a presidential veto, the chief weapons of Congress in this field are publicity and appropriations. It was through these two channels that Congress played a part in bringing about a termination of the military involvement in Indochina. Theoretically, there should be no problem, if laws are carefully drawn, but they are not always so drawn. Then, too, many laws are purposely drawn in general terms to allow a very considerable measure of administrative discretion. Laws whose chief content is the declaration of objectives and the creation of instruments to carry them out lend themselves readily to subsequent administrative modification of these objectives. The administration of certain laws may legally be entirely correct; while at the same time, administration may be in such a fashion as to incorporate the philosophy of the administrator rather than of Congress. Price controls, for example, can be administered to limit profits more than—or less than—wages. Moreover, Congress may never have made its intention clear in the first place. With so many laws actually matured in the bureaucracy, the Congress can never be quite certain what "sleepers" or hidden powers and meanings may be concealed within the text.

In Britain what seems to be a relative absence of such problems is probably accounted for by two circumstances—the general loyalty of the civil servant to the intent of the minister and the desire to save him embarrassment; plus the assumption on the part of the government of public responsibility for all the consequences of a given law, even though it may not have realized them at the time of passage. Separation of the executive from the legislative under the American system lessens the former's loyalty to the Legislative Branch, while at the same time it gives greater subsequent assurance that such deviation from understood intent will be ruthlessly exposed in floor debate and committee investigations. Retribution for non-compliance can be exacted through cuts or directives in appropriations.

A word of caution should be added at this point against crediting as valid all accusations in Congress as to distorted intent. It is not an uncommon practice for individual members or groups, unable to secure the general support of their colleagues, to charge such distortion, on points that were perhaps not even foreseen, let alone specifically passed upon at time of enactment. It is also standard tactics of the opposition to try to pin the badges of illegality and irresponsibility upon the party in power in the executive. These charges may or may not be true, especially to the extent alleged. Nonetheless, the nature of government today is such that a large measure of discretion must inevitably fall to the bureaucracy; and it is surely of importance that the way be open and used to prevent this discretion being employed contrary to the intent of the body passing the original law.

Crude peculation in the administration has not been a serious problem, and in any event is more likely to be uncovered by the ordinary internal accounting controls rather than by Congress. Scandals involving the Bureau of Internal Revenue, whereby tax favors may be extended for various considerations, represent a more difficult type to detect. An approach to problems of this kind which, at one time, attracted considerable interest is the formulation of a code of ethics for all public officials.[3] This code would go beyond the law, and serve as a crystallized norm for all public officials in place of the confusion we have already mentioned.

In 1966 the Senate set up a Select Committee on Standards and Conduct, and rules were established with regard to the Senate and its staff. The House did the same the following year. Both rely on the concept of disclosure of sources of income other than congressional salary. Similar arrangements have been proposed for the great bulk of government employees.

As already noted, the weapon of congressional investigation is an essential one. Leaving investigations wholly to the executive is an invitation to inertia if not a temptation to cover up errors, serious and minor. The American electorate rightly honors its crusaders and this puts a premium on success in this regard by a member. Congressional investigations not only have their own special staffs, they also have a considerable measure of concrete assistance in obtaining information from inside the executive and from members of the public. Such investigations are peculiarly adapted to those situations in which no law has been violated, but in which there has been an apparent indifference to public trust. By focusing on ethics rather than legality, they can perform the highly important function of crystallizing opinion on what things are or are not "done." This is not to say that all investigations are noble in motive or nobly conducted. Many fall far short of such standards. Yet, Madison's point made almost two centuries ago retains much of its pristine validity: the American system harnesses the self-interest of different institutions to check each other in such a way that perhaps the people so governed are better served than they would be by concentration of power and responsibility.

Efficiency as an objective of control requires more precise definition. Actually three principal values seem to be involved in this concept. The first is economy in financial terms, or, more fundamentally, in the use of men and materials. The second is effectiveness, that is, the performance of functions and meeting of goals as entrusted, accurately, expeditiously, and in full measure. The third has to do with coordination, the integrating of the several parts and objectives in such a fashion that there is no incompatibility or lost motion. A word is in order concerning each of these three.

Concerning economy we have already indicated the role played by the Appropriations Committees. The cuts imposed by Congress at the behest of the Appropriations Committees in the estimates that have already been approved by the Office of Management and Budget are occasionally fairly substantial; though some cynics doubt how far they go beyond what the agency succeeded in including originally in excess of what was vitally needed—expecting cuts in any event. As regards specific items of extravagance, the direct observations of congressional committees are supplemented from time to time by tips or information from many sources both within and outside of the government. Efforts to establish cost figures based on work load have made some progress in the so-called "performance budget." The staff work of the committees constitutes another invaluable aid. Yet, when all is said and done, Congress is still largely on the defensive as against a department, especially the departments of Defense or Health, Education, and Welfare, because of the sheer magnitude and technical nature of their operations. The secrecy surrounding many military matters constitutes another hazard. Nevertheless, as Senator Proxmire showed in recent years, an impact can be made by the possession of facts and persistence. His crusading on cost-overruns and other dubious fiscal practices in defense set the stage for curbing extravagant defense expenditures on the procurement of new military weapons and equipment.

The effectiveness of administration is a subject of constant congressional concern. Much criticism is informal, by telephone or otherwise, and the matter is settled "out of court." It should be borne in mind at this point that far more than is the individual member of Parliament, the member of Congress is looked to by his constituents for redress of grievances or as the recipient of suggestions for improved public service. The President is also written to on matters of this sort. By and large, the agencies are extremely sensitive to criticism, even by a single member of Congress. Thus, there goes on through various channels a continuous barrage of reactions from those affected by, or from those noticing, ineffective or faulty operations. Conversely there are instances of praise and gratitude as well.

Sometimes criticism reaches the stature of a full-fledged investigation. The investigation may be by the standing committees charged with responsibility for the field, or by one of the Committees on Government Operations, or it may be by a special committee created for the purpose. The investigation is an exceedingly flexible weapon of control. It can range widely; it can focus narrowly. It can be very simple—the result of a mere request on a committee's part for explanation of certain matters—usually, but not always, resulting in a single public hearing. On the other hand, as in the case of the recall of General MacArthur or the Watergate affair, hearings may go on for months and pass in review matters of the highest importance. Or the investigation may be continuous over a period of years as, for example, that by the committee presided over by the then Senator Truman during the war, which ranged widely over much of the war effort or the crime investigations of a Kefauver or a McClellan. It should be borne in mind that the standing committees of Congress are specifically charged under the Legislative Reorganization Act of 1946 with "watchfulness" over the corresponding agencies in the bureaucracy and, over the years, this function has come to be more fully exercised.

Of late, much attention has been directed both in the White House and in Congress as to whether an agency has in fact been effective in attaining its original goals. This has been true notably in the area of elimination of poverty and effective or compensatory aid in the education of children from underprivileged and minority groups. Certain specific programs have been under heavy fire as ineffective, and in some instances have been curtailed or eliminated on this ground. The end results are not yet in sight. A major problem is obviously the vested interests of entrenched bureaucracy.

A committee is often composed of members largely chosen from regions whose economic interest is coincidental with the purpose that created the agency for which the committee is responsible. In that case, the committee is likely to be especially zealous to see that the work is well performed; but it is also likely to be less ready to criticize policy recommendations. Pressure groups in this and in other fashions find their spokesmen in Congress. They serve as ready and alert vehicles to see to it, as far as agitation, criticism, and questions will do the job, that the group's interests are furthered up to the intent of the relevant law. They will also see to it that these interests are not harmed by a hostile administration without a clear showing of authority therefor. Finally, it should be repeated that the influence and activity of the Appropriations Committees extend considerably beyond economy. In the language which the committees write into appropriations bills and reports, in criticism, in informal guidance, or explicit directives, controls are exercised in a most powerful fashion over administration, organization, and policy.

On balance, Congress is reasonably successful in its efforts to keep the Executive Branch more sensitive to public opinion than otherwise would be the case on the basis of presidential direction alone. In its questions and investigations it sometimes goes far beyond what many regard as appropriate. Congress has in many instances itself been wasteful of time and effort. The weapon of investigation has at times been irresponsibly exercised. Yet, the public interest aroused, the quality of alertness created, the sense of accountability generated are surely assets of very great value. Over and above this there exists an impressive record of concrete reforms and results; and, conversely, of vindications of agencies through criticism being pursued to a conclusion, a record that makes the general verdict on the particular matter unmistakably favorable.

We leave for later discussion * the type of control that looks toward coordination.

* Cf. chapter 11.

The problem of the political power of the Executive Branch especially at election time is one on which congressmen are divided in mind. The temptation to profit thereby themselves is considerable. On the other hand, there are many campaign and election practices that are illegal, and others that are distinctly frowned upon by more than merely the members of Congress whose hold on the electorate is impaired thereby. The manipulation of administrative decisions and activities to create favorable impressions and results at election time evokes an uneasiness even among some of the President's party. It can bring criticism rising to rage on the part of the opposition.

A word is certainly in order concerning one of the most controversial aspects of congressional control of the executive—that is, the manipulation of the executive bureaucracy for the political purposes of the White House. The issue is always imminent. In the Watergate affair, and related matters, it burst upon the nation in a spectacular fashion, with the airing of the possibility of economic and tax favors in return for campaign contributions and in the involvement of the Internal Revenue Service, the FBI, and the CIA in highly dubious activities.

The Watergate affair had a counterpart in the intense congressional interest and intervention in the Executive Branch over the issue of the loyalty of government employees a quarter of a century earlier. The premise then held by the majority of Congress was that the "free world" was at war, a "cold war," with the "Communist world," a premise first advanced incidentally by the Executive Branch. A strong case was made out at the time that the enemy bloc had in fact resolved upon our ultimate destruction by whatever weapons it could employ, including internal subversion of the government and widespread espionage. Under these circumstances, it is not surprising that those in Congress who accepted this premise (and almost all did) felt impelled to take whatever steps were thought to be necessary to assure that there were none in critical and sensitive positions who might owe allegiance to the enemy. Once the process began, however, the fears of people were too often exploited for sheer sensationalism, not to speak of political purposes, with many innocent government employees and others suffering the consequences. Even at the height of this so-called McCarthy era, the majority sentiment in Congress still tended to be for giving the benefit of the doubt to the individual in a noncritical position, but it insisted that the doubt be resolved against the individual in a sensitive and critical position. To understand the congressional attitude the aforementioned underlying assumption must first be met squarely. Congress undoubtedly forced the pace, once the issue burst on the public, but the executive was likewise committed to the view that no Communist should hold an appointive office.

We may summarize the problem by saying that there is agreement that Congress has and should have a highly important role in the control and oversight of the administration, however much people may differ on the proper extent of such control and the skill and objectivity with which Congress in fact exercises it. The investigation is an inevitable response of Congress to the dangers of a technical monopoly on the part of the bureaucracy.[4]

The prescription of administrative standards is another matter. What is in question is not declarations of policy such as "appointment solely on merit" or "full reporting." It is when standards become detailed, with salary scales, retirement, accounting procedures, purchase and disposal of supplies, and similar administrative areas meticulously set out in statutes, and frequently with the laws thereon differing quite irrationally in different departments. These differences may have arisen through differences in the committees that brought in the original bills or through different times and personnel of the same committee, or differences in the influence of the employees concerned. For example, it is difficult to defend on rational grounds the singling out of the postal employees or the so-called "blue-collar" workers for unique treatment, as against the classified service.

However, the fact that laws of this kind may be intricate in their detail may leave a false impression concerning the origin of such detail. For the most part these laws are matured not in the congressional committee but in the department or agency of the administration appropriate thereto. Most bills relating to personnel originate in the Civil Service Commission, often it is true aided by at least some prior consultation with the Post Office and Civil Service Committees. These Committees reserve full right to amend the Commission's version and usually exercise it. The chairmen often differ, and differing versions thus find their way into the two houses, ultimately to be resolved in conference committee, with the executive tactfully but often effectively pressing its point of view. So also bills relating to procurement or disposal of supplies and property or accounting are apt to be formulated in great detail in the legal or accounting or budget offices of the agencies concerned. They are submitted to Congress for review and formal sanction.

The Appropriations Committees occasionally attach stipulations to bills which have the effect of prescription of standards. Some of these may be designed to force a shrinkage of staff or expenditure. Others reflect policy verdicts. They are often criticized by the administration as not leaving leeway for adaptation to individual circumstances or as being illogical in their incidence, except, of course, when they make provision for some power which was not obtainable from the authorizing committee.

Finally, Congress has retained a large degree of power to make specific administrative decisions. The most frequent are those associated with appropriations, public works, and confirmation of appointments. The appropriating process lends itself to specific decisions not merely in the detailed sums appropriated or denied but in the accompanying text of the committee reports. Specific books for overseas informational use may be frowned upon; higher salaries may be allowed specific positions; authorized activities may be sharply curtailed in specific aspects; funds for construction of veterans' hospitals may be tied to specific locations. These and other normally administrative decisions may result from use of the appropriating process to indicate policy judgments or to express the localism inherent in congressional structure.* *United States v. Lovett* [5] has curbed the use of the appropriation bill for direct removal of individuals, but more subtle tools remain.

Akin to this administrative detail are the numerous immigration and other special or private bills which pass each Congress. The amount of time that Congress spends on such individual decisions may easily be exaggerated. Relatively few members take part in the subcommittee discussion which reviews or screens them, and the members have staff assistance also. In these and other administrative matters in which congressmen intervene formally or informally, one sees a working out of a congressional philosophy that most laws designed to promote general objectives need adjustments to fit particular situations; and that the individual congressman has the responsibility of making such adjustment possible as far as his constituents are concerned. For the most part, such intervention is based on humane considerations; in some instances it reflects the economic interests of constituents or districts; in still other instances, campaign contributions or a legal retainer to a member's firm or a friend may have been not without at least unconscious influence. In any event, the practice of private bills, in its end results bears a curious resemblance to the effect on specific administrative decisions which British members of Parliament produce through the instrumentality of the question hour. Interest in the effect of administrative decisions on persons is widespread in Congress.

The formal confirmation of presidential appointments has been explored and discussed quite thoroughly many times. We have little to add, except to note that in the Ninety-third

* See chapters 7 and 15 for background.

Congress when evidence of an increasing degree of contempt for the powers of Congress on the part of the executive was detected, the Senate leadership with overwhelming support from both parties advised committee chairmen to consider the use of the power of confirmation as a counterweapon against executive contempt for Congress.[6] The response was immediate, and effective. Pledges were obtained from all major presidential appointees to the effect that they would be responsive to requests for appearances and information to the committees.

The confirming power, firmly exercised, assures the spotlight on the earlier record of at least the upper ranges among the appointees and can serve to put a philosophic commitment on the record. Patronage has been excoriated and defended in a multitude of quarters. The firing of employees has been "complicated" both ways by congressional interest—or usually by the interest of individual congressmen. Some employees have incurred enmity; others are admired. Congress protected a J. Edgar Hoover from the enmity of an attorney general. At the same time, it makes difficult the retention of a staff member who has lost the confidence of powerful congressmen as in the case of Lewis Patrick Gray, III, whose name as Hoover's successor had to be withdrawn by the President.

Apart from government employees, there are many other instances of Congressional interest in individuals. Certain orders concerning the deportation of aliens are subject to being overruled by the non-vetoable concurrent resolution. We have already mentioned individual immigration bills as granting exceptions from normal procedure. Much of the grist of congressional investigations has to do with *persons*—invasions of privacy, undue influence, loyalty, and other matters. The widespread interest on Capitol Hill in formulating rules of committee procedure and ethics springs largely from practices in connection with hearings which were widely regarded, at one time, as unfair in their impact on individuals.

For a long time Congress retained virtually the entire responsibility for final decision as to the internal organization of departments and agencies. The rigidities arising from such procedure have been greatly lessened, yet with ultimate congressional authority safeguarded. Initiative for proposing structural rearrangements has been explicitly vested in the executive, yet the executive has had very great assistance in the studies leading up to such proposals by the two Hoover Commissions and many other inquiries into the organization of the Executive Branch. The Hoover Commissions were "mixed" commissions, partly appointed by and from Congress, partly by and from the executive, partly chosen by each from outside citizenry.

Under the reorganization acts, either house of Congress retained the right to reject a presidential reorganization proposal by majority vote within sixty days of submission. Not every plan so formulated under these laws was adopted nor necessarily should it have been, but the method itself was conspicuously successful compared to any previously used.[7]

Efforts to recast administrative models often have foundered on the shoals of bureau support within Congress buttressed by clientele support among the electorate—examples of the power and autonomy of the "whirlpools" referred to elsewhere. Nevertheless,

> In performing these [administrative] activities, Congress is acting where it is most competent to act, it is dealing with particulars, not general policies.... Committee specialization and committee power enhance rather than detract from the effectiveness of the committees as administrative overseers. In addition, as the great organized interests of society come to be represented more directly in the bureaucracy and administration, the role of Congress as representative of individual citizens becomes all the more important. The congressman more often serves their interests by representing them in the administrative process than in the legislative process.[8]

The relationship of Congress to administration is far more pervading and complex than is indicated within the confines of this particular chapter.[9] We have run across it and shall run across it in almost every major consideration in this work—in the executive–legislative struggle and cooperation, in appraising the staff services of Congress, in connection with the pressure groups, the parties, localism, and international policy. All these matters lend color to the theory that separation of powers and checks and balances under our Constitution are the most powerful, the most all-pervading of its principles, save only the principle of the direct election of our officials. From these principles evolves much of the interlocking pluralism in decision-making which has been held to be both the genius and the despair of the American system.

NOTES

1. Holbert N. Carroll, *The House of Representatives and Foreign Affairs*, rev. ed. (Boston: Little, Brown, 1966), p. 367. See also J. M. Smith and C. P. Cotter, "Administrative Accountability," *Western Political Quarterly* (December 1956), pp. 955-66; (June 1957), pp. 405-15.
2. The ensuing pages draw heavily on Ernest S. Griffith's *American System of Government*, 4th ed. (New York: Praeger, 1965), chap. 10.
3. The names of Senator Douglas of Illinois and Representative Bennett of Florida were associated with this concept in the early 1960s.
4. An excellent analysis of this oversight function is found in George B. Galloway, *History of the House of Representatives*, (New York: Thomas Y. Crowell, 1961), chap. 10.
5. 328 U.S. 303 (1946).

6. *Congressional Record* Feb. 5, 1973, p. S.2054, Refusal of Cabinet and Other Officials to Testify Before Senate Committees":.

> WHEREAS, The Constitution of the United States, Article II, Section 2, vests the President with the power of appointment 'by and with the Advice and Consent' of the Senate;
>
> *Whereas,* on behalf of the Senate, Committees of the Senate are authorized to summon witnesses to appear and testify on the business of the Senate;
>
> *Whereas,* appointed officials, subsequent to Senate confirmation, have refused on occasion to appear and testify before duly constituted Committees of the Senate:
>
> *Resolved* by the Democratic Majority of the Senate:

> (1) That a prerequisite to confirmation is the commitment of Presidential appointees to appear and testify before duly constituted Committees of the Senate in response to Committee requests.
>
> (2) That all Senate Committees bear a responsibility to determine, prior to confirmation, the commitment of Presidential appointees to comply with committee requests to appear and testify before Committees of the Senate.
>
> (3) That Committee reports to the Senate on all cabinet designees and such other appointees as deemed appropriate should contain an evaluation of their commitment to respond to committee requests to appear and testify before duly constituted Senate Committees.

> *Resolved,* further, that the Majority Leader is requested to report the adoption of this resolution to the Majority Conference and to communicate its contents to the Leadership of the Minority, to the Chairman of the standing Committees and to the President of the United States and otherwise to seek cooperation in its execution.

7. The Reorganization Act (63 Stat 209, as amended by 85 Stat. 574) expired on April 1973. Although efforts were made to extend, in both houses, this delegation of authority to the President appears to have reverted for the time being to the Congress.

8. Samuel P. Huntington, "Congressional Responses to the Twentieth Century," in David B. Truman, ed., *The Congress and America's Future* (Englewood Cliffs: Prentice-Hall, 1965), p. 25.
9. A standard work on the subject is Joseph P. Harris, *Congressional Control of Administration* (Washington: Brookings Institution, 1964). The analysis therein is considerably less favorable to Congress than is that of the present authors.

CHAPTER 10

The Pressure Groups
and Congress

Among the most difficult problems of statecraft today are those which concern the relationship of the government and the group. We recognize our society as having centers of free and organized activity all over the place, and for the most part are happy that it is so. Neither the anarchy of the theoretically possible complete individualism nor the monolithic society of the dictatorship exercises very much hold upon our people. In general, we prefer to see our society as one of tremendous vitality and ferment—many individuals leading and bending others to their more clearly thought and strongly felt objectives; groups autonomous within limits, their drive and energy in the end operating (to a very considerable extent of their own volition) for the common good; and government the necessary integrator or adjustor where conflicts arise—either between individual and individual, group and group, individual and group, or individual or group and the general welfare.

The deeper origins of such a society have often been explored and need detain us only long enough to summarize the argument and to underscore a certain inevitable quality therein. Basically, the origin lies in technology, in the premium put upon differentiation in the economic processes of production, distribution, and to some extent consumption.

The economic advantages of specialization over the self-contained and self-supporting household economy have long been accepted. The derivative effects of such specialization are first of all sociological, and then as a corollary, political. Within a specialized group—dairy farmers, bricklayers, bankers, doctors, steel manufacturers, steelworkers—the initial earlier impact or emphasis on competition with its individualistic connotations has long since been accompanied and more and more overshadowed by an awareness of the common interests of the group as a whole over against other groups or society at large. More sophisticated reasoning has enabled the members of many of these groups to differentiate between the two—to compete vigorously among themselves but also to join forces in areas of common interest to attain common ends.

Moreover, group consciousness and group action have arisen in a period and in a society whose economic philosophy was at first the rather crude utilitarianism of Adam Smith and Spencer, that is, the universal identification of self-interest with the common good. Later, the more penetrating concept of *function* in a great society emerged, in which each group became more and more conscious of its contribution to national productivity, wealth, and well-being. The Rotary Club and other service clubs mark the full flowering of the mores created by this line of functional thinking.

Members of each of these groups commonly found themselves associated with each other, usually socially as well as in economic activities. They thus developed like patterns of thought. These patterns included a rationalization of their occupation in terms of its necessary contribution to the welfare of society, a derivative alarm at and resistance to anything that thwarted such a contribution (measured, of course, by the prosperity of their group), the cloaking of the public pronouncements of such alarm and resistance in usually perfectly sincere terms of the general good, and (and this is of cardinal political importance) an eventual full-fledged campaign of political action designed to use the instrumentalities of government to further their ends.

In many areas, these objectives did in fact coincide with the public interest, as, for example, the eight-hour day, the furtherance of agricultural experiment and research, the protection of products against adulteration or misbranding, but in other areas their social value was more problematical. These less fortunate developments were chiefly in state action designed to foster scarcity and consequent higher prices than would otherwise have ruled, and some would add state acquiescence in such wasteful and shoddy concepts as built-in obsolescence and nonreturnable containers. Long-range and secondary effects cannot be overlooked in a full appraisal of the relationships of such actions or nonactions to the public interest. Programs such as crop limitations with parity prices, the closed shop with union control over admission to the union, insistence upon basing point pricing so as to permit identical bidding and division of markets, retail price maintenance and private pollution at public expense, strip mining without restoration of the terrain—these and many others are certainly of mixed social consequence. But those who sustain them do not think so, for they have long been accustomed to identify their own prosperity with the common good under each and every circumstance.

The sociological consequence of differentiation is dispersiveness; the political consequence is the dispersive state. That is to say, the dominant characteristic of society and state alike is this pattern of organized group activity, often but incidentally in the interest of the whole, and often in conflict with such interest. This spontaneous pluralism is technological and sociological in its origin. It may be irreversible, but it is capable of being understood. The problem of statecraft is clear. It is how to adjust the intergroup conflicts and how to integrate group action into an over-all program in the common interest. The catch is how to do so without destroying or curbing unduly both the individual and group drive and spontaneity which are the lifeblood of our dynamic society. The ultimate judgment on how so to adjust and so to integrate lies with Congress. It is an inescapable responsibility of the first magnitude.

The political insistences of the groups do not stop with legislation. The legislation customarily creates a continuing instrument in the shape of an executive agency to further the objectives sought. Sometimes these agencies are arbitral in character, to adjust conflicts between groups; more often they represent the incorporation into the governmental structure of the principle of continuous intervention. Such is the Department of Agriculture. Such is the Civil Aeronautics Authority. Such is the Federal Highway Administration. Such is the National Labor Relations Board, whose members by an informal understanding for a number of years were "cleared" with the great union organizations. This is not the whole picture, of course, for the very cloaking of these officials with the mantle of the public interest itself affects their behavior and modifies their previous predilections. Yet, the pattern of the Executive Branch, insofar as this group influence is one of its major aspects, represents for the most part a pattern of agencies and clientele. It is the dispersive expression in administration of dispersive politics. Dispersive politics in the end is the logical and inexorable outcome of a dispersive society.

Congressmen are themselves the products or creatures of this same dispersive society. Yet, when they commence to serve, they come face to face, more quickly and readily than their constituents with the latter's narrower experience, with the nature of this problem as it confronts government. Many more Congressmen than one generally appreciates come to realize that the common good is not, as some would have it, totally bound up with the success of business; nor is it bound up, as others would have it, merely with high prices for agricultural products or a continuing lifting of minimum wages. In short, the common good is not assured by giving to each group more or less what it wants without regard to broader social consequences. To many a member of Congress, his problem appears to be that of picking and choosing; of granting to the insistent groups those portions of their demands that in fact minister to the common good. As for the remainder of these demands, by one device or another he would foster a masterly inaction. Organized groups on the other hand seek to put a member on record, to concentrate on obtaining his loyalty to their *total* program, to punish and reward accordingly.

The congressman cannot escape the fact that he is a product of this dispersive society—elected by his state or district as its representative, elected in all probability because he is "one of them," his opinions largely the product of their social milieu, his mores theirs. Even if his subsequent education and experience have given him a broader view, a deeper insight, he will not normally stray too far from the pattern of thought of his district or he will not return. The good he would do he cannot always do openly, and perhaps not at all. Yet, he can and does defend himself in his own conscience by the belief that he is aware of the nature of the problem and will push the public or general interest as far as he can and still remain in office—till the happy day in which he can push it still further. He will do so in the context of what is tolerable to his constituency.

Comparatively few members are aware that there is also an over-all, integrating role to be performed in the government. The automatic adjustment of a flexible economy is still a widely held belief even though the sudden shock of an energy crisis as in 1973 coming on the heels of international currency disorders and a rapid inflation can shake this belief considerably. Whether such an integrating role is to be performed by government directly and within the government by still another agency is discussible. That it must in fact be performed is held more and more widely by students of political economy. The congressional role in the matter will be treated more at length in a later chapter.* At this stage the problem is merely noted.

By and large, what is the pattern of the impact of these special interests or pressure groups in and upon Congress? It is so complex that only the broadest of generalizations can be safely made.[1] There are major groups with great political power. To the old standbys of business, agriculture, labor, and veterans must now be added the aged, the blacks, government employees, consumers, environmentalists, supporters of Israel, peace fronts, the "patriotic front," and "citizens lobbies." Certain of the professions, notably the lawyers and doctors, are influential within a narrower field.

Of course such a picture is a gross oversimplification. Business is by no means united except on a limited number of issues. Exporters and importers often conflict. Rival forms of transportation bring pressures and facts to bear upon the same congressional committees. Big business and little business lobby incessantly and not always for the same ends. To some extent, the same is true of agriculture. The farm organizations seldom speak with a wholly united voice. Rivalries between the erstwhile labor federations had their congressional expression. To a greater or lesser extent the whole intricate pattern of our dispersive society has its counterpart in the pressures that beat upon Congress.

In fairly obvious fashion this relates itself to regional groupings. Urban–rural conflicts are everywhere evident-so much so that those districts and states which are fairly equally divided between the two are more often the most unstable politically, in comparison with those primarily rural or urban. Within a metropolitan area, white suburbia competes with inner-city black power. The industrial East and Middle West follow much the same pattern of group structure. The South still is more conservative than other parts of the nation with interstices of populism and some influx of laborite liberalism and the new

* Cf. chap. 11.

element of enlarged Negro participation in politics. The Prairie States still have a smoldering agrarian radicalism from their debtor days and are in no sense clear-cut Republican or Democrat. The Mountain States have a coloration of their own, centering around the scarcity of water, mining, the frontier traditions, and now environmental protection. This uniqueness finds political expression in the activities of the great water resources construction agencies and the environmental agencies of the government. The Pacific Coast States are more complex, and consequently, perhaps, more involved in controversies over issues and personalities rather than along party lines.

Economic and sectional patterns reflect themselves within Congress in a number of ways. Among the most obvious is the seeking of memberships on committees which consider measures most decisive for the particular region or economic group whose views are represented by the member. Members of the Committees on Agriculture are almost wholly from the farm states. Both Interior Committees drew their membership predominantly from west of the one hundredth meridian. The Labor Committees are chiefly a mixture of members from regions dominated by organized labor and members from areas whose mores are those of conservative capitalism. Of the members on the House Merchant Marine and Fisheries Committee, a preponderance are from seacoast and lakefront districts. The pattern is less clear in the great business committees of Interstate and Foreign Commerce, Banking and Currency, Ways and Means, and Finance. Here the individual member may be explainable, but the total membership is complex. The importance attached to committees, especially to the latter two, results in a heavy representation from among the senior and more experienced members. All pressure groups struggle for sympathetic members on Appropriations Committees in both Houses and the House Rules Committee.

The ways in which individual members can represent or favor the groups assisting their election are numerous.

Committee action is influential, though not necessarily decisive. Committee hearings can favor the presentation of witnesses whose views are shared by the committee members. Helpful questions may be asked, or embarrassing ones. Attendance and attention may be discriminating. A negative reaction from a committee to a given measure is normally equivalent to a veto, though an affirmative report may not carry equal assurance of its final passage.

Members specialize and members bargain largely in fields determined by their constituents' interest and interests. Votes on the floor do not necessarily split on party lines. On the contrary, more often than not, they express or reflect a combination of economic interests involving a member's district and a more detached view on the part of those not intimately concerned with the measure in question. It is the presence of this latter group that on the one hand, it is true, is an invitation to logrolling and trading of votes, but on the other hand contains the best hope of the public interest prevailing in amendments or rejection or acceptance of a measure. This is the shifting group that can provide the margin to counter the special economic or regional interests so frequently expressing themselves in the committee memberships.

The strengthening of party discipline would not, in itself, guarantee the dominance of the general welfare as is commonly argued. It could lead just as readily to party bargains with special interests in exchange for support. On the one hand, party discipline might readily express itself by forcing into line in support of a bargain those who might otherwise be in a position to exercise a degree of detachment and independence.* On the other hand, the party would have to answer to the public for its role in any given vote in a way which it is not now required to do.

In concluding this portion of our analysis we again direct attention to the phenomenon of "government by whirlpools."

* Cf. chapter 16.

Our dispersive society and our dispersive politics are such that among their greatest realities are these associations of like-minded individuals—individuals with a common background of experience, a common set of mores, and common objectives. The spokesmen of the group are not only those paid to speak, or even the members of the group itself in a narrow sense. Spokesmen are also found among the people whose own prosperity, whose standing in their local community, are at least indirectly determined by the flourishing of the groups. They are also the government officials whose clientele are represented in these groups. They are the members of Congress from the states and districts whose experience and attitudes are woven from the same fabric and who accurately "represent" their district, by experience and conviction as well as by election. In the innumerable conferences and associations, formal and informal, between these various types of persons interested in common objectives, much of what we call government policy is matured. This is the heart of the dispersive state; it is the bedrock or grassroots expression of an inherent pluralism in an industrially mature society. How and how far a more general interest can utilize, discipline, or curb these special interests in the governmental process is a supreme test of a people's economic and political genius. It faces the President in his dealings with the bureaucracy no less than it faces Congress, but it is the latter with which we are most concerned.[2]

Congress over the years has evolved certain devices designed to limit the effectiveness of group pressures to those measures thought to be socially useful. Principal among these is the congressional hearing. A congressional hearing is a two edged instrument. It may serve the purpose of the witness in giving him an opportunity to present his case directly to the decision-makers. On the other hand, under questioning by a skilled exponent of the public interest, such sophistries and rationalizations as may underlie even the most plausible presentation may be exposed. This questioning is especially effective if the member or members are armed with the necessary factual as well as analytic basis for such cross-examination. Sometimes such information is forthcoming from an executive agency, sometimes from an opposing pressure group, but more and more it has come from one or another of the congressional staff sources.

Moreover, publicity remains one of democracy's best and most appropriate weapons in other parts of the congressional setting. Lobbies are an integral part of the give and take of politics—an influence in making public opinion and legislators' decisions. They are useful; they are also in many of their aspects dangerous; they are also at times a plain nuisance. In any event, Congress, following the lead of several of our state legislatures, has expressed a formal verdict that, whether useful or harmful, there would be much gain and little if anything lost, if the weapon of publicity were brought to bear upon them and lobbies were compelled to declare themselves. The Legislative Reorganization Act of 1946 contained provisions requiring registration, declaration of organization, membership, and personnel, and listing of the principal sources of financial support. This portion of the act was not drawn carefully and a number of lobbyists have escaped through its interstices. There have been subsequent inquiries into the law and many proposals for changes, but, to date, it remains unchanged.

The most recent effort to shed light on pressure groups is the Federal Election Campaign Act of 1971. This law represented the first significant revision in the Federal Corrupt Practices Act in several decades. While it did little to limit the use of contributions to political campaigns by pressure groups as a means of strengthening their influence, it did aim at full disclosure of the source of campaign contributions. As might be expected, those groups with a special interest in the impact of legislation, business, farm, labor, various professional associations, and similar cores of economic power were revealed to be among the largest contributors to political campaigns. So far as can be seen, and the evidence is not yet conclusive, the new law has had little effect on this source of heavy pressure on the Congress. On the contrary, whatever its intent, its effect to date, if anything, may well have been to discourage the small contributor with a minimal interest in legislation and the quasi-volunteer and local participants in Federal election campaigns. Without further changes in the direction of limiting the cost of campaigns and bringing about some equitable means of financing—public support or otherwise—election campaigns are likely to come increasingly under the control of special interests and the wealthy with all that implies for the political process. Revisions in the law in 1973 seemed to move in this direction but they remain to be tested in practice.

Not only in political financing but in its internal processes, Congress has responded increasingly in recent years to public pressures to conduct the public business in public. Open door mark-up sessions of committees are more common than in the past. But, whether open or closed, members frequently join in searching for ways and means of circumventing the undesirable portions of the legislation pressed by the various special interests. Sometimes vagueness of language is deliberate, to allow the administration of the measure leeway in interpreting the public interest. Informal understandings may be made with members of the counterpart committee in the other house as regards what will remain and what will be eliminated in conference. Conference committees almost always confine their activities to closed executive sessions, and modifications in the public interest are apparently much more frequent than the more highly publicized logrolling. Regardless of personal views, conferees are supposed to fight for the positions taken by their respective houses. Inevitably, however, in bargaining such zeal can be affected to a greater or lesser degree by the beliefs of the conferees themselves as regards specific provisions. Executive sessions have normally, as an important part of their agenda, considerations of tactics and strategy. Informal, unofficial meetings, by no means always confined to members of a single party, are frequently held prior to formal meetings, if it is felt that others on the committee must be circumvented or placated to obtain the necessary majority for the bloc in question.

Inaction or delaying action are tactics frequently used to trim down the demands of special interests. A chairman may put off calling a committee meeting. A quorum may suddenly evaporate. Hearings may be prolonged. In the Senate the filibuster with its various modifications may occasionally perform this type of function. Loading a bill with controversial amendments is not unknown as a means to assure defeat. The President's veto, known or understood in advance, is still another device. If an appropriation is called for, it is not always forthcoming. Time and again a "gravy clause" inserted at the behest of a special interest by one house or the other is eliminated in the conference committee of the two houses, and the broader public interest prevails. There have been times when implicit if not explicit understandings between committees have been reached with regard to which house will "play politics" and which "statesman." Sometimes the latter consists merely of an informal assurance that the measure will be bottled up in committee, or will still be left on the calendar at the end of a session. A filibuster may be incubated in the Senate, allowing the House to gain such kudos as may derive from a favorable roll call—without the nation having to be subjected to the passage of the measure in question.

We have also mentioned how the Rules Committee of the House may at times be used to "bottle up" or grant an unfavorable rule. Often, such tactics represent the quiet "better judgment" of a majority of the members, a majority which on roll call might be converted into a minority through political exigency. We have written earlier of the respect paid to committee recommendations. At this point a distinction should be drawn between the "clientele" committees and those with a more broadly based membership. Recommendations from the former are more likely to be subject in the Senate to floor amendment and in the House to be held up, or made subject to agreed-upon changes, by the Rules Committee. For example, during the decade of the 1940s the House Veterans' Affairs Committee was largely the spokesman of the veterans' lobbies. Only the Rules Committee stood between its recommendations and embarrassing floor roll calls. Similarly, the Agriculture Committees have found their recommendations substantially altered by floor amendments. So, too, bills of the Finance Committee and the Foreign Relations Committee in the Senate.

Party loyalty at the behest of party leadership occasionally allows a member to vote his better judgment as well as his poorer, provided the calls are not so frequent as to cast doubt on his independence. The reputation for a degree of independence is a political asset, especially if the results happen to coincide with the desires and program of politically powerful elements in a member's constituency.

If the foregoing description of legislative maneuvering appears a bit cynical, it is not so intended. There are many views of the national interest and no member or group of members has an infallible touchstone. Moreover, the member who eagerly takes a stand on every issue in accordance with what he believes to be the public interest, if it is repeatedly at odds with the interests of significant elements in his constituency, may not survive the next election. Far too many in the electorate feel so intensely on some one issue that a member's total record is ignored. If a member can block action on such an issue by some means other than a direct vote, the nation is more likely to have his services beyond the end of his present term, and he believes that this fact vindicates the necessary tactical obfuscation or "stealthy statesmanship."

The issues of civil rights and gun control are specific cases in point in which the inner struggles of conscience vs. constituency have been very marked in many members. For many years, legislation on these issues was delayed by various parliamentary devices. When it finally began to emerge, it came forth in forms which eased this conflict.

The real nub of the matter is this. While for the most part the beliefs of members sincerely reflect the beliefs of the electorate in their district, especially in the battle of economic interests, nevertheless a process of political and economic education inevitably sets in from the first time a member, or would-be or future member, gives his attention to national issues. He sees that there are two sides to a question; and, as the years pass, he sees also that there is a transcending public interest greater than and perhaps different from either side or even any compromise between the two sides. This realization comes to different persons at different times. It comes with different issues to different persons. To some it never comes. Moreover, the realization rarely, if ever, comes to any one member as regards all issues. Each inevitably has certain blind spots, the product of environment or the penalty paid for not enough time to study. The blind spot is not a defect of motive; it is a flaw in the nature of our society.

But to many members, now on one issue and now on another—and generally to a different set of members on each separate issue—this realization of the contradiction between the special interest and the general interest surely comes. Their horizons broaden as they witness the conflicts of interests and as they give thought to deeper analyses of problems and the findings of research. On given measures, because of the political and economic composition of their districts, many members enjoy the luxury of voting their convictions without incurring the hostility of any politically significant special groups among their constituents. Still others vote their convictions in any event and take the political consequences. Not infrequently these consequences vindicate their courage, but also they often bring defeat. Still others merely let their convictions dilute the intensity with which they support a measure favored by the insistent group or groups on which they are dependent for reelection. Such low-temperature support may then be the kiss of death for the measure in question. In this setting one must not judge too harshly those other devices whereby with seemingly less courage but frequently with a wisdom which foresees a better, long-range result, members of Congress circumvent the special interests in order to further the general good as they see it. With group interests frequently so evenly divided politically, the number who so vote or so act need not be very great to be in fact decisive. In the House there are easily twenty or thirty whose votes on most closely argued questions are not predictable in that they habitually approach such questions without earlier commitments or mind set. Whether the strengthening of party discipline would inhibit such statesmanship (as by and large it has in our past history), or enhance it, as much of the writing in political science would seem to indicate, will be considered presently. The recent revival of the caucus in the Congress is something of a test although its votes are far from binding.

Broadly speaking, Congress may be thought of as performing, deliberately or otherwise, a kind of "filter" function in its dealings with the pressure groups and the special interests. The vitality and energy of these groups represent an asset in our national life; their deliberations and decisions make up much of our highly valued pluralism in their multiplication of decentralized centers of power and decision-making. Yet, their dispersiveness, their limited view, and, often, their greed or special zeal mean that many of their demands are contrary to the general welfare. To filter these out, while not curbing the creative vitality of the system—this is the role of Congress. As we have seen, many are the devices by which such filtering has become possible.

We conclude this chapter as we began it, by underscoring what is really at stake in the Congress of a dispersive government and society. Insistent minorities in the form of special interests or pressure groups, by their organized power of political reward or political punishment, can force their will against even a majority if the "temperature" which which that majority feels the opposite is mild and if it is unorganized. Congressmen who fail to comply with the militant minority do so at their peril. But even if two or more powerful groups make common cause—as, for example, labor and agriculture or labor and business—there may still be a general interest contradictory to this alliance and perceived by those in Congress who are better informed.

How can or should representative government operate in such a society? That Congress is operating with increasing effectiveness and with an awareness of and conformity to the long-range public interest is the considered judgment of the authors. Congress has a right to be judged in large measure by its results. At the very minimum, some politics of the kind discussed in this chapter are probably essential to the member's survival in a society kept basically dispersive by its technology and its economic specialization.

NOTES

1. See Emanuel Celler, "Pressure Groups in Congress," *Annals of the American Academy* (September 1958), pp. 1-9.
2. Cf. J. Leiper Freeman, *The Political Process: Executive Bureau—Legislative Committee Relations* (Garden City: Doubleday, 1955).

CHAPTER 11

Economic Planning and Congress

Four substantive fields in particular raise serious questions as to the competence of Congress to deal with them. These are economic planning, foreign policy, national defense, and science. They are alike in that they require *expertise* of a high order. They are costly, together involving the bulk of the national budget. To a major extent they overlap or are interrelated, each one with each of the others. At least the last three involve considerable classified material. In one fashion or another they figure in most governmental decisions. The role of Congress in each merits separate treatment, and this and chapters that follow consider each in turn.

In the discussions thus far, and notably in Chapter Six, the groundwork for this consideration has been laid in general terms. Congress has through specialization on the part of its members, and through its increasing command of expertise, attempted to meet the onslaught of a technical age and at the same time preserve the reality of representative government.

* * *

The passage of the Employment Act of 1946 was evidence of the realization in Congress that government has a responsibility to contribute toward the full functioning of the national economy. In the original Senate version there was present the concept of continuous and, if necessary, vigorous intervention to promote and sustain full employment; but the House, and ultimately the conferees, shied away from such an aggressive approach as marking a path down which the nation was not yet ready to travel. However, as a very substantial residue, there survived a Council of Economic Advisers in the Office of the President and a Joint Committee on the Economic Report in Congress, a name subsequently changed to Joint Economic Committee. The former was to make a continuous audit of the economic state of the nation, and report to the President. The President, with such additions, deletions, or modifications as he saw fit, was to transmit a report at least annually to Congress. The Joint Committee in turn was to express its reactions and reflections on the President's report to the Congress.

The core idea in 1946 was not that of broad governmental planning and intervention but of providing stabilizing factors whereby the economy as a whole—relying primarily on private enterprise—might move forward in orderly fashion. Programs as articulated in party platforms, presidential messages, and congressional agenda only incidentally and obliquely deal with these factors—the individual items which they contain partaking more of the character of relief or support for various groups than of the needs of the national economy. If party government and responsibility are strengthened, it remains to be seen whether or not the end results will be a further intensification of these dispersive factors and a reduction of the correctives of those independent elements in Congress who are able to view the effect of a given proposal on the political economy of the nation as a whole.[1]

There is, entirely apart from economic programs of the kind mentioned, a type of governmental economic intervention which deals with aggregates and over-all relationships—with saving and consumption, with saving and investment, with cash and installment buying, with bank debits and bank reserves, with resources exhaustion and conservation, with taxation and borrowing, with the government zone and the private zone, with the purchasing power of other nations and our own, with exports and imports (including the invisible items), with wages and profits (as affecting some of these relationships), with inventories at the several stages and consumer purchasing, with price level and available purchasing power.

Of something of the same nature is the function of integrating the individual items of a program-approach. This was the crying need of the New Deal, which in its early years was the outstanding example of what a party program would be like as regards internal contradictions. Almost simultaneously it invoked measures designed to stimulate exports of our agricultural products and measures raising their prices so much that they began to be priced out of the export market. With the Federal Reserve policy it urged a loosening or expansion of credit. It raised the threat of public housing which frightened the private builder at the time; it stimulated the same builder to build by extending his credit. It prosecuted for antitrust violations; it promoted such combined action under the National Recovery Administration (NRA). Thus did the dispersiveness, the conflicts, and the contradictions in society and politics translate themselves into a series of contradictory, dispersive, and conflicting governmental actions.

Four decades later the crying need for integrated action which plagued the New Deal is still with us. To harmonize the several parts of government programs and to deal with the over-all forces affecting our economic life—these are the two aspects of what we here emphasize in this chapter on economic planning.

Economic planning is no easy task, even for an omniscient dictator. For a democracy it is considerably more difficult. The insistences of a dispersive society themselves constitute the major political obstacles. So accustomed has each group become to the utilization of government to carve out for itself a greater share of the national income regardless of consequences that over-all coordination is most likely to seem a thwarting or blocking of the very heart of what the group deems important to itself, and what it has rationalized into identifying with the national welfare.

Moreover, even the expectation of intervention may precipitate complications. In the early days of the Korean war, for example, when wage control and price control were merely authorized without being used at once, wage contracts presumably fixed for a much longer period were quickly reopened. Prices advanced without corresponding justification in increased costs. Inasmuch as both of these steps were taken in order to anticipate the controls, inflation gained another notch. Uncertain and reluctant intervention can produce a similar result, as witness the behavior of prices in the light of indecisive government action in the years after the termination of the Vietnamese intervention.

Last, but by no means least, there remains the disturbing suspicion that economic intervention in reality marks still another mile—perhaps the last—down the long descent into statism. Especially would this be true, it is argued, if such intervention should take the form of further additions to the already dizzy heights of government expenditure. A time may come in the United States which has already appeared in certain other nations, a time at which it becomes political suicide to tax at the rate necessary even to carry current expenses, not to mention debt repayment. Indeed, in the 1970s, we may have already entered on a period of steadily mounting deficit financing which is bringing in its train a steady currency depreciation with its attendant evils and the threat of ultimate crash.

Without passing judgment on the soundness or unsoundness of the arguments against this line of thinking, it should be borne in mind that governmental action of some sort becomes in this day and age a political imperative in the event of a recession or depression or indeed any significant economic crisis. Note, for example, government's urgent intervention to counter isolated falterings in the economy such as the Penn-Central Railroad bankruptcy and the threatened failure of Lockheed Aircraft Corporation. In the fuel crisis of 1973 the intervention was massive, with the energies of many departments and agencies and the Congress geared to alleviating the impact.

So, the question which confronts the Congress is not whether there will be government intervention but how much and what kind of intervention? Perhaps both the friends and enemies of so-called economic planning therefore might agree that at least that measure of integrated foresight should be forthcoming which would see to it that contradictions and cross-purposes are removed from any program adopted by government. It was this modest amount of coordination of government programs within the pattern of free enterprise that was originally contemplated in the 1946 Act which established the Council of Economic Advisers and the Joint Economic Committee.[2]

Nor must one suppose that economic foresight of this character is only governmental or that the indicated actions to sustain or restore prosperity are likewise only governmental. Working through organizations like the Committee for Economic Development, industry has shown marked ability to organize its economic thinking. Examples of similar attitudes can be found in labor circles.

The most effective role in this realm hitherto has been performed in Congress not by party leadership but by individual members operating in committee or in floor debate and voting. It is at just these points that independent thought is most significant, especially in calling attention to harmful effects of measures designed to carry out the wishes of major pressure groups. For a party as such to do this may be to invite the implacable hostility of the group in question. For individual members to do the same thing, especially if they are from districts in which the group in question is relatively weak, is much more feasible. Such members, possessed of the facts, influence the votes and action of others, and a measure in question may be amended, postponed, or defeated outright.

Needless to say, more than the efforts of individual members is needed to undertake the formulation of affirmative action for dealing with over-all aspects of the problem. While individuals of independence may block or modify harmful economic elements in legislation, they are ill-suited to mature, or at least to put through, constructive measures. For these there must be some institutional expression in the structure and workings of Congress. Party policy committees are advocated by many to perform this role, particularly if their membership goes beyond the personnel of one house, or even of Congress. The Senate (Republican) Policy Committee for many years revealed potentialities in this respect, partly because of its membership and partly because it had equipped itself with able staff. The majority (Democratic) policy groups almost of political necessity, in economic matters, generally followed presidential leadership under Roosevelt, Truman, Kennedy, and Johnson, though from time to time they influenced materially the channel such leadership took. When the Republican, Eisenhower, was in the White House, there occurred the emergence of the Democratic Majority Leader of the Senate as a rival spokesman on economic and other questions in the person of Lyndon B. Johnson, who had in this role the full support of the Speaker of the House, Sam Rayburn.

During the Nixon administration, systematized efforts were begun to delineate party positions in the Senate by Democratic Policy Committee consensus wherever the Committee could discern substantial agreement among its members, and subsequently these efforts were joined with those of the House Democratic Leadership to set forth party positions on various questions.

The Legislative Reorganization Act of 1946 called for a legislative budget or fiscal program with a joint committee to formulate it. This arrangement was designed to provide that at some stage the provisional totals of appropriations and revenues should be reviewed together and consciously related to each other. The proposal which was sound in objective was not consummated until the second Nixon administration. Under the twin executive pressures of impoundment and crit-

icism for "reckless spending," as well as continuous budgetary deficits and the erosion of legislative control over fiscal
policy, Congress passed the Congressional Budget and Impoundment Control Act of 1974.[3] The measure represented a
sweeping change in the way in which the budget is processed. It
provided, for the first time, a central locus for examining the
sundry presidential proposals and legislative actions which in
the end result in government expenditures. It created budget
committees in each House and established a nonpartisan congressional budget office to provide the expert fiscal and technical staffing for Congress which, when added to that already
available in the Congressional Research Service and the General Accounting Office, permits a technical confrontation with
the executive Office of Management and Budget on a more or
less equal basis. At the same time, the legislation established a
simple procedure for dealing with the problem of impoundment of appropriated funds permitting either House to reverse
such a presidential action by a simple majority vote.

The legislation also changed the beginning of the fiscal year,
commencing in 1976, from July 1 to October 1, providing in this
connection a timetable system for review of both revenues and
expenditures in juxtaposition. As such, the work of the new
budget committees directly affects the jurisdiction of all committees and in particular those which have traditionally dealt
with fiscal questions, that is, the Appropriations Committees
and the Senate Finance and House Ways and Means Committees. As of this writing, it remains to be seen how the respective
roles of these various cores of power will evolve under the new
law. Nevertheless it can be said that the groundwork has clearly
been laid by this legislation for an integrated congressional role
in economic planning, inasmuch as the manner in which monies are raised and expended by the Federal government under a
budget of several hundred billion dollars is a critical factor in
that question.

A complete picture of the role of Congress in economic
affairs would call attention to other committees that necessarily

deal with important sectors of the national economy—Interstate and Foreign Commerce, Foreign Relations, Foreign Affairs, Small Business, Banking and Currency, Labor, Public Works, Interior and Insular Affairs, Agriculture, Merchant Marine and Fisheries, Post Office and Civil Service, Government Operations, Veterans Affairs and others which, concerned as they are with governmental structure, personnel, or expenditure, exercise important influence on the political economy of the nation. Yet, these committees are by nature separate if not dispersive. Many of them are problem and clientele committees, with over-all matters inherently less easily fitting into their thinking. The Foreign Relations and Foreign Affairs Committees, moreover, have been of declining importance in the realm of expenditures as the world has moved away from a heavy dependency on U.S. economic aid.

Finally, there is the Joint Economic Committee, created as part of the Employment Act of 1946. It is not a legislative committee in the sense that it may sponsor legislation. Narrowly interpreted, it would have only the responsibility of commenting on the President's *Annual Report.* A broad interpretation of its function would take in a responsibility for advice or even leadership in Congress in the whole economic sector of our national life. Here if anywhere might have been the most likely and logical place for over-all considerations to emerge, if not the specific legislative acts to give them form. Yet, as it has developed, in practice, the committee is relatively unintegrated into the legislative mechanism. With the creation of the budget committees its role is likely to become even more ambiguous. It might be made more effective if the President's Economic Report were presented in July or later so as to give the committee more of a chance to influence legislation at the opening of the next session of Congress. A better integration of its membership with the major congressional committees would also help.

It must always be borne in mind that many members of

Congress, although less than in the past, are still reluctant to accept the fact that our economy is not self-adjusting and that the organized intervention of powerful private groups, such as labor unions or the trade associations, monopolies, and an expanding international factor, have introduced rigidities and uncertainties with which the ordinary day-to-day operations of the market cannot deal. The impacts may be inflationary, or they may prolong a depression. In either event, community intervention is inevitably called for at the policy level. Members of Congress who are not economists may not be aware that savings and investment or spending and saving are by no means self-adjusting at the ratios necessary to keep the economy on an even keel. What the average member usually does sense, however, is that there are certain harmful effects attendant upon measures sometimes laudable in purpose; he senses that governments elsewhere are making administrative decisions affecting our private economy; he sees inflation and recession and wonders if these are necessary. He sees our system of private transportation disorganized almost overnight and our economy disrupted by a war in the Middle East and an oil embargo. Out of elements such as these in his frame of reference it is possible to derive a measure of attention and support for an instrument focusing on over-all or interrelational economic policy.

It was precisely elements of this kind illuminated in the petroleum crisis of 1973–74, which permitted the majority and minority leaders of the Senate to attempt a new approach to the problem of government's role in the operation of the economy. The two leaders suggested that there was a need for an instrumentality which would bring together the Executive Branch, the Congress, and relevant nongovernment elements to provide the necessary "foresight" to guide government's intervention with a view to mitigating or preventing crises in materials supply and other aspects of the economy. On that basis, they convened a series of unprecedented meetings with the leadership of both parties in the House and with the President's leading economic advisors.* Out of these meetings emerged for the first time a recognition that there was a need for a predefined and integrated course of government economic action which might well be based on the combined judgment of both branches of government and nongovernment elements.[4]

Much remains to be done by way of realizing the implications of these various relationships and new proposals. Executive and Congress alike are only on the threshold of making the necessary adaptations to the level of mature economic thinking now available—thinking which, if translated into policy and action, can make it possible for our nation to adjust effectively to the ever-changing economic needs of the people. The politics of the special interests, the vested interests of the dispersive state, are ready to block such an outcome. On the other side of the ledger, however, is the need of all for a strong and unified nation.

NOTES

1. See also in this connection the study made by J. Roland Pennock of the power of agricultural interests in Great Britain under the parliamentary system, "Agriculture Subsidies in England and the United States." *American Political Science Review* (September 1962), pp. 621-33.
2. Herbert Stein, a chairman of the Council in the Nixon administration is quoted in an interview with Wassily Leontief as saying "if in place of the powerless and understaffed Council of Economic Advisers we had a well staffed, well-informed and intelligently guided planning board, the mess in which the country finds itself today could have been avoided." *Challenge* (White Plains, N.Y.), July–August 1974, p. 35.

* The Secretary of the Treasury, the Director of the Office of Management and Budget, and the Chairman of the Council of Economic Advisors.

3. P. L. 93-344.
4. See "Toward National Economic Foresight" a statement by Mike Mansfield, Majority Leader of the Senate to the opening session of the Joint Leadership–Executive Branch group, reprinted in *Challenge* (White Plains, N.Y.), July–August 1974, p. 62.

CHAPTER 12

Congress and International Policy

Until Vietnam, a constitutional myth had become almost universally accepted. It was to the effect that the President is for all practical purposes completely determinative in our international relations with the possible exception of the Senate's role as obstructor. There have been times in which the myth has been not far from the truth. Conspicuously has this been so in the events leading up to the American entry into many, if not most, of its wars. Franklin D. Roosevelt certainly controlled the American end of the events bringing the United States into its status of belligerent neutrality during World War II. More dramatically, it was Truman's decision to use U. S. forces in Korea, a decision, broadened and sanctioned by the United Nations, out of which stemmed so many subsequent international happenings. A succession of Presidents accelerated the commitment in Vietnam almost without restraint until, in the end, a half million Americans became engaged in hostilities without the direct sanction of Congress, not to speak of a constitutional Declaration of War.

In the material that follows there is no implication that the initiative in international policy does not normally lie with the President. It is he who has access to the immense intelligence network of the present day. It is he who possesses the instruments of negotiation. It is he who commands the Armed

Forces. These factors alone would be sufficient to make his role the dominant one.

Yet, notwithstanding the power of the presidency, the initiatives of Congress have played an integral part in matters of foreign policy, as for example in foreign aid and in ending the military involvement in Vietnam. At an earlier time, Congress was influential in setting the pace of the "cold war" and the evolution of Far Eastern policy. The very power of the President in foreign relations creates an inherent uneasiness in Congress and leads to the search for ways and means not so much to circumscribe the President as to insist on a sharing in crucial decisions.

Far from being passive or obstructive in international affairs, Congress has been searching for and finding ways of making itself felt in a constructive fashion. This search has led to a reexamination of congressional powers in terms of their applicability to foreign relations. Thus, the treaty ratification process as it involves the Senate is cited as a means of curbing excessive usage of executive agreements. The congressional war-making powers are invoked to justify curbs on unilateral presidential commitments abroad which in the end might lead to war. Oversight checks on the Department of State have been established which require annual authorizations of the department's appropriations.

The executive must always reckon with the possibility that Congress will refuse to "go along," by nonratification of a treaty, by failure to appropriate funds, by nonimplementation of an executive agreement, by declining to confirm a presidential choice for an important office. This is nothing new. Much more dramatic have been efforts by Congress to guide international policy, either by further stimulating or accelerating an already noticeable trend or by altering its course altogether. That Congress can nullify, that it can support, is well established; that in the mid-twentieth century it can change the direction and compel innovations in international policy is not too generally understood. Yet, the story of the disinvolvement in Indochina is largely one of congressional initiatives pressed on a reluctant executive.

There are reasons that make an enhanced congressional role inevitable. These reasons lie deep in the area of social change—on the domestic front involving a rising and articulate discrimination on the part of the electorate, on the international scene marking the advent of a diplomacy interlocked with political, economic, social, and cultural factors. Popular support and popular participation call for congressional leadership and conviction as well as for presidential negotiation with other heads of states.

Moreover, treaties are relatively less important in international policy than formerly. Of at least equal importance are certain obvious contemporary characteristics and instruments. These may be conveniently described under four headings—not necessarily mutually exclusive in particular instances. First are the bilateral and multilateral trade and economic agreements, including the so-called reciprocal trade agreements which led to U.S. participation in the General Agreement on Tariffs and Trade (GATT). Also included in this category are agreements for commodity stabilization and exchange support.

This first type passes rather easily into the joint project, distinguished from the first group more by its magnitude than by any difference in legal status. However, its customary legislative implementation may center more around the amount to be appropriated than around the formalities of approval. The great joint projects are the Marshall Plan, exchange stabilization, military aid, and programs of investment in and technical aid to less developed areas.

This type is not sharply distinguishable from still another type, participation in regional and international organizations. The United Nations and its affiliates remain a major sphere of our continuing international activity. The Organization of American States is also of major importance, though relatively speaking it is overshadowed by the larger world orientation. The Southeast Asia Treaty Organization was formed after the Korean War at the height of the hostility toward Mainland China, but has been of declining importance for many years. United States entry into these international groupings required some form of congressional approval, and effective continued participation must be sustained by at least congressional acquiescence and appropriations.

International activity requires money, and it also requires any number of instances of subsequent integration into legislation. The military significance of the cooperation and united action among the nations of the Atlantic Pact continues to occupy congressional attention, with much stress in recent years on a reduction of U. S. participation and costs.

Finally, it should be noted that the cultural leadership with which this nation emerged from World War II contains a more subdued but still powerful thrust. That, too, is sustained by Congress. The democratic way is part of the cultural impression which is asserted: the way of freedom, of equality of opportunity, of participation. So also are capitalism and economic development and growth. So also are our educational system, our humanitarianism, and our religious institutions and beliefs, and increasingly our new-found awareness of the need to control the devastation wreaked on the natural environment by economic growth and increasing population. We continue to use cultural leadership in an effort to raise the standard and quality of living of people everywhere. The Voice of America, the Peace Corps, the Fulbright exchanges, the social and political aspects of aid policies in Southeast Asia are the most obvious concrete examples of ways and means.

It is with reference to an international policy with characteristics such as these that Congress must perforce function in the present state of world affairs. No President alone can create, install, and execute these programs; no secretary of state unaided can carry conviction; no constitutional theory of the role of the executive can create *faits accomplis* which

Congress is legally bound to honor. Such an international policy will succeed only if there is a deep, underlying solidarity of popular support—a solidarity which Congress can develop as well as register. Whatever the current value of these programs, at the time they were adopted they represented an attempt to fuse a sense of world responsibilities with the attitudes of the people of the nation. In that respect they were at least as important to us as to the nations to which they were directed.

It has often been stated that a nation's international policy is an extension of its domestic. Certainly the fear of the growth and the aggression of communism has been a prominent factor, in part selfish, in most of our post-World War II international activities. More clearly than before, it has become apparent to us that to unchoke the clogged channels of international trade will contribute to our domestic prosperity and so is in our interests not alone because it stimulates our export trade or meets our needs for raw materials. A belief in free and representative government is also a part of the picture. Deeper yet are religious and ethical ideals and standards such as the sacredness of the individual and the brotherhood of man. We hesitate to utilize official channels in this regard, because of our tradition of the separation of church and state. But foreign policy is not confined to official organs, and is made by churches and trade unions and corporations and business and professional associations and other voluntary bodies, and the official can and does sometimes favor the unofficial and operate along parallel lines.

In such a setting, congressional support is absolutely essential to the pursuit of foreign policy. Treaties to these ends must be ratified. Appropriations must square with pretensions. Exhortations and alliances alone are not enough. Congress must be satisfied before it appropriates billions of dollars for foreign aid, with the concomitant increases in the tax burden and indefinite postponement of coveted normalcy at home. The role of military affairs in our international relations

Congress tends to understand or, at any rate, to accept. Post-World War II experience with the potency of economic factors in national strength has made these factors also part of its thinking. Nor are formal political alliances, international organizations, and international law alien to congressional patterns of thought. Congress can debate them and understand them. It can raise basic issues.

But what of these great and less clearly understood new elements in the international scene—the cultural, the psychological, the ideological, the protest and, on occasion, riot and revolt abroad? Can Congress understand their significance? Even if we grant that the President and the State Department may be better equipped to cope with the significance of these factors—and this is by no means certain—do the Department of Defense, the Department of Commerce, the Department of Justice understand them? Above all, do the representatives of the people in Congress assembled understand them? Do our editors, our educators, our labor leaders, our clergy, our businessmen see their ramifications? It is not the place of this study to pass judgment on issues but to analyze the setting; and it is clear that more and more Congress must and does understand what is involved.

In this connection, members of the Foreign Relations Committee have issued individual studies of policy after missions abroad. Staff personnel have been dispatched to areas of particular interest for on-the-spot reports. Various committees of the Senate have undertaken, either themselves or by delegation or contract, full-scale impressive studies, inquiries, and investigations. Some have been of regional design; others have dealt with long-range goals, still others have considered the process of foreign policy formation. Vietnam and China policies, two areas especially sensitive politically, were subjected to reviews which proved in both instances to be precursors of a change in the direction of national policy. Notable congressional studies in the reduction and control of armaments and the organization for national security will hold their own with the best that have been forthcoming from any source. These studies laid the basis, among other things, for the organization of arms control policy in the Executive Branch. The fact that a congressional committee stepped in where the Executive Branch was reluctant to go illustrates its balancing, supplemental, or corrective role in the American system of government even in international affairs. An interesting by-product was that when the Executive Branch did give attention to these matters, there was an informed group in Congress ready to share the deliberations and, as in the Test Ban Treaty or the restoration of ties with Mainland China, to give effective support to its efforts.

To say these things is not to say that there are not debit items in the ledger also or that Congress was united in these matters or that the executive was blind. These illustrations are presented rather to document the existence of an affirmative congressional role and to indicate how much there is to be said for such a role. This bipolar generation of policy may be complicating but it may also be invigorating. In the end, it may make for the adoption of a sounder policy than would result were the executive alone responsible.

The ways and means of exercising world leadership culturally and ideologically, insofar as these are governmental matters, remain fluid and uncertain. Insofar as they are governmental, they must have the assent and support of Congress if they are to succeed—a support that goes beyond appropriations and includes much of our internal behavior as well as external action. When to put conditions on our aid to other nations and of what nature they should be, whether this aid should be in loans or grants, what metes and bounds to impose on the Voice of America, what foreigners to entertain and how, what technical processes and ideas to export and how, what to learn from other nations, how to yield something of what we think is best in the interest of a pooling of the creative ideas of others as well as ourselves, how to stir the somewhat lagging spirit of allies—these and other issues have come upon Congress, making its role in international relations the most difficult it has ever been asked to perform.

Mention has already been made of the desire of Congress to find ways and means of exercising congressional initiative in international affairs. That this is at times looked at askance by the Executive Branch on the assumption of superior knowledge or on the basis of its proving an embarrassment or from its sense of invasion of prerogative is well known. Such lack of enthusiasm is at least understandable. Yet, when Congress does so exercise initiative, it may well be because its majority is registering some great upsurge of popular opinion—one of those waves of political intuition which are not infrequently sounder guides than more sophisticated reasonings. Such was the search of so many within and without Congress for alternatives to the exercise of the veto in the United Nations—and even for a world organization minus the Soviet Union some years ago. Such may have been the tide of hostility to China a few years ago and then the reversal of that tide. Some would read the same meaning into congressional activity looking toward the strengthening of Israel.

The harder and more realistic line in foreign aid certainly owes much to the criticism, prodding, and legislating of Congress. At this point, these and the others mentioned are cited primarily as examples of attempted congressional initiative in a field hitherto regarded for the most part as traditionally and constitutionally the prerogative of executive leadership.

The vehicles or instruments through which Congress exercises its degree of leadership and guidance are chiefly appropriations, laws, resolutions, hearings, and debates. Of these, the appropriating process is more likely to be a tool of censure or disapproval than to be an affirmative instrument. Attempts to add something in this field are few and far between. Riders and provisos are not infrequently used as in the earmarking of certain funds in a total program or stipulating certain conditions for use of the funds. Displeasure with particular activities, such as propaganda broadcasting, can be quickly registered in the curtailing of funds or in efforts to close out programs completely. The same tactic has been used to keep a relentless pressure on the Executive Branch in order to bring about a reduction of U. S. military contingents abroad. Riders and provisos were used to end direct participation in the war in Indochina to rebuke Soviet policies regarding Jewish emmigration and to register anger toward Venezuela and Ecuador for their participation in the Petroleum Producer's cartel (O.P.E.C.). Congressional investigations may serve to curtail certain undesirable activities, but this may be at the price of a resultant executive timidity and reluctance to operate on the scale or with the imagination necessary to bring maximum results.

Proposals for actual legislation in the field of international affairs originate sometimes with the executive, sometimes in Congress. They are particularly significant in connection with economic aid and cultural relations. Provisions for foreign scholarships and fellowships, the Pan American Highway, the International Development Fund, and the Asian Development Bank, have legislative rather than treaty bases. So also has foreign military assistance. In preliminary negotiations and in amendments the congressional contributions to the content of measures of this sort are likely to be fairly substantial, even if in the first instance they originated with the executive.

Resolutions are usually largely congressional in their origin, and are perhaps the chief affirmative tool available to Congress. Such were the Connally and Fulbright resolutions, opening the way for participation in the United Nations.[1] At times they constitute a kind of advance pledge of congressional support or opposition with regard to the object of a State Department negotiation previously announced or about to be undertaken. A pledge in advance was extended by the Senate in connection with the restoration of German sovereignty and by joint resolution sanctioning the use of the armed services in the defense of Formosa. In 1957, the use of force in the Middle

East was endorsed, if the President felt it to be necessary. Endorsement of a strong stand in Berlin and on Cuba was forthcoming in 1962. The most celebrated advance pledge in recent years has been the Tonkin Gulf Resolution. This was subsequently used as a rationale by President Johnson for the military intervention in Vietnam, much to the chagrin of Congress which then turned around and repealed it. Resolutions go far to reveal to other nations the pattern of legislative response to our official positions. They have the virtue of suggesting a unified executive–legislative position to other nations. They sometimes have the drawback of overstating the position.

Though the devices carry no formal authority, the mere holding of hearings or even speeches in either House may exert considerable influence in the highly sensitive field of international relations. Many hearings constitute a sharp post-audit of foreign policy. Others indicate that Congress is interested in or concerned about a certain subject as, for example, the operations of multinational corporations or U.S. activities in Laos. Speeches, especially by influential members, are listened to outside the United States as well as within our own official circles. The price of coffee, the adherence of Great Britain to the Common Market, the plight of refugees, Arab–Israeli relations, fraternization with Latin American dictators—these will serve as examples of fields in which speeches have been influential. Dangers obviously lurk in such uncoordinated efforts, and they may easily complicate or even block carefully prepared negotiations. They can also be helpful in supporting them.

It is especially worthy of note that Senator Fulbright, as Chairman of the Foreign Relations Committee, did not hesitate to question a number of executive policies, especially during the Johnson and first Nixon administrations. In the course of the debates thereby evoked, it became clear that the chairman of this committee had not been consulted or informed prior to important decisions, as had usually been the case in earlier administrations. This breakdown in communication led to a conflict between the Executive Branch and the committee which lasted until the designation of Henry Kissinger as Secretary of State.

What Congress appears to be seeking through the application of various legislative techniques to international questions is to forge tools whereby it can, if not wrest the initiative from the executive, at least share it to the extent that it can influence policy sufficiently in the informal initial stages and thereby make its will felt affirmatively in the end results. In other instances, monitoring or setting metes and bounds of executive action is the objective. Congress has learned this much at least from history: that our nation's foreign policy over the years has been seriously handicapped through failure of executive-legislative rapport. It is not willing to solve this problem through following the executive wherever it leads. It is rather seeking to fill this gap or remedy this defect by positive means.

During much of the post-World War II period, Congress has been particularly interested in finding ways of insisting upon certain conditions as the price of foreign economic and military aid. Speeches and resolutions, even appropriations riders or preambles to acts, have all been used as vehicles to convey congressional warnings or viewpoints or to set metes and bounds for the Executive Branch. Embarrassing as these restraints may have been, if Congress believes that conditions are in fact an appropriate quid pro quo of an agreement on aid, trade, or whatever, who shall say it is out of its province so to declare?

Vietnam opened the door for a reassertion of a strong if not coequal role for Congress in questions of war and peace. Operating on the theory that formal congressional declarations of war had become obsolete and treaties only slightly less so, by the end of the decade of the 1960s the Executive Branch claimed almost an absolute presidential authority to make commitments abroad by executive agreement and to use the Armed Forces in support of those commitments. Except, perhaps, for the appropriating power, the role of Congress in these matters was dismissed as almost irrelevant.

As public pressures on Congress mounted for the conclusion of the indecisive military involvement in Vietnam and Southeast Asia, however, Congress began to rediscover and assert its constitutional powers to influence the course of policy. The legislative effort began modestly enough in 1969 with limitations on the use of funds for various aid and military activities in Southeast Asia. In the ensuing years, additional restrictions were placed on legislation necessary for the continuance of military activity. Each drew the reins a little tighter on what had begun as the virtually unbridled use of military power by unilateral presidential command. It took a long time, but in the end the full phase-out of direct U. S. military activity in Indochina was achieved by legislative means.[2]

While moving against the specifics of the Vietnamese war, the Congress also sought to deal with the broader question of unilateral executive usages in foreign relations which committed the nation to courses which might irrevocably lead to military involvement. Again, the effort began modestly enough. In 1969, the Senate passed the National Commitments Resolution which merely stated the view of the Senate that:

(1) a national commitment for the purpose of this resolution means the use of the armed forces of the United States on foreign territory, or a promise to assist a foreign country, government, or people by the use of the armed forces or financial resources of the United States, whether immediately or upon the happening of certain events, and (2) it is the sense of the Senate that a national commitment results only from the affirmative action taken by the executive and legislative branches of the United States government by means of a treaty, statute, or concurrent resolution of both houses of Congress specifically providing for such commitment.[3]

At first, the Executive Branch chose to ignore the resolution as not only of no legal validity but also as representative of the views only of the Senate of 1969. Nevertheless, the Congress reiterated the views by direct reference to specific situations as, for example, in regard to base agreements with Spain, Portugal, and Bahrain.

The movement to reassert legislative prerogatives in basic questions of war and peace culminated in the passage of the War Powers Resolution in 1973 when two-thirds of the House joined two-thirds of the Senate in overriding a presidential veto of the measure.[4] The War Powers Resolution acknowledges the right of the President to use the armed forces abroad under his own authority as commander-in-chief but calls on him to report at once in writing to the Congress when he does so, setting forth the circumstances and the authority for his actions and the estimated scope and duration of the commitment. He must continue, furthermore, to report periodically as long as the use of the armed forces continues. Unless Congress takes affirmative action to endorse the President's course, he must end the use of the armed forces within sixty days, with thirty days more allowed for withdrawal. At any time, Congress can order the pull-back of the forces by a concurrent resolution.

The War Powers Resolution represented the most sweeping reshuffling of powers in foreign relations in several decades. It was buttressed, moreover, by a host of other congressional actions which on a smaller scale had the effect of increasing the congressional contribution to the design and management of our relations with the rest of the world. Most of these changes originated in the Senate which, traditionally, has played a more conspicuous role in foreign affairs than the House. As noted, many were fall-outs of Vietnam but others were part of the general and progressive awakening of the Congressional Branch of the government to its own constitutional powers.

Does Congress in fact know enough in the field of foreign relations to sustain this trend? Over the years certain of its members have been or have become specialists. Its committees have staffs of comparable ability, if not of comparable size, to those of the executive. The frequency of committee meetings is noteworthy. In 1973 the House Foreign Affairs Committee met forty-six times; the Senate Foreign Relations Committee, 107 times. Meetings of subcommittees should be added to these figures. There were 207 in the House and fifty-seven in the Senate. Partisanship is minimal on foreign policy questions. These considerations and others would argue that, regardless of the implications of the Constitution as drawn and perhaps as intended, House and Senate alike need not hesitate to exercise initiatives—save only that they exercise these responsibly.[5]

That such a sense of responsibility is overriding is the unmistakable verdict of the years since 1940. Both the House Foreign Affairs and the Senate Foreign Relations Committees have operated in a bipartisan or nonpartisan manner. The Senate committee in particular has developed a tradition in this aspect of its operations. The Republican Chairman Vandenberg under Democratic President Truman boasted of forty-seven critical occasions in the Eightieth Congress on which the Committee was unanimous or near unanimous. The most persistent and influential committee critics of the Vietnamese policies of the Democratic Johnson Administration were Senators Mansfield and Fulbright, both Democrats. President Johnson turned frequently to their Republican counterparts in a search of support for his policies but with little success, insofar as Republican members of the committee were concerned.

The practice of nonpartisanship in foreign relations has survived serious strains such as Vietnam and lesser in the form of failures on the part of the Executive Branch to consult before making controversial moves. That it has done so is indicative of the sense of responsibility which permeates congressional consideration of this subject. To be sure, Presidents normally can count on some greater support from their own party on questions of foreign relations. It is also worth noting that chairmen of the committee from the opposition party (when it was in control of Congress) have been able to demand greater policy concessions than those of the administration's own party.[6] If the over-all story be viewed, however, the give-and-take between the branches of government has been remarkable and partisan voices and action have been but minor elements in the total picture.

It can be said that any administration can get as much cooperation from Congress as it is prepared to pay for by sharing the power of decision. The State Department, for example, did keep Congress acquainted with the developing issues and associated members of Congress with the actual negotiations in the framing of the United Nations Charter. Its ultimate acceptance was nearly universal. In regular briefings of the committees, often in executive sessions, in facilitating congressional visits to the locale of international issues, in naming congressmen as delegates to conferences—in these and other ways the department can effect a congressional relation with international policy which contributes to its implementation. Regrettably the practice of serious prior consultation was all but abandoned during the war in Vietnam and was not resumed until the second Nixon administration.

There are a few other aspects of the role of Congress in foreign affairs which are worthy of notice before concluding. For one thing, the House has assumed a new importance in this whole field. The House Foreign Affairs Committee was formerly regarded as a minor committee. Now membership on it is highly coveted. The shift from emphasis on treaties to emphasis on programs and policy has had as its by-product also an enhanced House responsibility. The economic and the ideological have joined the political and military. Appropriations, ordinary laws, and joint resolutions all require bicameral action, and appropriations bills are initiated in the House.

The staffs of the two committees and of the Congressional Research Service, as well as the staffs of special committees in the foreign field, have played an important though undetermined role in the total operations. In the pioneer congressional staff work preceding the adoption of the Marshall Plan after World War II, for example, some thirty experts worked on all legislative aspects of the problem. Independently of, but in close touch with specialists in the Executive Branch, they provided a significant input of expertise into the formulation of policy. This new staff competence, like the committees to which it was responsible, operated without thought of partisanship. That pattern, once established, has governed practices ever since in both Houses and, of course, extends to the principal research arm of the Congress in this field, the Foreign Affairs Division of the Congressional Research Service.

For the most part, the State Department and others in the executive cooperate with congressional staffs in making available to them departmental files, although when communication between the President and the Foreign Relations Committee virtually broke down over Vietnam staff relations were similarly strained. Notwithstanding the degree of give and take which has been established in foreign affairs, there is still some reticence on the part of the Executive Branch. Second only to the military, moreover, our State Department experts have expected in the past to be listened to and not subjected to rival interpretations or advice. Back of this expectation lie not only greater access to confidential information but also a constitutional theory of great prestige, that it is the Executive Branch which is solely responsible for foreign relations. Indeed, members can still be found in Congress who subscribe to the theory. However, these members are now distinctly in the minority. The difference today is that Congress can confront the department as an equal, not merely constitutionally but in its command of competence. In no small degree this is accounted for by staff facilities. If Congress is to continue, as it doubtless will, to play an affirmative role in international affairs and likewise to play its constitutional part as the indispensable partner in the policies of the executive, then the availability of staffs to explore alternatives, to analyze executive presentations, to aid in the organization of hearings, to conduct inquiries and investigations overseas, to provide unbiased, thorough information quickly—this availability is a prerequisite.

Staff does not function in a vacuum. Its usefulness depends entirely on the presence of members who are competent to draw on this source of skill. Fortunately, there are members of both Houses who have now devoted many years of study to, or who have had many years of practical experience in, some area or problem in international relations. There are other members who between sessions have traveled as serious students of a problem or problems about to face Congress.

The practice of growing U.S. participation in interparliamentary meetings is also of relevance to the role of Congress. Members of Congress now regularly attend the meetings of the International Parliamentary Union, the NATO parliamentarians association, and annual Mexico–United States, Canada–United States parliamentary meetings. Special parliamentary visits are exchanged with many other countries. In this fashion, the United States reveals an element of its government which is of importance to others in making judgments of its policies. Similarly, members of Congress learn to appraise other nations and developments abroad in a more accurate perspective.

When President Nixon reestablished contact with Mainland China after a lapse of a quarter of a century by a visit to the People's Republic in 1972, the next official mission was undertaken by the two Senate leaders, Mansfield of Montana for the Democrats and Scott of Pennsylvania for the Republicans. That, in turn, was followed by a visit of the bipartisan House leadership.

One more aspect deserves comment. Foreign policy is in fact made in many departments of the executive besides the State Department. It is made in Defense, in Commerce, in Agriculture, in the Central Intelligence Agency, in Justice, in Labor, in the cultural-relations program of the Library of Congress, in many other agencies in at least a minor fashion. So also among the corresponding committees on Capitol Hill.

The effect of the projection into the international sphere of our policies in trade, the military, atomic energy, food supply and raw materials, cultural relations, immigration, shipping, labor standards, and many other spheres is to project international considerations to some extent into the deliberations of many congressional committees.

We are a world power. Our cultural leadership, our military strength, our political influence, to some extent even our economic power, initially were not sought. There probably never was a more reluctant assumption of world leadership than that of the United States prior to our entry into World War II. Other peoples have tended to personify us in the shape of the individual who happened to be our President at a given time and have assumed that the voice of the President was necessarily the total voice of America. Yet, these other peoples that make up the world need more than an understanding of our President: they need to understand the position of our representative body, the Congress. It is significant that after the Watergate affair had dealt the image of the presidency a staggering blow resident diplomats in Washington redoubled their efforts to understand the role of Congress. What they discovered was that the Republic has Congress too among its institutions of leadership—incorporating not only the hesitations and cross-purposes of its people but also their sense of responsibility and the agreement on objectives and methods which the people's assembled representatives have produced following study and discussion.

NOTES

1. Senate Resolution 192; House Concurrent Resolution 25: Seventy-eighth Congress, first session.
2. See P.L. 91-121; P.L. 91-171; P.L. 91-441; P.L. 91-668; P.L. 9-652; P.L. 91-672; P.L. 92-226; P.L. 92-156; P.L. 92-129.
3. S. Res. 83, 91st Congress, 1st Session. See Holbert N. Carroll,

The House of Representatives and Foreign Affairs, Rev. ed. (Boston: Little Brown, 1968).

4. P.L. 93-148.

5. An informed evaluation of the readiness and competence of Congress to exercise a more vigorous role in foreign relations is to be found in an article by a former chief of the Foreign Affairs Division of the Congressional Research Service, Dr. William C. Olson. See William C. Olson, "Congressional Competence in Foreign Affairs" *Round Table,* No. 250 (April 1973), pp. 247-58.

6. Cf. Malcolm E. Jewell, *Senatorial Politics and Foreign Policy* (Lexington: University of Kentucky Press, 1964), p. 146. The entire book is an illuminating study of events and political forces in the Senate from 1947 through 1960.

CHAPTER 13

Legislative Responsibilities
in National Defense

The authority of technical competence has no sphere more formidable than defense and warfare. Weapon systems are out of date before they leave the drawing board. The possibility of mutual annihilation is with us at all times. The very capacity for control of lethal weapons may already be a fantasy, rendered obsolete by the possibility of minuscule construction and the ease and speed of conversion and production. Moreover, defense policy must be formulated and adopted, not only in a nuclear age, but also in an ideological age—an age in which ideologies clash amid the revolutions of rising expectations, the revolts of color and class, and rapid population growth.

How does, how should, Congress operate in defense policy in such a setting?

As in foreign policy, so also in defense the Constitution seems deliberately ambiguous and ambivalent. Overlapping functions were assigned to Congress and the executive. While the Constitution made the President commander-in-chief, it gave to Congress the power "to make rules for the government and regulation of the land and naval forces." No authority on constitutional law has been able to draw the line between the two. Congress must appropriate, but the executive may successfully plead national security in refusing to disclose ways in which substantial portions of the money appropriated are to be or have been spent.

In this setting there have grown up images in the two branches, each of the other. To the professionals in the Armed Services, Congress has often appeared, with the possible exception of the Armed Services Committees, as a group of fumbling amateurs, interfering where it should not interfere, making it difficult for those who know the answers to put them into operation.

On the other hand, from the perspective of Congress, the defense establishment often appears to be a group of big spenders divided into warring factions, protecting vested interests and personal empires, indifferent to national needs other than defense, and habitually trying to handle rather than persuade the Congress as the representatives of the people.

Each sees itself as dedicated to the national interest, conscientious and hard working, trying to arrive at the best answers to overwhelmingly difficult problems in a world that at any time may crash around it.

There is an element of truth in all these images, truth of the favorable as well as the unfavorable. This is the setting in which Congress works out its role in the defense picture.

Of national security itself, Congress also has an image—a composite image which has grown gradually. There is, for example, the suspicion that "generals either fight the last war when seeking manpower or the war several generations ahead when seeking vast appropriations for the development of exotic new weapons. Basically, it was the mistake of the French General Staff between World Wars I and II that alerted Congress to the first danger. The Maginot Line became a symbol carrying with it a warning against the vested interests and thought-patterns of earlier wars. After this came Pearl Harbor, and from it an idea emerged of noncommunication between branches of what is now the Defense Department. To this was added an impression of the danger of slackness or laxness. Yet, as World War II progressed, counteracting these unfavorable images there arose a growing confidence in the Armed Services leadership, in military commanders such as Marshall, Nimitz, Eisenhower, and Bradley.

Nevertheless, Congress went counter to their pleas after World War II and forced a drastic pace of demobilization. To be sure, Congress was reflecting the mood of the times. Nevertheless, the concept of military service as a professional career was spattered and the armed forces fell somewhat into disarray.

When simultaneous with this course there came, not peace but Cold War, the triumph of Chinese communism on the Asian Mainland, and the Korean War, Congress shifted gears once again. Almost as in remorse there came a series of actions, risking corruption, delegating vast emergency powers over the nation to the President, and an enormous growth in military appropriations. It was as though Congress was determined to build an Armed Forces not only "second to none" but vastly superior to all and to maintain that level until there were no other centers of great power remaining elsewhere in the world.

As the dimensions of the cost of this determination became evident during the Eisenhower administration, there was some backtracking and retrenchment. There was talk of a "bigger bang for a buck," a reference to a greater reliance on nuclear weapons. On the other hand, the Kennedy campaign for the presidency was waged on the need for a restrengthening of the Armed Forces, particularly with respect to the need to be able to conduct a limited war, a war short of nuclear. This concept was converted by the armed services into planning for what was known as a strategy of preparedness for two and a half wars. To put it another way, what was sought of Congress was support to enable the nation to conduct a simultaneous nuclear conflict with the Soviet Union and China and a limited war with some other less powerful entity. The costs of this concept were astronomical.

Vietnam and Indochina turned out to be the setting for a "half-war" which became, in time, a huge military quagmire. In a decade, our military commitment grew from aid and a handful of advisors to Vietnamese forces to a peak deployment in Vietnam of well over half a million U.S. personnel in April 1969. Fifty-six thousand Americans died in Vietnam and more than 300,000 were wounded. The costs which ultimately will tally in the hundreds of billions did much to damage the stability of the nation's economy and to depreciate its currency. The nature of the war and its pursuit were such as to tear at the social fabric of the nation. When the war was finally brought to an end by diplomacy after the accumulation of intense congressional pressure, the strategic concept of the two-and-a-half wars began to be brought into question. Its validity became increasingly difficult to maintain in the light of the Nixon policies of rapprochement with the Soviet Union and China. At the same time, U.S. nuclear superiority disappeared as Soviet power in this area grew. Notwithstanding the nuclear nonproliferation treaty, moreover, nuclear weapons capability appeared in several additional countries and became a factor in the strategic Middle Eastern situation where the United States is deeply involved.

These, then, are some of the principal impressions in the composite image which Congress holds of National Defense, impressions to be reckoned with as responsible for initial reactions, if not ultimate congressional decisions regarding the defense establishment. It is well before probing the congressional role more deeply to call attention again to certain general developments within Congress, to the setting in which defense decisions are made. First is the fact of specialization. In defense matters, Congress, for practical purposes, is the Armed Services Committees of the two Houses, the Joint Atomic Energy Committee, the relevant Appropriations subcommittees and, in a peripheral sense, the closely related committees in the field of foreign policy. Second, nonpartisanship has characterized these committees and Congress as a whole in defense matters. The party of the President would normally assume the responsibility for carrying the President's program, and the party opposite to the President might be expected to be the most articulate in criticizing it. As a practical matter, however, a long tenure of Democrats in the leadership of Congress and, in particular, of its Armed Service Committees has produced significant variations on what might be expected. Those who have carried the burden of presentation of the military programs have been Democrats of these committees under both Democratic and Republican Presidents. At the same time, the largest and most articulate group of critics of the programs have also been Democrats, notably in the Senate.

It should be noted that the growth of competent congressional staffs, already discussed, has taken place in the defense field as elsewhere. A few such specialists may seem insignificant compared with the vast research and analysis personnel, and all the contractual research which goes to buttress it, in the Defense Department and other parts of the Executive Branch. Yet, when such specialists are added to years of committee service on the part of members themselves, it becomes possible for a committee to probe, to bring together material, to sense the architecture of the issues, and hence to review and analyze military policy, if not to initiate it.

Substantial research has been precipitated in the congressional committees, notably in the Senate, to fill the gap in defense-related fields where for many years the Executive Branch showed little interest, fields such as long-range foreign policy, disarmament, weapons evaluation, contracting procedures, volunteer vs. draft personnel systems, and the processes of defense and foreign policy formulation. Independent congressional interest in these matters has continued and grown. The Congressional Research Service and private research facilities have been enlisted to supplement the congressional staffs. The resources of the General Accounting Office have been increasingly used by committees and members to probe waste and inefficiency, notably in foreign aid and in various practices of the Defense Department.

It is clearly difficult for Congress to make affirmative policy decisions in opposition to a hostile executive. It tried to do so by increasing the size of the Air Force some years ago, but the Bureau of the Budget impounded the extra money appropriated. The next year, on congressional insistence, the money was spent; but less was asked for the following year. Even though a forced change of fundamental policy may be difficult if not unsuitable for congressional initiative, such change by no means exhausts the possibility of congressional correctives.

Correctives from Congress are needed because there are built-in dangers tending toward adherence to the status quo in the present system. There is the built-in danger of pressure from the contractor who has a vested interest in the continued use of his product. There can be a similar vested interest on the part of those in the Armed Services who have committed years of their lives to the mastery of a particular weapons system. There are ties of long-standing personal acquaintance between military personnel and civilian suppliers. A vested bureaucratic job interest is lodged in maintaining the size of the military forces and the civilian component of the Defense Department.

In one sense, Congress plays something akin to the role played by Her Majesty's Loyal Opposition in the British system of government. Many of the major decisions of the Joint Chiefs of Staff, by the time they reach the National Security Council or the President, are decisions in which the intradepartmental criticism and opposition that attended their formulation have been filtered out.

Congress has the function from time to time of retracing these arguments. That is one reason why there are frequent inquiries and expositions by committees and individual members. It is also the reason why, by statute, high-ranking members of the armed services are required on demand to speak freely their own minds on these subjects to Congress.

This practice is frequently resented and is always risky. Yet, Congress believes that the issues involved are too great, the national safety is too important, not to have the benefit of conflicting viewpoints and all possible information. So it is regarded as a proper function, this role of going over the ground again to make sure that the original decision was in fact the correct one. Sometimes, it has been pursued in significant debates in the Congress, often in rare executive sessions of the entire Senate. Basic executive decisions as, for example, in the case of the ABM (antiballistics missile) are not often overruled by this process but the congressional influence may often be seen in subsequent modifications of policy. In any event, Congress and the public each time are better informed thereby and better prepared to cope with subsequent defense issues.

Assuming staff work well done and a candid presentation, the time once was that the executive could anticipate congressional acceptance and the requisite appropriations. It used to receive these endorsements almost as a matter of routine. No longer is that the case. In the wake of Vietnam and the enormous defense costs which it precipitated, the questions in Congress over defense policy, organization, procurement, and practices have grown more and more widespread and penetrating. Congress appears, at this writing, to have reached the conclusion that it was too trusting, too self-effacing in this admittedly highly complex technological field.

Military defense is, also, more and more seen in Congress as only one aspect of national security and its costs are beginning to be weighed in relationship to other facets of national security, including internal social well-being. The tangible effects of this shift in terms of cost reductions are still limited but the days of almost automatic acceptance of Pentagon premises and promises have gone.

After manpower costs, the point of greatest congressional leverage in the control and reduction of the defense budget lies in close scrutiny of innovations or alterations in weapons systems. In 1959, the Congress required that all such changes be authorized specifically prior to appropriations. Aircraft, missiles, and naval vessels were listed in 1962, and in 1963 the research, development, and evaluation stages were added. This has resulted in greater and more intelligent focus in the hearings and inquiries prior to the initiation of programs.

The problem of waste and inefficiency in defense also has its congressional aspect. Congressmen are responsible to their districts and states. This gives them an undue or subjective concern as to the location of navy bases, army camps, air-fields—not to mention the awarding of contracts to firms which are in their constituencies. It is often almost impossible to close down an installation without the consent of a particular committee. For a period the House Armed Services Committee was characterized as primarily a "committee on real estate." A public administrator naturally regards such matters as costly and dangerous intrusions into administration.

Sometimes it seems as if it is Congress, rather than the executive, that holds on to the past too long. Most striking and most obviously contrary to the preponderance of military authority is the emphasis laid by Congress on the state-sponsored National Guard. It is not that a case cannot be made out for the Guard, even at its present strength; but there is a strong suspicion that it is the local loyalties of Congress and tradition rather than military judgment that account for its devotion to this branch of the services.

What may be fairly said on balance? Less preeminent since Vietnam, one school of thought believes that Congress not only does not, but also should not, play any significant role in defense policy. This doctrine rests upon an alleged executive monopoly of *expertise* and the existence of so much classified information, and also upon the record to date. In this view, Congress would be granted a role in matters such as economic mobilization, selective service, reenlistment incentives, veterans' legislation, and other instances in which cooperation of the civilian arm is important or is affected. Indeed, Congress has always been most active in this "nuts and bolts" aspect of defense. It does take initiatives in these fields and, increasingly on the basis of oversight, is legislating with greater specificity on policies involving recruitment, careerism, grade distribution, education of officers and men in military and nonmilitary subjects, morale, racial strife, and drug addiction.

Those who hold the view that activity of this kind is about as far as Congress should go, if, indeed, it has not already gone beyond its competence, have failed to take into account certain factors already mentioned. Congress does have expertise in members who have pursued questions of defense and military strategy for many years and in a much broader perspective than those whose lives have been dedicated strictly to military pursuits. Congress can also draw on the competence of its own staff and the congressional support services such as the General Accounting Office and Congressional Research Service. It can obtain tips from within the Executive Branch from those who have been overruled as well as from the expert witnesses among military critics and retired military men. It, too, can draw on the "think tanks" by contractual arrangements if it chooses to do so. Its vested interest in the military status quo is likely to be less inhibiting than that of the permanent defense bureaucracy, civilian and military.

It is not civilian "supremacy" that is the main issue in the role of Congress in its confrontation with the Defense Department. This is conceded, at least, in principle by all concerned. Rather, it is the inability of the Executive Branch itself to structure into its procedures an effective, responsible, even daring criticism of the status quo or a system for continuously challenging today's decision in the light of the rapidly changing technological and international circumstances. Within the uniformed armed services themselves too much ought not to be expected in this regard. The reasons are inherent and obvious. They lie in a hierarchical system of organization with place and promotion dependent heavily on conformity and tradition, in interservice rivalries and jealousies. Outside civilian secretaries and assistant secretaries might serve the purpose but their tenure probably does not average more than two or three years, scarcely enough time to find one's way around the Pentagon. The Office of the President is a possible location for such built-in criticism, and to some extent has been used as such, as witness the activities of the Office of Management and Budget and several ad hoc special commissions, not to mention the President's Assistant for National Security. But in the long run this is a function that must at least be supplemented by and often performed by Congress with the aid of agents such as the committee staffs, the General Accounting Office, the Congressional Research Service, and, as they develop, the new budget committees and Congressional Budget Office.

To accelerate the implementing of decisions already made, to review controversial decisions for their soundness, to force decisions in areas in which there have been none (or only conflicts), to weigh military security concepts in the light of the total needs of national security and the changing international situation—these are the major elements in the role which an informed Congress can play in addition to a continuing concern with the housekeeping of the Department of Defense. Such a role deserves the respect of all concerned; it should be welcomed by the armed services themselves. They can assist its performance best by that combination of candor and humility which first seeks to convince rather than bypass, and, failing to convince, reexamines its own record and decisions to see if perchance these may have been wrong. To quote Holbert Carroll, "Regardless of the depth of its involvement, whether it chooses to monitor, to attempt to govern, or, more commonly, to blend the two tendencies in varying proportions, the Congress participates significantly in the shaping of national security policies. No major legislature in the world can match the extent of its participations." [1]

NOTES

1. Holbert N. Carroll, "The Congress and National Security Policy," in David B. Truman, ed., *The Congress and America's Future* (Englewood Cliffs: Prentice-Hall, 1965), p. 152.

CHAPTER 14

Policy Roles in Science

The explosion of knowledge in the natural sciences has sent its reverberations throughout the Federal government. As a matter of fact, most of the American expression of this explosion has been nurtured by the government itself. Research and development appropriations in 1973 amounted to $16.8 billion and seem to be rising inexorably. Defense accounts for the greater part of this sum but space research is not too far behind, and research in nuclear energy and public health and medicine are of billions of dollars magnitude. Most recently, public anxieties over the pollution of the environment and the adequacy of energy supplies have emerged to add vast new sums to the cornucopia of Federal research and development funding. We have been witnessing a quantum leap in the development of applied science, growing out of a combination of the climax of an educational system, the urge of weaponry, man's insatiable curiosity, his desire to live longer and better, and exploding populations throughout the world. At the same time, we are also catching the first glimmers of the dangerous consequences of this development in the form of a breakdown of man's relations with his natural environment.

In such a sphere, can Congress really function? What are its roles, if any?

Not that the problem is intrinsically new, or even different from what Congress has been grappling with for many decades—save only in the whirlwind speed of its development and the cascades of its specialized details. We must start with the members themselves in facing the congressional role. Less than ten percent in the Eighty-ninth Congress were either scientifically educated or vocationally oriented toward science. The Ninety-second Congress included only thirteen members who might be categorized as scientists or engineers. In themselves these numbers are utterly inadequate to assure competence in monitoring the technical details of every project in every agency, not to mention the problem of inter-relating the projects. But bear in mind that Congress is not charged with the mastery of science, only with developing science *policy*. In that perspective, the number of members already science-oriented need not be any larger.

The role of Congress in science is the role of value judg-ments, of selection of objectives from among alternatives, of evaluation of results. Its role is also to provide or evaluate appropriate forms of organization and procedure, to ferret out moribund practices or vested interests, to balance or stimulate the flow of manpower, to look for secondary or derivative effects of decisions, to consider not only the needs of the living but also of those yet to be born.

Even these tasks would lie beyond the competence of Con-gress without some degree of specialization among the mem-bership and sufficient professional support from technicians independent of the Executive Branch.

So new is the explosion in science that it is not possible to go beyond citing a few examples of congressional efforts to act effectively in this field. Congress as a whole still suffers from the same trauma which pervades the public at large, as it views something too great really to comprehend. It may well be that the combined power of the defense establishment, the indus-tries dependent thereon, and the scientists, research corpora-tions, and university personnel and equipment spawned by both will prove too much for Congress and President alike to control. In this connection it is significant that President Eisenhower made an aspect of this danger—the danger of a powerful military–industrial complex—the principal theme of his farewell message at the end of two terms in the presidency. Nor is the scientific power structure confined to a defense orientation. Research in outer space also has a momentum and magnitude of its own. So, too, has medical and health research. The heart of the congressional role may well be in the fact that in all these matters Congress has considerably less vested interest than the bureaucracy and its outside affiliates, although, here too, some congressional interest does already exist in the form of plant locations, employment opportunities, and professional, scientific, and university pressures. Nevertheless, it may well be the more hopeful branch of government whenever questions arise involving the shrinking and redirection of the apparatus.

Turn first to the choice of objectives. With costs mounting as they are, disciplined value judgments concerning alternative uses of billions of dollars are clearly within the prerogative of Congress. The major choice is obvious. The Soviet Union and the United States, for example, have begun to discern that they must choose between unlimited achievements in outer space or military overkill capacity on the one hand, or, alternatively, such programs as grappling with the problems of an urbanized society, safeguarding the natural environment, and cooperation in raising the living standards of the "have nots" the world over. Now that we have reached the moon and bypassed Venus, will billions more spent on reaching Mars be more valuable than similar billions in seeking new sources of energy, on agricultural productivity, population limitation, oceanography, or weather control—without even leaving the natural science area? Now that we have intercontinental ballistic missiles with an accuracy of a five mile radius several thousand miles away, will we spend billions in a search for an accuracy of two miles? Or will we use these funds to reduce pollution and clean up the rivers and lakes of the nation? With ever increasing frequency, this kind of question comes before the Congress for decision.

A search for consensus in objectives and the sifting of the evidence on which to base its decisions challenge Congress's best efforts. Until recently, Congress dealt mostly with the fringes, being inclined to leave to the Defense Department, for example, the choice of weaponry. Some congressional effort also consists in an "egging on" of certain scientific agencies to spend more and faster on research. In the past, the favorite candidates for increases in appropriations were the military services and the space agency, along with the National Institutes of Health. More recently, these have shared the spotlight with environmental protection and the development of energy sources.

Turn next to the evaluative roll of the Congress. The most usual congressional concern thus far, apart from appropriations, has been in the field of organization and procedure. This is not surprising, considering the number of executive agencies with important science responsibilities. Duplication, lack of coordination, and confusion exist in situations of this type, and the Executive Branch is often either unable or unwilling to do much about it, except under congressional prodding.

Among the congressional achievements in the field of the organization of science must certainly be placed the National Aeronautics and Space Act of 1958.[1] The Soviet Sputnik traversed the heavens in September of 1957. Congress moved into action, thereafter, first to spur the executive and then to develop its own policy. Early in 1958, it delegated responsibility to two "blue ribbon" special committees, headed respectively by Lyndon Johnson, then the majority leader of the Senate, and John McCormack, the majority leader of the House. The two committees probably held over fifty sessions, and the end result was the act setting up the National Aeronautics and Space Administration. Preliminary studies were made by the Congressional Research Service, whose staff subsequently cooperated with committee staffs in organizing the hearings and analyzing data.

It is worthy of note that congressional initiative was also primarily responsible for establishing the Office of Science and Technology in 1962 in the Office of the President, which was recently allowed to lapse. On the other hand, the reconciliation of conflicting interests in the formation of the Communications Satellite Corporation was largely undertaken in the Executive Branch prior to any submission to Congress.

The longest continued special relationship between Congress and the executive in science policy has been in the field of atomic energy. The organic act setting up the Atomic Energy Commission charged it with the responsibility of keeping the Joint Committee "fully and currently informed with respect to the Commission's activities." In large part, this legislation represented an attempt by Congress to fulfill what it regarded as its normal responsibilities in the light of the secrecy involved at the time. What was not practicable for the entire body was feasible for a smaller group, and the Joint Committee device was chosen.

Since the inception of the Atomic Energy program, the Joint Committee and the commission have worked together closely, though by no means always harmoniously. Differences of opinion arose concerning security precautions and the manufacturing of the hydrogen bomb—to mention two of the earlier problems. The committee's views eventually prevailed. Under the chairmanship of Senator McMahon, the committee kept up a continuous pressure on the commission for expediting its activities. In turn, the committee assumed substantial responsibility for securing ample appropriations for the commission's work, and in general identified itself with and rose to the defense of the latter.[2]

Congress has always concerned itself with persons, and scientific manpower has been a focus of attention. The development and education of scientists has been aided with liberal funds, but the congressional concern has not stopped here. Questions of in-breeding, of undue concentration in certain universities, of the danger that ideas from outside the "establishment" will not be given due consideration have all fallen within its purview. The Government Operations Committees as well as the Science Committees have sponsored such investigations.

How have Congress and its committees equipped themselves to deal with these esoteric subjects? The story follows similar lines, differing not too much from other legislative and investigative fields. The great majority of committees at least occasionally are faced with decisions requiring scientific data for intelligent consideration. As noted, three committees, the Senate Aeronautical and Space Sciences, the House Science and Astronautics, and the Joint Atomic Energy, are primarily science policy oriented. Since the awakening of the nation to the problems of pollution, the Senate Committee on Interior and Insular Affairs, the Committees on Commerce, and their subcommittees, Public Works, and the House Committee on Merchant Marine and Fisheries have drawn heavily on scientific knowledge in legislating. Committee staffs have become competent in setting up hearings and analyzing material. A few subcommittees have perfected the panel technique in one form or another, whereby highly competent witnesses, perhaps the best the nation has, are consulted prior to policy decisions. Care is taken to include a cross-section of points of view. Committee prints and documents testify to the high order of the work being done, including the capacity to state issues and basic data in language intelligible to nonscientists.[3] The Congressional Research Service had about forty specialists in 1973 in the Science Policy Research Division operating in support of the committees and individual members.

An Office of Technology Assessment, established under the Technology Assessment Act of 1972, introduced a new element of major significance into the evolution of the machinery for evolving science policy in the Federal government. In the first place, as a congressional agency, it has provided Congress with a substantial increase in access to technical knowledge in dealing with scientific questions.

In the words of the act, this agency is designed to equip Congress:

(1) with new and effective means for receiving competent, unbiased information concerning the physical, biological, economic, social and political effects of . . . (technological) applications, and

(2) [to] utilize this operation, whenever appropriate, as one factor in the legislative assessment of matters pending before the Congress. . . .[4]

The office is governed by a Joint Congressional Technology Assessment Board which is bipartisan in membership. It is amply financed and operates with a substantial staff which, in turn, can contract for additional scientific skills from outside government and can also draw on the resources of the Congressional Research Service and the General Accounting Office.

At the time of this writing, the Office of Technology Assessment is still in the formative stage. Nevertheless, it is apparent that it offers to Congress a major new bureaucratic source of scientific information. How the Office of Technology Assessment will develop over the years remains to be seen. At this point, however, it is possible to concur with the evaluation of its potential which was set forth by the Congressional Research Service in August 1973 in a report which concluded that:

If an appropriate policy and organizational framework backed with adequate resources is established, the Congress can have a new and valuable input to its deliberations and actions. . . .[5]

As for the future, in science and technology also, as in foreign policy, defense, and economic planning, the principles of separation of powers and checks and balances would appear to be serving well. Though the task of formulating and executing science policy is colossal and intricate, the presence of a Legislative Branch amply supported by scientific and technological experts, which must be convinced on the basis of facts and analysis can make for that consensus in the nation as a whole which will assure sound foundations of public support. Likewise the legislative presence as subsequent monitor may well be decisive in disciplining the vested interests that inevitably cluster around the nest in aggregates of great power and money. That this monitor may also command as witnesses those in the electorate at large who may feel aggrieved by or profoundly doubtful of executive policies must be reckoned as a major asset in the process.

NOTES

1. The standard work on the legislative history of this act is Alison Griffith: *The National Aeronautics and Space Act* (Washington: Public Affairs Press, 1962).
2. For a full story of these relationships, see Morgan Thomas, Atomic Energy and Congress (Ann Arbor: University of Michigan Press, 1956) and Harold P. Green and Alan Rosenthal, *The Government of the Atom* (New York: Atherton, 1966).
3. See, for example, U. S. Congress. Senate. Committee on Interior and Insular Affairs. *Congress and the Nation's Environment. Committee Print* (Washington: U. S. Government Printing Office, January 20, 1973), pp. 1136.
4. United States 86 Stat. 797.
5. U. S. House of Representatives Committee on Science and Astronautics, *Office of Technology Assessment, Background and Status.* Report to the Committee . . . Ninety-third Congress, First Session, prepared by the Science Policy Research Division, Congressional Research Service, Library of Congress, Serial F. p. 5.

CHAPTER 15

Congress and Localism

Today Congress finds itself charged with greater responsibility than in the past for safeguarding the vitality of state action which is the operative reality behind the legalistic phrase "states' rights." Closely related to this is the role played by Congress in seeing to it that state and local needs, interests, and peculiarities receive recognition in national measures and the administration thereof.

Our founding fathers thought they had built our Federal structure truly and well. Nation and state, each in its sphere, were autonomous. To those who feared the encroachments of the larger unit, it was pointed out that to the nation were entrusted only certain strictly limited powers.

Now few of these powers were such, or originally such, that they touched directly the daily life of the ordinary individual. Hence, the practice grew up of assuming that it was the responsibility of the states and the cities and the local units to provide regulations (if regulations were necessary) and services for all the ordinary, multifarious relations and aspects of everyday life—health, education, local business, most utilities, labor, the home and family, most public works, recreation, poor relief. So it continued for a hundred years more or less, though toward the end of the nineteenth century disquieting signs were already noted.

The distribution of powers was to be safeguarded not only by the Constitution itself, and by Congress operating in observance thereof, but also by the Supreme Court, its living exponent and guardian. Before proceeding to a detailed consideration of the congressional role of state protector, it is worthwhile briefly to recapitulate the values traditionally associated with state and local vitality so as to recapture some portion of the old sense of its importance in the event that the lure of a rampant centralization may have eroded our former faith. These traditional values were many. They included the opportunity to experiment, given the necessary prerequisites of taxable capacity and civic vitality. They included the facility offered to differentiate governmental activities in accordance with differences in population and environment. By developing functions in the smaller units, the size of the central establishment could be kept down, and the terrific managerial and political problems associated with big government were lessened accordingly, or at least became less acute than they otherwise would have been. Above all, local responsible experience was educational in the best sense of the word. Mistakes and successes were brought home to an electorate not too large to understand the manageable issues facing it. Responsible fiscal experience was thereby gained through learning the simple lesson that activities voted must be or at least ought to be paid for by taxes. This is a slender thread at best that limits what voters want to that which is practicable in terms of their own efforts; and the thread has already snapped in many nations and among peoples who have gone far along the treacherous path of insisting upon their wants and dodging the sacrifices involved. Some believe that we, too, are in this unhappy state, but to the extent that we are not, surely a large share of the credit for this belongs to the fact that we have been educated to responsible political behavior in the school of local self-government.[1]

We venture to quote at this point from a *Report* of the Intergovernmental Relations Commission:

Experience amply justifies the view that our federal system, with the degree of flexibility that it permits, can be adapted to crises of the present and future as successfully as it has been to those of the past. As an instrument of positive government, it possesses—at least for a nation as large and diverse as ours—a clear advantage over a strongly centralized government. In helping to bolster the principle of consent; in facilitating wide participation in government; in furnishing training grounds for leaders; in maintaining the habit of local initiative; in providing laboratories for research and experimentation in the art of government; in fostering competition among lower levels of government; in serving as outlets for local grievances and for political aspirations—in all these and many other ways, the existence of many relatively independent and responsible governments strengthens rather than weakens our capacity for government. On the whole, therefore, the enduring values of our federal system fully warrant every effort to preserve and strengthen its essence.

But for local and state self-government to continue to possess the vitality necessary to fulfill this role, they must continue to have a zone of discretion and creative action in a sufficiently large sector of governmental activity to be real, to attract the interest, to enlist the participation, and to command the loyalties of their citizens. Merely to act as agents of a central government that has made all the significant decisions is not enough, even though officials are still locally elected.

It is therefore of cardinal importance for us to realize that as far as the field of statute law is concerned, we no longer live under a genuine federal system constitutionally speaking. The freedom and autonomy of the states have lost most of their assumed constitutional protection. What they do, the decisions they make, the laws they pass, are now largely on sufferance— protected not by the Supreme Court but by the restraint of

Congress in not passing such laws as would wipe out the discretionary element in their remaining functions.

In the generally costly area of public works, the states and cities find themselves hard pressed for revenue. While the property or real estate tax seems still to be peculiarly theirs, it is one which is engendering increasing hostility at the same time the national government is steadily encroaching upon one field of revenue after another of those that remain. On the one hand, this lessens the capacity of the smaller units to undertake activities on their own initiative. On the other hand, the fact that the Federal government returns large sums as subsidies, under conditions set by it, lessens local discretion by the same act that it enlarges local resources. The effect is the same, even though it is frequently the locality rather than the Federal government that presses for the subsidy legislation. Hence, in those proposals in which national standards are tied in with grants-in-aid, the average member of Congress calculates the fiscal effects on his district or state, and hostility to centralization tends to be inevitably modified if the financial aspects appear advantageous.

In the social sphere state autonomy has subtly but none the less surely been undermined by the spending power. The Court stated explicitly in *United States v. Butler*[2] that "the power of Congress to authorize expenditures of public moneys for public purposes is not limited by the direct grants of legislative power found in the Constitution." This had in fact been inferred as implicit from the very earliest days of the Republic. Grants-in-aid of such functions may be made conditional upon the performance by the states of the functions in question in accordance with the stipulations of the central agency.[3] Apparently there is inherently no constitutional limit to the transfer of discretion through conditional grants-in-aid in matters such as education, health, libraries, relief of distress, recreation, police and fire protection, or even the courts, if Congress shall similarly appropriate and decree them to be matters of national concern. It is perhaps gratuitous to point to other court decisions under other clauses of the Constitution where the trend is in the same direction. At one point, equal and even identical educational facilities were required of the states for all races under the Fourteenth Amendment.[4] In its later rulings on segregation the Court stipulated that this "separate but equal" doctrine was superseded, and states had to move to integrate their school systems.[5] Then, too, the court has consistently held that nonspecified powers presumably retained by the states are legitimate subjects of international negotiation. No stop has yet been put to this use of the treaty provision to extend Federal activity. In resisting for many years the ratification of the Genocide Convention, the Senate's objections were directed not to the substance of the treaty but to the fear of executive legislation through this avenue.

It is not that the Supreme Court's interpretations make it the villain in the play. After all, those laws enlarging the sphere of the national government and lessening that of the states were passed by Congress in the first instance. Emphasis is placed only upon the fact that of the original two safeguards of operative federalism, that is, of the court and the Congress, the latter has assumed an enhanced importance.[6]

One cannot look to the Executive Branch for any assurance of protection of state and local autonomy, although since 1964 both parties have extolled its virtues, and in the Nixon administration an attempt was made at least to identify the White House as a leader in this respect. The permanent Federal bureaucracy is another matter. Here and there a bureau or department chief may have a genuine conviction in the direction of local autonomy, and for a while his agency may show remarkable restraint in seeking additional power at the expense of states and local units. Such a line of thinking has at times been not without its influence in the Department of Agriculture, the United States Office of Education, and the Federal Bureau of Investigation, to mention but three examples. But in the long run, the scales are inherently weighted

otherwise. Bureaus and their clientele believe in the importance of their objectives. They see, or think they see, that these
objectives would be more easily attained if power and discretion were transferred to them from the states and localities. If
some lingering doubt exists regarding the constitutionality or
even the wisdom of coercion in a given bureau's particular
field, then the alternative of the conditional grant-in-aid offers
itself. The state or locality may be persuaded—some would call
it bribed—when it cannot be forced. Into the scales in many
instances is thrown the importance attached in bureaucratic
circles to size of staff and budget, to power for its own sake—
very human, no doubt, but irrelevant to the real issue of local
vitality and autonomy.

As for the President, he is nationally elected. It is he in our
system who is expected to represent the national point of view
rather than that of a state or locality. His campaigns are on this
note. So, too, as a practical matter, is his constituency. He may
pose as an opponent of big Federal government or Federal
spending, but in the end his emphasis invariably will be on the
unities, upon the goals that have the widest national appeal. It
is so easy to make a case for the point of view that we are one
people, that the health and education and welfare of the people
of Mississippi are of importance to New York and the nation.
Yet it was written in another connection:

> Any legislative act but concerns a number of individuals,
> and must rest for its ultimate sanction upon their will. Ini-
> tially, or at any given instant, progress may be given the
> appearance of acceleration by central mandate—yet if the
> various human beings concerned or the various communi-
> ties involved are not convinced, further and still further
> mandates must be the rule—until the government becomes a
> kind of central dictatorship, and the local life is gone.
>
> Each step taken by individual or local initiative means
> individual or local growth in consciousness and knowledge.
> Initially, the way is slower; ultimately, the results justify. It is

easy, but it is also dangerous, to dictate reform or change in advance of individual or local willingness. It is difficult, but the gain becomes the greater, to raise a whole people to a conviction for progress. . . .[7]

If we regard our nation as in one sense the sum of its several parts, then a strong case can be made out that, from this perspective, Congress is more "national" than a Washington-centered agency in the Executive Branch. Surely both viewpoints are needed in arriving at an ultimate consensus on distribution of power and responsibility.

The economic and social forces are for the most part on the side of centralization. Business and labor are organized on a national scale, and from a practical standpoint the furtherance of their interests or the regulation of their conduct to be really effective must more and more frequently be on a scale commensurate with the problems involved. Transportation and communication are nationwide. The great river basins usually know no state boundaries. Population is increasingly mobile, and local and state loyalties are lessened thereby. The schools of Oklahoma educate the future workers of California. We have been through two world wars and two major Far Eastern wars, all in the space of a half-century. These experiences have expedited and intensified our national outlook. Finally, many matters vital to our individual welfare must now be settled at the international level, and only the nation can negotiate them.

All these things have been said before, either with approval of the trends or with regretful resignation.

Yet, there is still very great state and local vitality. While widening the bounds of permitted Federal action, Supreme Court decisions have also widened the bounds of state action. Thus, state and local activities continue to mount along with Federal, even in the unsubsidized and uncontrolled sectors. State expenditures were $2,734,000,000 in 1932. In 1953, they were $14,677,000,000; in 1958, $23,536,000,000; in 1963, almost $40,000,000,000; and in 1972, $72,483,000,000. If the problems of the revenue base are solved, much of the argument for centralization because of inadequate local resources would disappear.

After several years of active debate and discussion, Congress passed a revenue-sharing bill which represented a compromise between proposals of the Nixon administration and members of Congress, as worked out by Wilbur Mills, the long-time chairman of the House Ways and Means Committee. The Mills' bill as it was called became the State and Local Fiscal Assistance Act of 1972 and it was signed into law by President Nixon, symbolically, at Independence Hall in Philadelphia on October 20, 1972.[8]

The bill opened the way for the solution to the perennial problem of the fiscal vitality of state and local units by authorizing out of Federal revenues a sum of $30 billion to be distributed in annual disbursements of $5 to $6 billion over a five-year period ending in 1976. With minimal controls, the states were authorized to use these funds as they saw fit to support a wide selection of essential state functions and for capital expenditures.

It remains to be seen whether this long-sought approach to the Federal role in state affairs will "restore real partnership to the American government" and "place decision making in the right hands."[9]

After an uncertain start, accompanied by complaints from the state governments that grants-in-aid were being curtailed simultaneously with the promulgation of revenue sharing, the new program appears to have been absorbed into the mainstream of state–federal relations with few ripples.

That this program was adopted at all is reflective of the fact that both of the major political parties are predominantly state and local, even though more and more of the major issues are becoming national. Most important of all for our present consideration is the fact that congressmen, as individuals, tend to be more locally minded, on the whole, and apparently still wedded to the Federal system. If there are values in this system it would seem that in the last analysis it is to Congress and not to the restraints of the Supreme Court or the initiative of the President that one must largely look for preservation. It is to Congress also that one must look for recognition of the state and local viewpoint when national legislation is framed and passed. Indeed, most of the consideration of this question over the past decade leading to the passage of the Revenue Sharing Act in 1972 centered in the Subcommittee on Intergovernmental Relations of the Senate Committee on Government Operations and in the Joint Economic Committee.

Why has Congress shown on the one hand a greater watchfulness over local interests and on the other more resistance to the national approach in the handling of problems and also a greater devotion to state and local vitality? The reasons are many. In the first place, members owe little if anything to their national party organizations for their election. National headquarters will sometimes provide modest funds in aid of a local campaign. But on the Federal level the permanent Congressional Campaign Committees of the two parties are of greater significance in this respect. They undertake to raise and distribute campaign funds to their respective candidates. Speakers of national reputation are also detailed to help, but often as much or more for a presidential or gubernatorial candidate as for the congressional. Intervention by the President or by national headquarters may even be regarded, at times, as a liability. Much of the financial support for those campaigns is raised locally, although money has flowed in recent years in large amounts from interested business and labor union sources, notably into hotly contested elections, especially in the smaller states. In general, members wage their own campaigns, primarily aided by the local or state organizations.

In the second place, subject to the direct primary, the member is the nominee and frequently the product of the state or local party organization. In the case of members of the Senate, perhaps ninety percent held a prior public office, most usually that of governor, representative, or member of a state legislature. In the primary and the general election alike, locally important issues figure largely. Those issues on which the district or state are substantially united are taken for granted by candidates of all parties. If the locally favored position on one of these issues happens to be contrary to that of the national platform, or the President if of the same party, the candidate ordinarily explicitly dissociates himself from the national viewpoint on the particular issue. The presence of the direct primary tends to render ineffective attempts at national conformity, if contrary to local views. The net result in any event is a sensitivity to or sharing of the dominant local viewpoint on issues deemed locally important.

Moreover, all the time the member is in Congress his constituents and his local party organization maintain a steady stream of letters, telegrams, telephone calls, conferences, and visits to the end that he shall not forget what is important to his state or district. Visits home from time to time strengthen the same mood.

Curious anomalies follow from this close relationship between constituent and congressman, notably ticket-splitting. In 1948, Iowa elected a solid Republican House delegation but the state went for Democratic President Truman. In 1972, notwithstanding a landslide victory for Republican President Nixon, the Democrats actually increased their majority in the Senate. It is as if the people said, "We like the President's national program as a whole, but we want our own people there to see that our local interests are safeguarded by those who have proved that they understand us and are one of us." Invariably, within the President's own party are large numbers of senators and representatives who differ with him on many of the issues on which he makes his chief campaign. Here again local considerations are dominant.

How concretely does Congress give expression to this localism? It evidences itself in an emphasis on local interests in national legislation and the administration thereof. A most obvious example is that of securing public improvements for their particular state or district. This is a paradox, for it is national action and national money that are involved in local construction—but the motivation is primarily local. New post offices, veterans' or armed services' hospitals, public roads, grants for new schools or slum clearance, defense and aerospace establishments of one sort or another, and great water-resource projects—these are cases in point. Many of these are justified, and our nation as well as the locality is the better for them. Pure logic, however, might frequently have dictated their location elsewhere. Nevertheless, the values of diffusion are not inconsiderable and the localism of Congress must take credit for its realization. In some instances, national planning might well have overlooked certain worthy local projects. The other side of the picture, the waste and the politics involved, is well known and has been documented. At this point our interest lies in observing the phenomenon rather than in passing judgment on it.

In those instances in which there is actual Federal pressure or control, local and state governments can and frequently do obtain adaptations or modifications through intervention by their congressmen. Few are the laws in which administrative discretion is nonexistent.

Of a similar nature, though confined to the President's party, is the patronage element in Federal personnel. Apart from its use to strengthen the members' own political standing, there are two more general usages worth noting. By the so-called courtesy of the Senate, the senior (and sometimes the junior) senator of the President's party is consulted in regard to nominations of persons (civilians) from his state who require senatorial confirmation. If the duties of the position lie wholly within his state, the senator's concurrence in the nomination is customarily required. This applies chiefly to judicial appointments, but with the growth of government other nominees in this category outside the classified service and the military are numerous. The practice is defended on the theory that the senator knows his own state better than the President. One result is to strengthen the state party organization, irrespective of the effect on the party nationally.

Within the classified service which comprises the great mass of government workers, localism took a different form. This was the imposition by statute of an apportionment provision for employees in Washington whereby such employees were to be divided among legal residents of the states in accordance with the state populations.[10] For a number of years an attempt, not wholly successful, has been made to give effect to this provision. This of course was founded upon Congress's regard for state equality. It was defended on the ground that there were values in such a distribution—values of fair play, of widespread interest in and responsibility for government.

More pervading and fundamental, more far-reaching for good or evil, is the localism associated legislatively with regional economic interests. When Congress wrote the details of tariff acts, as was the case until the early New Deal days, it was each man for his own state or district. The St. Lawrence Seaway pitted the Great Lakes states against the Atlantic seaboard. The West as a whole has a vital interest in irrigation and the equalization of power resources and freight rates. With the increasing industrialization of the South, there has been a growing protectionist sentiment, notably with regard to textiles, in this traditionally free-trade area. The Tennessee Valley Authority enjoys almost unanimous support of the members from its area regardless of party or general economic orientation. The same is true of support of the performing arts insofar as New York is concerned. Thus, in part, this economic regionalism reflects itself in the form of seeking greater and greater Federal expenditures in the area, in part in promoting legislation deemed favorable to its economy. In either case the end result may be good or it may be bad, but at least it makes sure that attention will be given to each area. None will be overlooked, though the effort may be more successful in the case of those areas whose representatives belong to the majority party.[11]

Another widespread manifestation of this localism is the all-pervading rural–urban cleavage. Up until the reapportionments following the 1960 census, the Congress, and especially the Senate, was more inclined toward the rural than toward the urban viewpoint when the two were in conflict. Rural areas were in fact over represented. This was compounded by the relatively safe nature of many rural seats, with the resultant impact on the committee chairmanships and their attendant power. However, by 1966 the discrepancies in population of the various districts had begun to disappear in the House in view of a Supreme Court reapportionment decision.

The great cities may be a major factor in electing the President, but they count for less in Congress, where their voting power is felt by only a minority of the membership. Representatives from the so-called working-class districts in the House vote overwhelmingly for a particular point of view, and in an urban state like Rhode Island the same viewpoint is reflected in its senatorial elections. However, in the great majority of states and in a substantial majority of the districts, the combination of rural, suburban, and middle-class urban voters still outweighs the often very considerable labor element. The suburban and middle class cannot hope to win without the rural, and so at least until recently rural members tended to call the tune on matters which they deemed important.

The localism of Congress expresses itself not only in a watchfulness over local and regional interests but also—and this is more to the point in any consideration of the future of federalism—in many instances of reluctance to increase the extent of centralization if there is any other feasible way to meet a given problem. In Federal aid to education, for example, recent bills have provided explicitly that the grants to the states were to have no strings tied to them involving central controls. Until recently these measures failed of passage because some members felt the grant to be an entering wedge which later on would grow into a national system of schools —and Congress was not ready to amend the Constitution by indirection in this fashion. The emphasis until recently upon Federal aid to school building programs instead of to educational systems as a whole was in part an expression of distrust of the results of long-continued Federal subsidies. State unemployment-insurance systems still rule. Proposals for river-valley authorities either explicitly provide for retention of existing state and local powers or include regionally constituted advisory or policy boards or both. Interstate compacts remain highly favored as a device if at all practicable. The retention of local initiative, autonomy, and discretion could go even further now that Congress has realized more clearly that a large part of the problem which seems to call for action on a national scale is accounted for by the inequalities in taxable capacity and the absence of sources of local revenue and has moved to remedy it through revenue sharing.

A principal factor in bringing about this action was the creation in 1959 by Congress largely on its own initiative of the permanent Advisory Commission on Intergovernmental Relations. The work of this mixed legislative-executive-federal-state-local bipartisan committee laid the basis for committee study and eventual legislation on revenue sharing.[12]

Much of the problem centers around the multiplication of categorical grants in great detail. Efforts are being made in Congress and by the President to combine a number of these so as to allow much greater State and local discretion. The success or failure of this effort is of critical importance to our Federal system.

Congress tends to oppose a large bureaucracy, in part out of a desire for economy, in part because it senses that bureaucracy with its command of facts and acquaintance with problems is a formidable rival in the maturing of legislation—an area which Congress regards as largely its own under the Constitution. In part, however, it is because Congress knows from experience in the United States, as well as in other countries, that bureaucracy becomes an increasingly powerful force in the direction of the centralized state. Consequently, Congress may be expected to drag at the wheels of the onward march of big government and centralization—even though it may in practice prove impotent to reverse the trend.

The implications of this situation for party solidarity and discipline may also be noted at this point. So long as members are locally nominated and locally elected, just so long must they pay attention to local and regional interests. Here is a major obstacle to party solidarity, for the member or senator who puts party ahead of district or home state on a matter which the district or state regards as vital will probably not survive the next primary—not to mention the next election.

In conclusion, let it not be thought that there are not values, great values, attendant upon the national viewpoint in contradistinction to the local. All that is claimed here is that *both* are of value, and decisions ought to be made with a full awareness of both aspects and without the scales unduly weighted in either direction. It is the authors' contention that this purpose is best served if, as the founders of the Republic originally intended, a national and a state and local viewpoint are woven into the fabric of our government—and any action taken would represent an adjustment between the viewpoints. The President represents the national viewpoint. Is it not therefore all the more important that those elements in our government which by conviction sustain the values of local autonomy shall not be whittled down or eroded by so altering the structure, whether of party organization or of government itself, that this function is no longer effectively performed? Much of the genius of our Constitution lies in the way it allows no one center of power, no one group or point of view to ride roughshod over others, but rather fosters government by consensus, which encourages united action on the things on which there is unity but allows for diversity in other matters. In the total picture the values of decentralization would seem to be an essential factor in the strength of the nation—a part of our belief that operative pluralism is a major pillar and expression of the democratic way.

NOTES

1. Cf. Ernest S. Griffith, *The Modern Development of City Government in the United Kingdom and the United States* (London: Oxford University Press, H. Milford, 1927), chap. 11, for documentation of this paragraph.
2. 297 U.S. 1 (1939).
3. *Oklahoma v. U.S. Civil Service Commission,* 330 U.S. 127 (1947).
4. Especially under *Missouri ex rel. Gaines v. Canada,* 305 U.S. 337 (1938); *Sipuel v. Board of Regents,* 332 U.S. 631 (1948); *Fisher v. Hurst,* Chief Justice, et al., 333 U.S. 147 (1948); *Sweatt v. Painter,* 339 U.S. 629 (1950); *McLaurin v. Oklahoma State Regents,* 339 U.S. 637 (1950).
5. *Brown v. Board of Education of Topeka,* 377 U.S. 483 (1954).
6. But cf. Fellman, "Federation," *American Political Science Review* (December 1947), for the field of state interpretation of common law, in which the Supreme Court has shown more concern for the autonomy of the state courts.
7. Ernest S. Griffith, *The Modern Development of City Government in the United Kingdom and the United States* (London: Oxford University Press, H. Milford, 1927), II, 598.
8. P.L. 92-512. See U.S. Congress. Senate. Committee on Finance. Revenue Sharing. Hearings. 92nd Congress, 2d Session (Washington, D.C.: U.S. Government Printing Office, 1972), 636 p; See also, Senate Report No. 92-1050, 2 pts. House Report No. 92-1450 and Senate Report No. 92-1229.
9. Radio address by Richard M. Nixon broadcast by CBS radio network, October 25, 1968. Washington, D.C., Republican National Committee.
10. 5 USC 3306.
11. For a sophisticated discussion of Congressional–constituent relations in this regard see Lewis A. Dexter, "The

Representative and His District," in Robert L. Peabody and Nelson W. Polsby, *New Perspectives on the House of Representatives* (Chicago: Rand-McNally, 1963), chap. 1. Patterns of response of members differ widely, on the basis of a number of variables.

12. The Commission was established by P.L. 86-380. Cf. Neil S. Wright, "The Advisory Commission on Intergovernmental Relations," *Public Administration Review* (September 1965), pp. 193-202.

CHAPTER 16

Political Parties and Congress

Of all the subjects of contemporary controversy concerning Congress, probably none is more complex than the role of party. It enters into, if it does not pervade, most of the other questions. It is the principal factor in the organization of Congress. It is both a solvent and an irritant in legislative–executive relations. Its local roots reinforce the localism of Congress. Its looseness and vagueness are the despair of those whose minds run to comprehensive and integrated programs. The dispersiveness of our society with its insistent pressure groups finds party one of the mediums for attaining these group ends.

While the broader implications of party must necessarily be brought into review in order to understand its congressional impact, our chief concern lies with the place of party in the congressional scene. What role do these two loose confederations—Democrats and Republicans—whose elements at times seem to have little else in common but their name and their presidential candidate, play in Congress?

Historically viewed, the story of the past fifty years is undoubtedly one of weakness or even of disintegration as regards the hold of party on Congress. Emphatically we do not have integrated party government in this country now, whatever we may have had in the past. During most of the nine-

225

teenth century party discipline and solidarity had been part of the congressional picture. The binding party caucus was a vital factor. By 1900, in the House the Speaker had come to be in a position to punish, and did punish, any member of his party who had the temerity to break seriously with the party line. Except that the President tended to be more nationally minded than those of his party in Congress, there was for the most part agreement between him and them on most major issues. At any one time the great issues were very few in number, thus allowing a member to follow his party without too frequent a strain on his intellect or conscience. Today the issues are many and do not divide themselves neatly into alternative programs.[1]

Political behavior in the nineteenth century was more emotional than it is today. Party names were symbols to conjure with or be fought over. Torchlight parades, songs, and slogans worked up the kind of enthusiasms and loyalties that discounted reflective thought. The party with the greater enthusiasm might well be more likely to win than the one with the better argument. Today, we are a better educated and more sophisticated people and at least like to think that reason and argument, and not loyalty to symbols, are what sway us.

As disciplinarian, the party in Congress has fallen upon evil days; as an influence and organizer it is still one of the principal factors in arriving at decisions.[2]

In the first place, on it lies the responsibility for organization. In effect it elects the Speaker of the House and the rest of the House leadership and the Majority and Minority leadership of the Senate. It determines the membership of committees. Seniority within a committee modifies party control, but even seniority is itself subject to party acquiescence and control. In 1971, Senate Majority Leader Mansfield initiated the practice of submitting the entire Democratic membership slate for each committee, including the designated chairmen, to the party caucus for a vote of approval before presenting the lists to the Senate for election. Republicans in the Senate followed suit and a similar practice also began on the House side. This practice was repeated in 1973 at the outset of the Ninety-third Congress. The new procedure did not bring a serious challenge from any quarter to the preeminence of the traditional criterion of seniority in the selection of committee chairmen and members. Nevertheless, it did serve as a reminder of the ultimate sources of the position of the individual member in the congressional structure. He does not stand alone but in a party grouping. This point was driven home at the outset of the Ninety-fourth Congress by the House Democratic Caucus. Three long-time Chairmen, each the senior member of his respective Committee, were replaced in a sweeping "revolution," as it was termed at the time. That a similar upheaval did not occur in the Senate was generally attributed to an evolution in intra-party procedures in the direction of democratization which had begun several years earlier.

Party can be significant in the flow of legislative business because it is in the inner circles of the majority in consultation with the minority that the schedule is arranged. This is somewhat less important than might appear, because of the increasing tendency of Congress to stay in session around the year. When it comes to voting, party leadership is influential rather than coercive. It argues and pleads rather than threatens. Yet, in both parties there are many members who vote "with the party," especially if the issue involved is not one to which they have given any very serious scrutiny or is of little direct concern to their constituency. Party loyalty is less certain on major issues with a high degree of visibility. It is difficult to single this out as a factor, especially as so many of these members would doubtless have voted the same way had there been no party lead at all. Perhaps, the best summary would be to say that the leadership faces the problem of building majorities, even across party lines. This involves conferences and concessions, more than the exercise of power.

The effect of party on legislation is thus extremely difficult to appraise.[3] As regards members of the President's party, there is (even apart from coincidence of views) a natural desire to support a popular President and, at the least, to close ranks against the opposition.[4] At the very least he can count on his party in Congress to present his program, though not necessarily to support it in its entirety. Certainly under Lincoln, Franklin D. Roosevelt, and many other Presidents, the weapon of loss of patronage or the prospect of a reward in the shape of a future job or concessions were used to induce party support of the President's wishes. The practice is as yet by no means obsolete, although if poorly used it can build up resentment and probably lose votes as well as gain them.

The opposition party tends to function as much as a critic as a dissenter. When in a minority its members frequently endorse the objectives of a bill, vote for it in final form, but press for amendments on the way. It is unusual for the minority to propose a sweeping alternative for meeting the problem in question, but rarely does it deny the existence of the problem or deny that its solution lies in governmental action. Often it will go along with the major portion of the bill—albeit registering criticism of certain portions of it. This criticism is an important function, though it lacks the dramatic function of an alternative party program.

During President Eisenhower's tenure, the Democratic majority in Congress made a strong attempt to avoid being tagged as obstructive, but at the same time it sought to suggest identifiable differences between itself and his administration. It did not court the veto for the sake of an issue. After the election of Gerald R. Ford as Republican Leader of the House of Representatives, a similar policy of presenting alternatives to the Johnson Administration emanated from that quarter. The Democratic majority has done the same in the Nixon administrations.

Far more than is commonly realized, Congress is at heart bipartisan or nonpartisan and, if anything, becoming more so. So much has been made of the bipartisan foreign policy that it is not appreciated in how many other fields a similar approach is followed. Among the members of the Appropriations Committees, such differences as there are are frequently not along party lines at all. The House Interstate and Foreign Commerce Committee has prided itself for many years on its tradition of nonpartisanship. So also have both of the Judiciary Committees in much of their agenda. The revisions of the Social Security Act are generally nonpartisan in both the Ways and Means Committee and the Finance Committee. In most of the other committees large portions of legislation are approached without reference to party. In two-thirds to three-quarters of the committees, nonpartisanship in executive sessions, in particular, has been the rule. Differences of opinion there usually are, but not on partisan lines. The occasional measures singled out for partisan controversy make the headlines, but this should not obscure the fact that the bulk of the consideration of foreign affairs, housing, national defense, civil service, governmental reorganization, education, health, reciprocal trade, social security, water-resource projects, water and air pollution, atomic energy, transportation, taxation, agriculture, conservation, and civil rights is not partisan at all.

While the absence of sharp partisanship has been the prevailing atmosphere for many years, the party cannot be dismissed as a factor of great significance in the operations of the Congress. Indeed, its significance may recently even be growing. Partly in response to the presence of a Republican in the White House and partly out of concern for the declining influence of the Congress in the Federal system, Senate Majority Leader Mansfield began a systematized effort in 1969 to enhance the unity of the Democrats in the Congress. The effort involved initially a revitalizing of the role of the Senate Democratic Policy Committee. The Democratic Caucus and the Democratic Committee Chairmen approved, unanimously, a design for increasing party cohesion by establishing party positions for the guidance of Senate Democrats in accordance with the following procedures:

DEMOCRATIC POLICY COMMITTEE PROCEDURES

(1) The Majority Leadership, that is, the Leader, the Assistant Leader, and the Secretary of the Conference, will try to meet with the legislative Committee Chairmen every six weeks for a review of the legislative situation in the Senate and for a discussion of any other matters of interest to the Chairmen.

(2) The Policy Committee itself will meet regularly for lunch every two weeks on Tuesday at 12:30 p.m.

(3) The Committee staff will prepare a special agenda for these meetings which will be separate from that involving the scheduling of routine legislation.

(4) The agenda will include a staff analysis of any significant emerging issues which will be identified primarily from these sources:

a. By reference to the staff from any Member of the Policy Committee;

b. By staff study of legislative proposals, statements or other actions of the Administration; and

c. By reference to this Committee from any of the legislative committees.

(5) The Committee will consider the issues which are thus brought to its attention for the purpose of determining whether they are of a significance and are likely to evoke sufficient party agreement as to warrant the taking of a Policy position.

In this consideration, the Committee will use for its information, staff briefings and memoranda and any other sources deemed useful. A legislative committee chairman will be invited, as necessary, to explain or elaborate on legislation which he believes warrants concerted support from the party.

(6) Votes will continue to be avoided, and the effort will be made to secure the widest degree of party acceptance of a position on any significant issue. When necessary, however,

the Committee will be guided by a minimum of a two-thirds vote in determining the issues on which a party position should be taken. Vote tallies will not be made public under any circumstances. Members of the Committee, of course, remain free to take any position on the floor on any issue.

(7) When the Committee sets a policy position, the Chairman will undertake to inform the full membership of the Majority by any or all of the following means: direct contact of members by the Assistant Leader and the Assistant Whips, calling of a party caucus, issuing of press statements, making of speeches on the floor, sending letters to members, and so forth.[5]

The process, of course, was entirely voluntary. Nevertheless, in the first session of the Ninety-third Congress, the Democratic Policy Committee and the Caucus adopted eighteen resolutions which covered a range of subjects that included legislative priorities, executive privilege, executive testimony before Senate committees, open committee hearings, the energy crisis, and inflation. Of these eighteen resolutions, Senate legislation or administrative action pursuant thereto was obtained in almost every case, with the great bulk of the Democratic members supporting the leadership positions.[6] The Democratic Caucus in the House is likewise meeting more frequently, and defeat of a proposal there may well kill it. Support in caucus is helpful but not decisive.

As for party cohesion between the Houses, during the Kennedy administration, Republican Senate Leader Dirksen and House Leader Halleck met on a more or less regular basis in press conferences at which they gibed at the Democratic administration in what came to be known as the "Ev and Charley shows." During the era of Speaker Sam Rayburn and Senate Majority Leader Lyndon B. Johnson, there was a great deal of consultation between the two men. It was, however, a personal rather than an institutionalized relationship, based on a common Texas political ancestry and a close personal friendship. Beginning in the Ninety-third Congress, Speaker Albert and Majority Leader Mansfield sought to regularize the contact by including the entire Democratic leadership of both Houses in monthly meetings, at which common legislative problems and other matters have been considered. From time to time, Democratic governors and mayors and the Democratic National Committee Chairmen have participated in these meetings. On occasion, joint majority statements of party positions have been released to the press.

For the present, the most that can be said with certainty is that contrasts between various Congresses as regards degree of party influence and solidarity suggest the presence of a number of important variables. Certainly the personality of the congressional leaders and of the President, the majority or minority status of a party, whether or not the two branches are in the control of the same party, the type of issue, the attitudes of particular committee chairmen, all play important roles. Parties still remain, essentially, mediators in seeking a consensus, rather than ideological rivals.

There is a certain premium on a measure of independence from party, especially if a member's own state or district agrees with his dissent. "Party loyalty" is far down the scale as a plus symbol of value, and independence, "unbossed," "thinking for myself," have correspondingly gained in prestige. Indeed, party loyalty contains within itself certain connotations of puppeting, a nonrational implication which can be a liability. This has gone along with the steady increase in split voting and independence among the electorate at large, the despair of the party organizers, but one of the chief factors making it necessary to nominate better candidates in large sections of our country than used to rule when the voters would swallow almost anything, if it bore the correct label.

The desirability of strengthening party ties and party discipline has received support from among political scientists. Entering into this line of thought is certainly an admiration for the workings of party government in Great Britain. It all seems so smooth and orderly. Programs are advanced and fought over. Her Majesty's Loyal Opposition criticizes and carries the debate and its alternatives to the hustings. Platforms mean what they say. An election really decides something. It is all very logical—unless one goes behind the scenes in England and finds such things as a bureaucracy maturing almost all legislation and increasing by leaps and bounds; the two parties outbidding each other with promises of governmental largesse, so as to attract marginal groups; a division of the nation along class lines; the sacrifice of independence of thought and action on the part of the individual member. Nor is there any real assurance that parliamentary or a near approach to parliamentary government in the American setting would develop British usages. Geographic, sociological, economic conditions all differ drastically.

In the United States, insofar as party divisions came to be logical in an ideological sense, they would also become nationally divisive instead of basically unifying as they tend to be today. Our present habit is of advancing by substantial consensus, stressing pragmatic rather than ideological considerations, of waging our political campaigns largely emphasizing the unities and not the divisions.[7]

To support nationally imposed viewpoints would be an invitation to many state and local party organizations to commit political suicide by renouncing indefinitely any chance of electing local candidates. To read members out of positions of influence in Congress for the party "irregularity" would almost certainly bring about a coalition in Congress for organizational purposes which would effectively hamstring what party responsibility now exists.

At the present time we have in the presidential years two platforms which of late have rarely shown substantial differences. Individual planks typically incorporate two or more impeccable principles which in their concrete application come into conflict and require compromise. This gives the party the best of both worlds. It attracts support from rival groups, each of which reads its own emphasis into the wording, and then leaves its leaders and members in Congress free to work out what they deem to be appropriate solutions, without violating their pledges. In any event, candidates for Congress feel quite free to contract out of one or more planks, if they so desire. Whatever the concrete position a candidate takes on the various issues, he goes to Congress with the confidence a man feels who has the electorate behind him.

One of the results of this convenient vagueness in the party platforms is that an attempt is made to appeal to all groups in our national life. Only straw men are denounced. Class appeals are conspicuously lacking. Racial appeals are for greater recognition of minority groups. Because of the breadth of appeal, the net result is that our national campaigns are essentially unifying. We have, as it were, a "government by consensus." No one group or region can have its way unless it can carry with it substantial fractions from each of the other great groups or regions.

There is at least an equal chance that, instead of nationally imposed party programs lessening the power of the pressure groups, they would in fact increase such power. The parties in search of votes might well embrace the special groups more than ever, with this additional and highly important further difference. They would in the new setting be able to coerce their members in Congress to go "down the line" for the pledges made to the special groups. No longer could coalitions of independents drawn from both parties block, as they now do block, the extremes of special legislation crassly favoring a special interest at public expense. The party would, it is true, have a "program," but it would in all probability still be a dispersive one and one which would lack the restraints now put upon it by independent voting. It might also seriously impair the tradition of government by consensus.

The values associated with independence are not lightly to be discarded. They may sacrifice the smoothness of operation and superficial logic of the monolithic party in the parliamentary system, but they do introduce a much wider variety of considerations into debate and decision. The result may be an illogical conglomerate, but our legislation may also be closer to the popular will, less full of bureaucratic blind spots, more thoroughly aired in hearings and debate. Who shall say? These are generalities whose only significance is to indicate the doubtful nature of the verdict.

One thing seems certain. The type of individual attracted to Congress in a setting in which he is committed in advance to follow his party would be different from many now in Congress. There would be little or no room left for independence of judgment. The independent on a given issue is in a position to criticize and vote against a special interest; the disciplined party man cannot do this if the desires of the special interest have been incorporated into his party's program. The opportunity to urge his views in the councils of the party is a poor substitute for the sacrifice of his freedom at the time of the final, responsible decision. It was our earlier contention that the social and economic structures of our districts and states are such that in connection with most legislation sponsored by a substantial group there are a very considerable number of members who can afford to speak out in behalf of the more general interest as they see it. If the party (or both parties) is committed to a group's program, this can no longer be done without risk of party discipline.

Similarly and more subtly, the values associated with the localism of Congress would seemingly be eroded in the face of binding national-party programs. It would not be necessary to postulate the rise to a dominant influence of the bureaucracy, as in England, to foresee this outcome, for Congress has expert staffs of its own. It is only that the strengthening of party responsibility as visualized by its advocates calls for a lessened role to be played by the state and local organizations and also for the greater influence on party programs of nationwide groups with large memberships. Both of these are centralizing factors. Government by consensus applies not only to the great groups but also to agreement among the regions and to the equilibrium between the states and the nation—that is, to the federal element in our Constitution. National party strength would move in the direction of seriously impairing these latter two.

Policy wise, we have in our Congress a government by shifting majorities, and not by party. In this type of government the individual's views have far greater play; and conscience, intelligence, and local concerns can be much more influential than would be practicable in a parliamentary system, in which party discipline is virtually a prerequisite to stability in government. Only separation of powers makes individualized voting possible, for the executive does not depend upon the legislature to retain its office.

The search for means of combating the power of the special interests and narrow sectionalism, and of securing the better integration of the several issues, is essentially sound. The solution offered, of greater party responsibility, even if it were to be effective in these matters (of which there is doubt), by no means exhausts the list of things that might be done. We have spoken of congressional staff aides largely in terms of their usefulness as a corrective vis-à-vis the executive. They are equally important in equipping Congress to deal correctly and intelligently with the recommendations of the special interests. It is trite to say that the ultimate answer to problems of this sort lies in the area of education and civic responsibility and integrity, but it happens to be true. As the knowledge of the nature of public affairs spreads, as the level of education moves higher, members and voters alike come to appreciate the secondary and often harmful effects of some of the seemingly plausible demands of the special interests. They come to appreciate the need for an inner harmony or compatibility in a legislative program, over against the dispersiveness which has prevailed in the past. Civic responsibility and integrity are more subtle things, less easy to teach, part rather of the mores of a people, the sphere of their religion and ethics. To the extent that they become influential they will tend to curb the selfishness of groups, to give courage to those who would fight against this selfishness, to lessen coerced or blind party loyalty and increase the responsible behavior of the individual member.

This approach and the values placed on independence cannot be carried too far. The existing party mechanism fulfills functions too important to be scrapped. This, perhaps, was the greatest evil of the Watergate affair. It brought public confidence not only in the presidency but in the Congress and the nation's political institutions and processes to its lowest ebb in modern times. Even then, few dared to ask what might be the alternatives to parties because the alternatives were too disastrous to freedom to contemplate. The fact is that the party mechanism remains an essential part of the American political process and it is still the best mechanism we have for soliciting and electing candidates. It singles out certain issues from time to time for public discussion. It forces the successful party candidate for President to present a program and the opposition party in Congress to assume some responsibility for presenting for discussion and possible enactment alternatives thereto. It assures an opposition that will criticize the President's proposals in their detail, even though it may support the objective and main provisions of many of them. By so much, it creates a reasonably effective mechanism to get things both discussed and accomplished—and without either the class bitterness or sacrifice of individual independence of thought which characterizes many other countries. Proposals to democratize party platform making and to utilize its machinery for more research and discussion at all levels are all to the good. These can increase the value of its contribution without impairing those values of our political and governmental structure that lie elsewhere than in party. Let the parties remain administrative rivals, but one should think long and hard before urging that they espouse rival ideologies. The genius of Congress lies not so much in the expression of the politics of conflict as of the politics of consensus.

NOTES

1. For an excellent summary of historical trends in party discipline, see Clarence Berdahl, "The Workings of Party Discipline," reprinted in Theodore Lowi, ed., *Legislative Politics, USA* (Boston: Little, Brown, 1962), pp. 113-32.
2. For an excellent study of contemporary leadership structure and operation, see Ralph K. Huitt, "Democratic Party Leadership in the Senate," *American Political Science Review,* Vol. 55 (June 1961), pp. 333-44; Margaret Munk, "The Origin of the Senate Floor Leadership," *U.S. Capitol Historical Society,* Vol. 2 (1974), pp. 23-42; Randall B. Ripley, *Power in the Senate* (New York: St. Martin's Press, 1969 [parts 1 and 2]); Randall B. Ripley, *Majority Leadership in Congress* (Boston: Little, Brown, 1969); Randall B. Ripley, *Party Leaders in the House of Representatives* (Washington, D.C.: Brookings Institution, 1967); Hugh A. Bone, *Party Committees and National Politics* (Seattle: University of Washington Press, 1958); Kenneth Bradshaw and David Pring, *Parliament and Congress* (Austin: University of Texas Press, 1972), chap. I.
3. For a thorough study of the period 1961-63 among House Democrats, see Lewis A. Froman, Jr., and Randall B. Ripley, "Conditions for Party Leadership," *American Political Science Review* (March 1965), pp. 52-63.
4. This is brought out empirically in David Truman, *The Congressional Party* (New York: Wiley, 1959), chap. 8. For an analysis of party leadership in the House as a whole see Richard F. Fenno, Jr., "Internal Distribution of Influence: The House," in David S. Truman, ed., *The Congress and America's Future* (Englewood Cliffs: Prentice-Hall, 1965), pp. 61-70.
5. *Congressional Record,* February 2, 1973, p. S-1917.
6. The House Democrats initiated similar practices at the beginning of the 93rd Congress, and a House Majority Policy Committee was established for the first time in 1973. The Legislative Reorganization Act of 1946 had provided for Policy

Committees in both Houses but only in the Senate was one formed initially.

7. Proposals which sustain the viewpoint of party responsibility were brought together in a challenging report of the American Political Science Association's Committee on Political Parties which is worth consulting for a different approach from the one argued here. See *American Political Science Review,* Supp. September 1950. For an exposition of a theory of parties which lies between this *Report* and the viewpoint expressed in this work, see Clinton Rossiter, *Parties and Politics in America* (Ithaca: Cornell University Press, 1960).

CHAPTER 17

Congress and the Education of the Public

The political education of the public is one of the recognized functions of Congress. How it is performed and ways whereby it may be better performed have been the subject of some research and more writing. While there is relatively little to add to what has been said elsewhere, an incomplete picture of Congress would result if no mention were made of it.

The channels for such education are many. More frequently than not, such political education is, as indeed it should be, a by-product rather than the chief end of congressional behavior. The chief ends remain: to put through or reject a policy or program, to solve a problem, and to retain the confidence of one's constituency. In the last analysis these ends are the consequence of legislative acts. The education of the electorate is chiefly relevant as it contributes to one of these ends, but regardless of whether or not it is consciously sought, it nevertheless takes place continuously.

Political campaigns to be elected begin the process of voter education, even though on occasion it may seem that their purpose is to confuse an issue rather than to clarify it. Members frequently make personal requests to each other to speak in one's district or state. This is usually, but not always, partisan. The Senate and House Campaign Committees of both parties maintain speaker schedules during election years for the same purpose, which is invariably partisan. In any event, the talk and commentary generated do add to the political ferment and, perhaps, to public enlightenment.

Floor debate and discussion attract the press. Self-governing press galleries exist in both houses for duly accredited correspondents. The debates—on foreign policy, on taxation, on national defense, on constitutional questions—attract attention in all the principal media of communication. Even though sessions of Congress are at present neither filmed, broadcast, nor televised, there are follow-ups by commentators or members themselves through all these media.[1] Floor debate thus projected into other settings obtains wide attention.

Second only to the publicity attending floor debate and frequently surpassing it is that accorded the committee hearings. The aggregate publicity of the latter almost certainly exceeds the former. The televised McCarthy hearings on subversion in the 1950s and the Watergate investigations of the Ervin Committees in 1973 attracted audiences of tens of millions and held their attention for weeks on end. Additionally, press coverage featured these events day after day.

The use of television is the most spectacular innovation in committee proceedings. Criticism has frequently been voiced at the amount of time often required of key administrators to appear before not one committee but several, with the inference that much of it is for purposes of publicizing committee members. While that consideration is no doubt present on occasion, the fact is that the public education function is better performed when press and other coverage of the subject matter at issue is assured by such means. Criticism has also been voiced that outside coverage is largely confined to the spectacular and that the solid substance of many hearings is correspondingly overlooked. This premium on the spectacular, it is said, tempts Congress to distort the nature and purpose of the hearings, which are supposedly designed to be informative to Congress. The point may be well taken, but if the public's attention is thereby attracted to an issue of which it was previously unaware and is induced to discuss that issue there is still some gain. These defects, if defects they be, lie as much with the press and the public, who demand such dramatization as the price of attention, as they do with Congress. The media make their own decisions on what to cover and what not to cover on Capitol Hill.

To the serious student, the records of hearings are mines of information. Here are set out in detail, and subjected to cross-examination, many of the basic data relating to the nature of our economy, the underlying factors in foreign relations, the future of our resources, the strategy of national defense, the problems of labor relations, and many another field of importance and interest. If even after such study the details still do not reach the general public, they are sufficiently used to be influential as background for much of our current writing—editorial, economic, and other. On the other hand, a number of the committees deliberately plan some of their hearings with the education of the public in mind and choose subjects and witnesses accordingly.

Due credit must be given to the publications of Congress. In addition to the record of floor debate, there are the transcripts of the hearings, staff reports, and published committee reports. A wealth of miscellaneous and fugitive, but often thoroughly important, material exists among the mass of inserts printed in the *Congressional Record* in addition to the floor debates. Congress, its committees and its staff agencies, publish frequent studies often of great educational value. With the growth of professional staffs, this type of educational document is increasing both in quality and in number. Many members make it a point to see that certain of these reports reach appropriate constituents.

As an educational instrument there should certainly be

included the various ways in which a member reports to his constituents. By radio and television, by press release and letter, by speeches and multiplication of personal contacts, members seem more and more to be associating their constituents with the problems that face Congress. A large majority report regularly by radio or television or newsletter or all three. Sometimes these explain the member's stand on a particular issue; at other times they invite constituent reaction. As the level of education of the electorate rises, and as media such as television make such communication more and more easy, we may expect this personalizing of political education steadily to increase. It helps the member on all counts; it builds up support for measures he believes in, it enables him better to understand the viewpoint of his district, it makes it possible for him to perform the public service of spreading the knowledge of public affairs, and it may help him to get reelected by becoming better and more favorably known. Precisely this last consideration has led to complaints and even court actions involving the use of the franking privilege and other instrumentalities of office for what, it is charged, are political purposes. The thin line is hard to draw. It is a fact that the functions of office do bestow certain advantages on an incumbent. On the other hand, there are disadvantages in incumbency which a challenger does not face. The spotlight is always on the member of Congress. His votes which at one time or another are bound to antagonize some in his constituency are spread out for all to see. His public and his private life must be lived in a goldfish bowl.

Political education is almost necessarily selective as regards the type of issue lending itself to the process. Highly technical subjects, however important, receive little publicity. Non-controversial subjects seldom spark much public interest. Subjects of interest to one group receive coverage by and for that group but are given little general attention. It is in the areas of great controversy or of general familiarity that most publicity is concentrated. Differences between the President and Congress always are newsworthy. In recent years, with one party in control of the presidency and the other of Congress, the media have telecast not only the President's State of the Union Messages but congressional leadership statements in response. The quiz of a man in whom there is widespread popular interest receives attention—whether the man is a cabinet official, a former White House aide, or a private citizen.

As a by-product, even normal congressional activity often makes a particular member himself newsworthy, especially in the Senate. This personal visibility in turn can be and is used for the further education of the electorate. Congress as a body may suffer, as Holcombe has put it, from "exhibiting its indecisions in public." Individual members may so conduct themselves as to draw ridicule as well as favorable publicity. All this is part of the game.

Political education resulting from congressional activity is not only selective, it tends to be disproportionate and even distorted. Nevertheless, in the aggregate, it is quantitatively very considerable and on balance one of the greatest assets we have in our functioning democracy. It has been performed of late with increasing responsibility, intelligence, and effectiveness. That is fortunate because political education lies near the heart of the democratic way.[2]

NOTES

1. Exceptions are made in the House of Representatives for Joint Sessions, usually on ceremonial occasions.
2. There is another dimension to public education with regard to the Congress which has to do, not with politics and issues, but with the nature of the institution itself, what it has been and is in the structure of the Federal government. In the Senate, a non-partisan Commission on Art and Antiquities exists for the purpose of preserving the Senate's collection of records, memorabilia, and artifacts and using them more effectively for the

edification and education of the public. The Architect of the Capitol has recently been charged by law to study the feasibility of "Sound and Light" exhibits at the Capitol, a process for dramatizing its history for the millions of annual visitors. The National Capitol Historical Society supports various projects for similar ends.

CHAPTER 18

Congress in a Crisis

Thus far the picture of Congress has been highly favorable as regards both function and behavior. However, many of the underlying assumptions have been those of a more or less leisurely age during which issues may mature and solutions for problems may obtain a broad base of consensus prior to adoption. But this is not the kind of age in which we now live. Its tempo is rapid. It moves from one crisis to another. It seems to require correspondingly prompt action on the part of government—in the international field because of the rapid emergence of crises in the multiplicity of unstable situations, in the domestic field largely because of a sensitive and interlocking economy. There is interference in one basic element in this economy, as in the energy shortage of 1974, and the impact is felt across the board. The public demand for action by Washington is immediate and powerful. Issues in their relationship to both the domestic and the international situation are of very great importance, not only to contemporary society but to future generations, not merely to this nation but to the entire world. Can government in general and Congress in particular muster the sustained high-level thinking and conduct that the great responsibilities involved seem to require?

In part, it is our Constitution with its checks and balances, its separation of powers, that is on trial over against the parliamentary or some other representative type. In part, the issue is more far-reaching, involving the success or failure of all representative institutions as against totalitarian systems and the success or failure of a free economy over against the communist or some other autocratic structure.

This second issue is partly a matter of having a better awareness of this nation as against impressions of other nations which may be misleading. At one time, for example, it was thought that the dictatorships of Italy, Germany, and Japan operated under very efficient political systems. The revelations of the inefficiencies, lost motion, internal friction, and other errors of these pre-World War II political structures are now a matter of record, exposed so that he who wishes may read and ponder. The gains, if any, from being able to move without having to reckon with opposition or criticism may well be outweighed by the losses resulting from not having the benefit of criticism and built-in correctives. This is obviously an oversimplification but contains an important truth. Reports of the performance of the Soviet system are mixed in character, although obviously the growth of its technological and industrial base indicates an immense capability in this aspect of its economy. Reports from China carry a heavy accent on dedication, innovation, and national self-reliance.

It should be borne in mind that in all these societies, mistakes are easier to cover up and critics of the status quo can be more readily shunted aside. Nevertheless, the extent of Soviet, Eastern European, and Chinese economic success has in a number of respects been noteworthy. We would be fooling ourselves if we disregarded their substantial achievements. In this connection, it is therefore all the more important that democracies, and especially our own democratic republic, shall in fact rise to the great demands of the age.

Criticism of our Constitutional system from those who uphold democratic values concerns largely the relationships between Congress and the President. Especially has this criticism centered upon the risks involved or revealed in a crisis situation. Without more power in the hands of the President or, as regards Congress, without more strict party discipline and stronger party leadership relating itself to the program of the President or party, it is alleged that Congress could not or would not act with the necessary speed. Indeed, Congress itself over the years appears to have accepted that premise. In 1974, a special Senate committee noted that as a result of 470 separate laws passed by Congress, a situation exists whereby the President may

> seize property; organize and control the means of production; seize commodities; assign military forces abroad; institute martial law; seize and control all transportation and communication; regulate the operation of private enterprise; restrict travel; and in a plethora of particular ways, control the lives of all American citizens. For forty years, freedoms and governmental procedures guaranteed by the Constitution have, in various degrees, been abridged by laws brought into force by states of national emergency.[1]

Much of the rationale for this vast delegation of power has to do with the "slowness" of Congress or its inability to act decisively in emergencies. The fact is that Congress is slow and deliberate and discursive rather than decisive not only by practice but by design. To be sure, legislation has been known to pass through its cumbersome procedures in less than a day in response to some overriding national concern, sometimes, one might add, with results which in retrospect are best forgotten. That is not, however, the normal or desired pace for the Congress.

There are times when the nation may count itself lucky that Congress does not move too rapidly. At one point in the early days of the airlines-hijacking era, for example, the Senate appeared to be on the verge of responding immediately to urgent demands of some members to issue an ultimatum to Cuba. Fortunately, the Senate's cumbersome procedures permitted calmer heads to prevail. The proposed ultimatum was not acted on at a moment of fiery emotion but instead shunted into routine committee channels where it disappeared and was never heard of again. It was subsequently learned that the plane's landing in Havana had nothing to do with the Cuban government but was, rather, the work of a United States citizen and that the Cuban government was prepared to make prompt arrangements for the return of the plane and its passengers.

In its present form, Congress is not intended to take urgent action and much less to administer the day-to-day affairs of the government. What can be done by the President with a stroke of the pen requires weeks of study in committees, followed by the agreement of a majority the Senate and of the House, and two-thirds of both if the President demurs.

Reforms of antiquated methods are possible, but as long as the role of Congress remains unchanged in a government of divided powers, an appreciable change in the congressional pace is not to be expected. To bring about a substantial speed-up would require a fundamental reshuffling of mission and methods, with the government moving in the direction of supremacy of the Legislative Branch in something akin to a parliamentary system.

The alleged extent of ineptitude and delay as Congress presently functions has been overstated through the news coverage which is given to its debates and other activity. Crises are dramatized, which, in turn, leaves the impression that any substantial congressional consideration, whether procedural or deliberative, is prima facie evidence of its inability to act quickly. In the process of dramatization, moreover, impressions of great controversy and intransigent partisanship are often created when the realities may be quite otherwise.

Significant changes have taken place in the relationship

between the branches since 1920. In the first place, as Corwin[2] has shown, the emergency powers permitted the President under the Constitution have been greatly enlarged, allowing for immediate action on his part, with Congress called upon later to endorse or reject such action. Indeed, this process has gone so far that, as mentioned earlier in the chapter, the trend now is to strip the Executive Branch of some of the powers transferred during the Korean conflict and various other emergencies.

In the second place, beginning with the first Legislative Reorganization Act of 1946, Congress has been seeking constantly to improve its organization and to streamline its procedures. These efforts, however, have been scarcely adequate to keep up with the enormous increase in business which confronts both Houses. There were, for example, 12,090 bills introduced in the Eightieth Congress. In the Ninety-second Congress, a quarter of a century later, the total was 25,354.

Congress is increasing the use of automation to facilitate procedures and to aid in its deliberations. Projects have been established in both Houses and in the Library of Congress which are providing increasingly for the consolidation and automatic processing of information for prompt congressional retrieval. Advanced electronic techniques are being applied for routine administrative work and for indexing, abstracting, and research purposes.

In behavior as distinct from organization, we have already noted the lessening of partisanship and the growth in consideration of legislation on a bipartisan or nonpartisan basis. This lends itself to high-level action commensurate with the importance of the problems to be dealt with. Watchdog committees such as the Truman Committee during World War II and the Watergate Committee have not uncommonly matched the occasion with their moods.

Actually, Congress is more and more shifting to reliance on research rather than controversy as the basis for decisions on issues and problems. The more facts that can be agreed upon, the less the remaining orbit for partisan or other controversy. The education of the electorate has increased and so has that of Congress. It could probably be demonstrated that Congress is today at an all-time high in the ability and sense of public service and integrity of its membership.

All in all, we seem to have learned something of a lesson. It was the Eightieth Congress, in control of the opposition party, that voted the President the most substantial program of international cooperation that has ever been voted any administration. Here was no paralysis, no deadlock, no jockeying for partisan advantage with great issues at a great moment. The Eighty-first Congress, in turn, quickly granted the President emergency powers in an economic and defense crisis—in fact, more powers than he had asked for. Here also was no delay, or dragging, or failure to respond to need. The Eighty-fourth Congress, again one controlled by the opposition party, moved rapidly and responsibly in international crises. The only arguments seemed to be concerned with which party most cooperated with the President, or whether Congress improved upon his program. In the Eighty-sixth Congress, it was Congress itself which sought acceleration and reappraisal in space, defense, foreign aid, and foreign policy generally—over against an apparently improvising and lagging executive.[3] While the presidency remained under the shadow of the impeachment proceedings in the Ninety-third Congress, there was little slackening in the movement of legislation and very positive support was extended to the President and the Secretary of State in their management of foreign relations and in negotiations with other nations.

The factors that made the difference in congressional–presidential relations after World War II as compared with those following World War I were not fundamentally accidents, such as differences in the personalities involved, though these played some part. The real differences are to be found in social trends, which are not likely to be reversed, unless, indeed, partisanship by some means or other finds itself strengthened. In that event, a unified party behind a President might be able to move faster. There is no assurance, however, that it would move more skillfully or with the large measure of consensus in a united nation which the present operation and usages of our Constitution appear to bring.

NOTES

1. Quoted by Ronald Goldfarb in an article, "The Permanent State of Emergency," *Washington Post*, January 6, 1974, pp. B1, B4.
2. Edward S. Corwin, *The President: Office and Powers*, 4th ed., rev. (New York: New York University Press, 1957), pp. 147-58.
3. For a particularly striking case study of this see Alison Griffith, *The National Aeronautics and Space Act* (Washington: Public Affairs Press, 1962).

CHAPTER 19

Congress and the Years Ahead

The time has come to bring together the various strands in our thinking. Of what sort is this government of ours, and what is the place of Congress in the over-all setting? Woodrow Wilson was able to speak and write of "congressional" government in his times. During the period 1933–72 there was certainly a temptation to speak of government as "presidential," based upon the ascendancy of presidential activity and leadership during these years.[1] The Vietnamese War and the Watergate scandal seem to be pushing the pendulum back toward Congress.

How long will it swing in that direction? How far will it go? At this writing, Congress seems intent on rediscovering forgotten powers and developing new usages. It appears unlikely that we will return to the Wilsonian concept of congressional government. Nevertheless, out of this search may well come a new equilibrium within the existing framework and behind the facade of the Constitution.

Let us summarize briefly our argument hitherto. The formal constitutional powers and position of Congress have changed but little, by either amendment or judicial interpretation. An exception is in the expansion assumed by the presidency in emergency situations, notably during the Great Depression and World War II and its aftermath. Even so, much of this expansion was present in embryo in the powers exercised by President Lincoln. The internal organization of Congress has changed measurably in the direction of clarity and fluidity. The latter is most noticeable in the diffusion of leadership, which allows considerably more scope than formerly for the individual member. The center of the stage is occupied by legislative–executive relations. These are an intricate pattern of conflict, compromise, and cooperation. On balance, each branch possesses under the Constitution a formidable set of powers with which it can press the other to take its point of view into account and hence assure responsible behavior. The nature of contemporary society with its premium upon leadership and rapid, informed action has given the executive an advantage in those informal factors which are frequently decisive in a power struggle. But Congress has restored the equilibrium somewhat by new legislation and notably by increasing its influence in foreign relations and in the control of the executive bureaucracy. It has also added to its professional staffs and expanded the legislative bureaucracy, thus better equipping itself in technical terms to meet the executive on a basis of parity, even in the matter of initiating or maturing alternative policies. Special importance also attaches itself to the appropriating process, which is developing uses more or less extraneous to its original concept. This process elaborated now into congressional budgetary procedures promises an even greater enhancement of the role of Congress in fiscal discipline and in over-all fiscal policy and the political economy. Various cooperative devices making for better executive–legislative relations are appearing, notably in the multiplication of informal contacts, some of which have become regularized. For the most part, these are still in the experimental stage.

The unifying factor of party government is less effective than formerly. Yet, here, too, there is clearly discernible in recent legislation on campaign financing the prospects for a resurgence of party influence. The burdens which the new laws place on individual or local group participants in the financing of individual election campaigns is bound to put a premium on centralization of campaign funding. It may also serve to increase the influence of special interests in the political process. Both factors can act to enhance the role of party.

A dispersive society reflects itself in pressure groups, each with its own program. Such programs tend to be incorporated in bureaus in the administrative structure of government, where the bureaus continue their active intervention in behalf of their clientele, with much freedom from even presidential control. Similarly, in Congress these dispersive elements are influential in committees and elsewhere, but there are also elements of independence in Congress that curb and filter their excesses considerably, elements which can operate only if there remains a degree of leniency in party discipline. The further problem of an integrated overall legislative program is not yet solved. Here again, recent developments in the democratic party structure in both Houses and between the two Houses for devising common positions on issues may contain the seeds of a solution.

Proposals to strengthen the role of party discipline, however, run up against the probability that this would weaken the very real independence of thought that has developed in Congress in opposition to the special interests and most certainly would accelerate the overall trend toward centralization of government.

An inherent localism in congressional viewpoint still makes it possible for it to do much in preserving state and local vitality and autonomy and in attending to local interests. Thus Congress is seemingly instrumental in the direction of attaining a reasonable equilibrium between the pressure groups and the general interest and between what should be done by the nation and what should be left to the states and localities.

Congress performs an important function in educating the electorate. It is utilizing new media to perform this function, as well as the time-honored methods of the hearings, reports, and floor debate. The hearings in particular have attained new stature as educators.

Congress has demonstrated its capacity to act quickly in a crisis and to sustain a mood of high purpose in an age of major problems.

In all the foregoing the importance of person-to-person relationships must not be underrated. When acquaintance ripens into mutual confidence, a situation influencing policy almost invariably occurs. By the same token, the shattering of trust, as in the Watergate affair, creates a mood of malaise in which every action of the Executive Branch will be subjected to greater scrutiny. What this may mean in terms of restraints on both the presidency and the bureaucracy is not yet clear. The critical internationally oriented departments of State and Defense and the Central Intelligence Agency, however, are likely to be brought more tightly under legislative control and the President's own immediate staff—heretofore beyond the reach of Congress—may also be kept under closer watch.

As for the future development of Congress, it is not necessary to speak in detail. Books have been written on the merits and defects of Congress and the several remedies that are prolifically suggested for the latter. Here let us speak in more general terms.

In the first place, there should be further experiment in the give-and-take of executive–legislative relations. Initiative in policy matters may appropriately be taken by either branch inasmuch as the measures originally suggested by each must be responsibly defended and justified before the other, else they will not become law. With the increased availability of staff to the Congress, this dual input of initiative has become increasingly possible. In international relations, a special case, the resolution furnishes an appropriate medium whereby Congress may initiate, correct, support, or guide the executive in those critical formative stages prior to matters hardening into a treaty or agreement. Personal contact and the cultivation of trust with candor by the President and Secretary of the State through frequent meetings with the congressional leadership of both parties and the appropriate committee members can also be of general value in this connection. In fields in which Congress wishes to experiment before it commits itself semi-irrevocably in detail, the "legislative veto" and authorizing legislation which contains terminal dates have already provided hopeful lines of approach to continuing cooperation. These practices deserve elaboration not only for facilitating action but in order to compel periodic legislative reexamination of grants of power to the executive.

The dominant position occupied by the pressure groups requires that their tremendous vitality be in fact channeled into the course of the public interest, that their conflicts be constructively resolved, that the overall economy be kept functioning, that the fiscal policy of the government be kept under control. This would seem to call for an influential position for the congressional instruments which are charged with the overall view, such as the Budget Committees, as well as the party leaderships. It also calls for constantly better staff work throughout the congressional processes, designed to uncover the secondary and long-run effects of legislative proposals and to buttress the increasingly large group of members who are seeking to understand such effects prior to debate and voting.

Because of the vast number of issues, and the difficulty of finding common denominators for party loyalty except by sacrifice of a member's discrimination and by compromise, the party's role in Congress should remain delineated in broad contours. The party is the instrument of inner structure. It is the instrument of mutual support. It is the instrument for examining the range of ideological views and geographic interests. It is not, and as yet shows little signs of becoming, the instrument of strict discipline on issues. Independence and cross-voting cannot and should not be eschewed. It is in accord with the rational and ethical elements in our culture; it allows more accurate representation for the states and districts; it promotes government by majority; it promotes intelligent criticism.

As a nation, we are suspicious of concentrations of unrestrained power, but we also profoundly believe in and have a genius for multiplying the areas of creative and spontaneous action. We seek the success of our economy in equilibriums between the great forces therein operating and not in the triumph of any one of them—in an equilibrium between capital and labor, between producer and consumer, between buyer and seller, between farmer and city man, between independent and chain store, between big and little business, between the needs of foreign defense and domestic tranquility and progress.

In government, we seek its effective operation, also in equilibriums and balance—between legislature and executive, between state and nation, between party loyalty and independence, between the vitality of the special interests and the overall viewpoint of the public interest, between a sound nationalism and world responsibilities, between radical and conservative viewpoints, between regionalism and the national view. We would not force or coerce any group or section to the breaking point. We would rather wait for some measure of support from within the major groups or sections before instituting important changes. We are equally suspicious of a too-dominating President and of a Congress which is deliberately obstructionist. We are repelled at the thought of inner strife. We do not want parties on class or ethnic lines. We give great scope to individuals, but we would hold them responsible.

The storms of controversy beat on Washington. Mayors, governors, religious groups, atheists, representatives of business, agriculture, labor, old people and young, unions of firemen, police, mail carriers, veterans, and war protesters flow in a continuous stream toward Capitol Hill. There the storms are quieted and the flows are deflected into the mainstream, and the genius of our government thus expresses itself in a kind of government by common consent.[2]

Our Constitution contains within it the principle of equilibrium but leaves to usage the great flexibility which alone makes this principle work. It embraces within its system of checks and balances the principle of responsible official behavior, but it leaves scope for creative leadership. We can move rapidly in a crisis, but we can also move surely step by step in those great tidal developments in legislation that the age of technology and power seems to demand. These then mark the role and responsibility of Congress in the years ahead: to safeguard the great constitutional principles of a responsible executive and a representative legislature, to preserve the vitality of our states and localities and of the functioning economic groups, to intervene in the social and economic structure when great national and international interests so require, to operate with independence and at the same time in interdependence with the Executive Branch at that high level of governmental action, rationally and ethically, which our education and our religious faiths have made an integral part of our culture.

NOTES

1. Roland Young, *The American Congress* (New York: Harper, 1958).
2. This is akin to the thesis developed in Herbert Agar, *The Price of Union* (Boston: Houghton Mifflin, 1950). See also the emphasis placed by James Burnham on what he calls "intermediary institutions" in assuming, not plebicitory majorities, but concurrent majorities, as the hallmark of constitutional government. James Burnham, *Congress and the American Tradition* (Chicago: Regnery, 1959), pp. 313-16 *et passim.*

Index